CRIMINAL MASTERMINDS

CRIMINAL MASTERMINDS

ANNE WILLIAMS,
VIVIAN HEAD
SEBASTIAN C. PROOTH

Futura

A *Futura* Book

First published by Futura in 2007

ISBN-13: 978-0-7088-0611-1

Produced by Omnipress, Eastbourne

Printed in Great Britain

Futura
An imprint of
Little, Brown Book Group
Brettenham House
Lancaster Place
London WC2E 7EN

Photo credits: Getty Images

CONTENTS

PART FOUR: SPIES AND DOUBLE AGENTS

PART FIVE: MURDERERS, OUTLAWS
AND THIEVES

PART SIX: TERRORISTS

PART SEVEN: SWINDLERS AND FORGERS

PART EIGHT: BANK ROBBERS

PART NINE: FICTIONAL MASTERMINDS

INTRODUCTION

In this book you will read about some of the most ruthless criminal masterminds ever to walk the face of the earth: Attila the Hun, Vlad the Impaler, Arnold 'The Brain' Rothstein, Lucky Luciano, Carlos the Jackal, the thirties' art forger Han van Meegeren and Frank Abagnale Junior, the con man and high-school dropout who managed to persuade the world that he had qualifications to practise as pilot, a doctor and a lawyer, among other professions. Along the way, we take a look at some of the female fiends of history, such as Countess Bathory, the sixteenth-century Slovakian murderess, who tortured hundreds of peasant girls to death in her castle, after indulging in her sexual perversions with them. There are also murderers, outlaws and thieves of the eighteenth century, like Jack Sheppard and Jonathan Wild, who terrorised the population of London, and when they were finally brought to justice and imprisoned, managed to escape repeatedly from high-security prisons. And there are the double agents of the Cold War years in the twentieth century, such as Kim Philby and the Cambridge Spies, the upper-class Englishmen whose apparent political allegiances to the Soviet regime are still not fully understood.

MORAL BANKRUPTCY

Then there are the outlaws who have gained a popular reputation over the years as romantic Robin Hood figures, like the Australian bushman Ned Kelly, who brought the plight of rural poverty among the settlers in the country to the authorities' attention, and who managed to evade capture for years but who finally met his end in a shoot-out with the police. Less romantic, but equally fascinating, are the accounts of nihilistic terrorists such as Abu Nidal and the Baader-Meinhof Gang, who sought to undermine the very fabric of Western democracy, for reasons that are hard to fathom. Like the Cambridge Spies in the UK, who colluded with the Soviet government against the West, these groups appear to have started out as politically motivated, only to degenerate into violence and moral bankruptcy.

Also included in this book, just for fun, are the most satisfyingly evil, devious criminal masterminds of all: those of the world of fiction, such as Blofeld, the James Bond villain; Fu Manchu, the evil genius of China and Fantomas, the ubiquitous, elusive French super-thief. In these fictional creations, we see the archetypal criminal masterminds – characters who are imagined as highly intelligent, gifted individuals, but whose ingenuity and cunning is used to wreak their revenge on mankind.

It is this aspect of criminal masterminds, whether real or fictional, that seems to fascinate us: that an individual can be intelligent, brilliant, a genius even, yet completely lack any moral sense that would encourage him – or her – to use their talents for the good of humanity. Indeed, there seems almost to be a popular fear that extreme intelligence may almost be supernatural, or at least unnatural; and that a high level of culture, sophistication and learning may sometimes go hand-in-hand with a desire to destroy lesser mortals in the service of a higher plan. The facts of human history seem in some ways to bear this out. Many of the leaders of the Nazi party in the Third Reich were highly intelligent, cultured individuals who greatly appreciated the art, music and learning that had characterised Germany over the centuries. Similarly, the leader of the terrorist group Shining Path in Peru, Abimael Guzman, was at one time a professor of philosophy and a highly respected political thinker. In addition, one can point to the Cambridge Spies as some of the most highly educated people in the UK, members of a class elite that traditionally held conservative views. Yet all these individuals used their gifts of native intelligence, education and social position, to ignore the dictates of decency, to treat their

opponents without mercy, to behave like the most common, violent street thugs, with no feeling for humanity. One can't help but ask 'Why'?

SOCIAL BACKGROUND

In a sense, the answer is blindingly obvious. Most criminals act out of a combination of greed, self-interest and lack of concern for others. The gains – and the risks – are clear enough. As Willie 'The Actor' Sutton allegedly put it, when asked why he robbed banks: 'Because that's where the money is!' Yet the picture that emerges from these stories is actually a rather more complex one.

As one would expect, the social milieu in which a criminal grows up usually has a major part to play in their career choice. For example, during the period of Prohibition, career opportunities in the legal world of business were few and far between for immigrant youngsters raised on the mean streets of North America's big cities, whether Jewish, Italian or German. No wonder that the more ambitious and ingenious among them, such as Meyer Lansky, Bugsy Siegel and Dutch Schultz, turned to bootlegging, drug running and the like to make their fortunes, rather than spend their lives working for a pittance in the same kind of dead-end jobs that their parents had to work at. For example, Meyer Lansky's father was in the New York garment trade, an exemplary immigrant

11

who worked extremely hard for a living, yet who barely managed to feed his family. His son, a bright, ambitious boy, was determined not to follow in his father's footsteps, and thus turned to a life of crime from an early age as a way of improving his prospects. Unlike some of his contemporaries, such as his friend Bugsy Siegel, later on in his life, Lansky had the intelligence to steer clear of directly involving himself with violence and mayhem, thus ensuring that he had a long and successful career in organised crime.

EMOTIONAL HISTORY

However, even with the mobsters, there are the exceptions. Arnold Rothstein, for example – perhaps the most famous criminal mastermind of all and the man whose legendary wealth and habit of carrying around large wads of cash gained him the nickname 'the Big Bankroll' – was the son of a wealthy New York Jewish businessman. The young Arnold could easily have chosen from a range of middle-class careers. So why did he choose to become a gangster instead? Perhaps it was for financial gain. Before he met his violent end, Rothstein had become an immensely wealthy man. However, his personal history shows that there were emotional reasons why he may have chosen to become a gangland criminal rather than a respectable businessman. From an early age, he had been rejected by his parents and felt that they favoured his brother. It may be that he took to crime as a form of rebellion against the family who had mistreated him, and against the Jewish culture that they were part of.

Certainly, this history is common enough among criminals from well-to-do families; although, here, once again, the picture is not always simple. In some cases, such as that of George 'Machine Gun' Kelly, one can't help feeling that, no matter what the circumstances, here was a young man bent on a life of violent crime, for whatever reason. Complex emotional needs and mental imbalance, also appear to drive much other criminal behaviour, from that of fantasists like Frank Abagnale Jr to that of lone killers such as the Unabomber.

THE THRILL OF THE CHASE

If social and emotional pressures play a part, what else makes a criminal mastermind? Intelligence, one might say. Yet curiously, once one analyses a master criminal's career, it becomes clear that in many cases, these individuals often avoid the most intelligent course of action open to them – to operate within the law, rather than outside it. Clearly, many of them have the brains to make their fortunes legally, or at least to 'go straight' once they have amassed money; but many choose not to do so. What emerges from many of these stories is that most high-profile criminals are not simply clever people prevented by their social or emotional background from becoming well-to-do citizens. It becomes clear that material gain is not the only aspect of crime that attracts them. They don't just want money: they want excitement, adventure, the thrill of the chase. They are, in essence, thrill seekers.

Christopher Boyce, who became a spy, selling secrets to the Russians, perhaps put it most clearly when he was asked the motivation behind his actions. In response, he said that he had become a spy because he believed that the American government was wrong. He also said that he liked the idea of getting some extra cash but, above all, that he had 'a lust for adventure'. This need for thrills is echoed by many other characters in the book: from drug barons like Ramon Arellano Felix to the 1960s bank robber Jacques Mesrine; from terrorists such as Carlos the Jackal to fraudsters like Frank Abalagne Jr. All of them, to a greater or lesser degree, are people who enjoy danger, who prefer to speed along life's highway than to take the journey slowly and enjoy the view. Those like Meyer Lansky, who prefer to keep a low profile, who like a quiet life and who invest their ill-gotten earnings cautiously and sensibly as soon as they can, are the exception rather than the rule. Only Lansky and, perhaps, Mickey Cohen – both gangsters from the Prohibition era – come into this rare category of cautious criminal masterminds.

... AND THE KILL

As well as the need to take risks, there is another, more disturbing, element to the make-up of a criminal mastermind. This is the need for another kind of thrill: that of the kill. The obvious examples here are the strangely charismatic killers who manage to attract their victims to them like moths to a flame. Men like Charles Manson, who showed signs of more than average intelligence and yet was a brutal psychopath with a list of horrifying murders to his name. In Manson's case, not only was he a killer, but he managed to influence those around him to commit the most appalling acts of murder. Also in this category are some of the outlaws, such as Bonnie and Clyde, who seem to have got their kicks from killing. (Some commentators have argued that Bonnie Parker was not a murderess, yet regardless of whether she pulled the trigger, she was clearly closely involved in the murders that took place, and very much attracted to a milieu of men who liked to kill for a living.)

Bloodthirsty drug barons such as Ramon Arellano Félix and violent mobsters like Bugsy Siegel are also among the criminals who seem to get a kick out of violent crime. So are the terrorists, such as Abu Nidal and Timothy McVeigh, who cold-bloodedly murdered innocent victims for their own political causes. In fact, there are very few types of master criminals – with the possible exception of fraudsters – who are in no way involved with violence. Even those whose exalted position among the criminal fraternity removes them from the scene of the crime, who do not have actual blood on their hands, are often responsible for murder and violence in an indirect way.

THE MODERN WORLD

Thus, it seems that the psychological profile of the criminal mastermind is a highly complex one. Greed plays a part, as does intelligence, along with the individual's social and emotional background; yet, more crucially, it is the need to take risks, and the thrill of the chase – of adventure, of danger and of violence – that seems to define the motivation of the master criminal. In this book, you will find out how the master criminals of the past and of the present responded to that urge.

What emerges is that most criminal masterminds don't want to lead an ordinary, humdrum life like the rest of us. Even if they could have their wealth on a plate, one senses that they would probably reject it. Clearly, in today's economy, in periods of economic boom there are many opportunities for sharp young men and women to make a great deal of money, whether in law, accountancy, business, the stock market, computers or any number of other growing enterprises in the modern world, without risking the penalties incurred by breaking the law. But even in the

PART ONE

ANCIENT
MURDERERS

ATTILA
THE HUN

Attila the Hun was king and general of the Hun Empire from AD 434 to 453. He is remembered as a cruel and predatory figure who appears to have been motivated by raw power rather than bloodlust, but he should also be remembered for skill in shaping a nomadic band of mercenaries into a successful fighting machine. The Huns themselves were surrounded by mystery, and it is believed that their origin was directly connected with two infamous people of the ancient Middle East – the Sumerians and the Scythians. They were fierce and superb horsemen who struck terror into both the Germans and the Romans. Atilla and his men became known as the 'Scourge of God' and their savagery and brutality became part of medieval history.

An ancient Roman practice was to hold a member of your enemy's family hostage, as a security that the conditions of treaties were upheld. Attila, himself, was no stranger to this practice, as he was held as a hostage by the Romans. During this period he was trained and educated by the Romans and also learned many of their secret methods of warfare. Once he was released, Attila vowed to avenge the nation he so despised, and put his newly acquired skills into use by forming an army. He realised that it would take incredible leadership skills to unite the Hun savages, and through his carefully planned training he managed to earn respect and loyalty from the various chieftains and warriors now under his command.

The Huns arrived on the outskirts of the Roman Empire towards the end of the fourth century. They were a wild band of horsemen who soon struck fear wherever they went. In their effort to reach Rome, the Huns crossed paths with the Ostrogoths and Visigoths, two major German tribes, invading their huge empires. The Germans had never witnessed such behaviour, describing them as 'barbarians with an appetite for raw meat'. They fought with complete disregard for their own safety, usually firing from a distance with sharpened bones fired from a shaft. When fighting in close combat the Huns would throw a net over their enemies, rendering them powerless to thrust their swords. When the Huns defeated the Ostrogoths, their king took his own life because he felt he could not stand up to the new ruthless rulers. The Huns then attacked the Visigoths, the majority of whom fled to the Roman Empire for protection.

However, the Visigoths and Romans were not a good combination and they remained firm enemies. In fact it was the enormity of the migration of Visigoth refugees fleeing the Huns that hastened the fall of the Roman Empire.

A NEW LEADER

Events took a downhill turn for the Romans when Attila the Hun succeeded Rugila to the throne in AD 434. Attila and his brother Bleda, who were sons of Rugila's brother Mundzuk, inherited the huge Hun Empire. Their new empire stretched from the Alps and the Baltic in the west to the Caspian Sea in the east. Attila, who was only twenty-one years old when he became king, was far more aggressive and ambitious than his predecessor, making him a rather unpredictable leader. Despite being young he was both brave and ambitious and was determined to be a powerful leader. He delighted in war and ruled with a superiority that scared even his own subjects. One of Attila's and Bleda's first joint actions was the negotiation of a peace treaty with the eastern Roman Empire. Under the terms of this treaty the Romans were forced to pay double the original annual subsidy of gold to the Huns to keep the empire from being attacked. The two brothers immediately started to strengthen and expand their kingdom, and bitter fighting broke out with their neighbours. Attila's Huns soon became a formidable fighting force, no longer the horse nomads of their ancestors. Attila, who wanted to be a sole ruler, solved the problem by killing his brother in AD 445.

For five years, Attila was true to his word and the Huns left the Romans alone, but a new emperor came to power and refused to pay the tribute to Attila and his army. This resulted in a series of battles in which Attila and his barbarians ruthlessly destroyed city after city, before finally reaching Constantinople. Realising that it was hopeless for his archers to try and penetrate the great walls of the city, Attila captured the vestiges of the Roman forces who had withdrawn to Gallipoli and killed every one of them. The emperor, realising that he had been beaten, agreed to pay the arrears of the tribute, which amounted to 6,000 pounds of gold. To make matters worse for the Romans, Attila now trebled the annual payment they were forced to pay.

ATTILA AND PRINCESS HONORIA

Although Attila was very unpopular with the Romans, he had caught the attention of one particular woman. Honoria was the sister of the western Roman emperor, Valentinian III. Her brother had placed her in exile in a convent for having an affair with an officer in her household, despite the fact that she was betrothed to a senator.

Desperate to get out of her plight, she sent a pleading letter to Attila with her ring, asking for his help. Attila, who could see the opportunity to gain a large dowry, approached her brother to ask permission to marry Honoria. At the same time he asked for half of the Roman Empire as a dowry, a request which, not surprisingly, was immediately turned down.

Despite a second attempt to win the hand of Honoria, his advances were once again spurned by Valentinian, which forced Attila into taking action. In AD 451, Attila amassed together an army of over 700,000 men and marched across Germany into Gaul. They burned and looted towns and raped, killed and beat the inhabitants – even the children and babies were not safe from their brutality. Churches and monasteries were razed to the ground without remorse, adding to the Huns' already menacing image. Atilla was a splendid spectacle in battle, riding a magnificent black horse ahead of his savage barbarians bearing grotesquely scarred faces, adding to the psychological effect they had on everyone they encountered. As Attila and his Huns marched across Gaul they left a trail of devastation, and it wasn't until they reached the city of Orleans that they met with any opposition. Orleans, like most major cities in those days, was surrounded by fortified walls. As soon as the inhabitants learned of the advancement of the Huns, they closed their gates and prepared to defend themselves.

Although Attila attempted to break down the defences at Orleans, he was thwarted by a large army advancing towards the city. The army was a mixture of 300,000 Visigoths and Romans, led by a Roman general by the name of Aëtius and the Visigoth king Theodoric. The Visigoths who, like the Romans, were determined to overcome the Hun army, had joined forces to try and defeat their enemy. Attila, on seeing the army, decided to take his forces and march to the neighbouring area of Champagne to a place called Châlons. The Romans and Visigoths pursued Attila and a fierce battle followed, with both sides fighting bravely for ultimate victory. The Huns managed to drive back the opposing army and in so doing killed Theodoric.

Aëtius now feared for his own life and felt it wouldn't be long before his own army were beaten by the Huns. However, the son of Theodoric, Thorismond, who had taken command of the Visigoths when his father was killed, led his army in a charge against the Huns. They were desperate for revenge for the death of their king, so they fought with extra courage and strength. They quickly managed to overpower the Huns and Attila decided to flee from the battlefield and return to his camp.

This was the first time that Attila had ever experienced defeat and with his army greatly de-pleted, he prepared for his own demise. On reaching his camp, Attila built a huge funeral pyre out of his belongings and wagons, which he was prepared to light and jump into the flames if the Romans came to attack him.

'Here I will perish in the flames, rather than surrender to my enemies,' he cried.

However, the Romans did not come, and the Huns continued their long retreat across the Rhine, struggling with the harsh winter conditions. Although Attila and his men were considerably weakened, they were not defeated, fighting had been their life and their spirits remained high.

ATTILA RISES AGAIN

In AD 452, with his strength renewed, Attila set out once again to claim Honoria as his bride and marched upon Rome with unrestrained anger. His first target was the city of Aquileia and at the sight of the warring barbarians, the people fled in fright to the surrounding hills and mountains. Others fled to the small islands of the lagoons lining the western coast of the Adriatic. Although many of the refugees returned to their mainland homes after Attila withdrew, the seed was planted for the founding of Venice.

Following the siege of Aquileia, Attila and his army marched towards Rome. Emperor Valentinian and the inhabitants of Rome were greatly alarmed at the approach of the fearsome Huns. However, just as Attila was approaching the city, he met Pope Leo I, who persuaded him to turn his troops back. In a surprising turn of events, Attila told his men that he no longer had any interest in marrying Honoria or gaining more land and called the attack off. The true reason for this change of heart will always remain a mystery, although there is evidence that many of Attila's men were struck down with the plague. It has also been said that the apostles Peter and Paul appeared to Attila in his camp and threatened him with death if he attacked Rome.

THE FINAL MARRIAGE

In AD 453, Attila married a very beautiful young girl by the name of Ildico, despite the fact that he already had numerous other wives. However, Attila never saw his wedding day out, because he died from the excesses of food and drink at his wedding feast. He fell into a drunken sleep lying on his back, and the blood from a nose haemorrhage flowed down the back of his throat and killed him. His royal attendants on hearing shouts from Attila's bedchamber, broke down the door and found Attila lying dead on the floor, with Ildico sobbing loudly still wearing her wedding veil. Then, as was the custom of the Huns, they cut Ildico's hair and then disfigured their faces grotesquely and smeared the blood on the face of the dead warrior. His body was laid out in a plain, silk tent for people to come and pay their respects. They enclosed his body in three coffins – one of gold, one of silver and one of iron – and buried him at night in a secret location in the mountains. When the funeral was over the Huns killed the slaves who had dug the grave so that the place of his burial would remain a mysterious secret. Today, Attila is remembered as one of the most feared men in ancient history.

GENGHIS KHAN

Genghis Khan was the founder of the Mongol Empire and a supremely capable military leader and administrator. He formed an ingenious intelligence network from which he was able to obtain valuable information against his enemies, and which helped him build his growing empire. However, history has shown us that Khan's enemies suffered greatly at the hands of this powerful ruler. His methods were ruthless and bloodthirsty, often massacring whole cities that tried to oppose him.

THE BOY GROWS UP

Temujin, as he was originally known, was born *c.* AD 1162, the son of a minor Kiyat-Borjigid chieftain, Yisugei. Legend tells the story that Temujin was born with a blood clot in the palm of his hand, indicating that he was going to be a formidable leader. When Temujin was only nine years old, his father was poisoned and his mother was left to raise him on her own.

Mongols grew up on horses and were used to hunting, and Temujin became adept at using the bow and arrow. They were a race of nomadic herdsmen who lived on the grassy plains just north of the Gobi Desert and south of the Siberian forests. They generally hunted in small groups and were led by a chief, or *khan*, living in portable tent-like structures called *gers*, or perhaps better known, as *yurts*. It was a tough existence and Temujin quickly learned the value of making allies to help him through the hard times. As he grew into a fine, strong, young man, Timujen gained respect through his bravery, intelligence and power of persuasion – in fact he scared the other khans with his ability to make others do what he wished.

As he grew into adulthood, Temujin made an ally of Ong Khan, an old friend of his father's. Ong Khan saw the potential in the young man and he asked Temujin to join him on a campaign against the Tartars of the west. The young man fought well and so impressed Ong Khan that he decided to adopt Temujin and appoint him his legal heir. Ong Khan's legitimate son, Senggum, was understandably put out by this decision and he attempted to assassinate his rival. However, Temujin was informed of the attempt on his life and managed to defeat Senggum and his supporters in a battle.

Ong Khan had spent many years building up a coalition of Mongols and other tribes and, on his death in 1206, Temujin took the title of 'Universal Ruler', which translates into Genghis Khan.

BRILLIANT ORGANIZATIONAL SKILLS

Genghis Khan continued to build up his army and destroyed what was left of any old enemy tribes. He also created a new body of law, which was something he worked on for the remainder of his life. As a teenager, before he became khan, Temujin's beloved young wife, Borte, was kidnapped. He was devoted to her and spent a long time trying to rescue her, which resulted in the massacre of an entire tribe. Because kidnapping of women had caused much feuding among the Mongols, as khan, Genghis made the practice illegal. He also declared that all children were legitimate, regardless of who their parents were, and he also made it law that no woman could be sold into an arranged marriage. Genghis Khan also made it a capital offence to steal an animal and regulated hunting so that meat was available for everyone. As he expanded his empire, Genghis Khan created order but, despite being a genius at organization, he still managed to terrify the continent stretching from Peking to the Crimea. If his opponents were not submissive and remained defiant, Genghis attacked. If, however, they agreed to his terms, he usually allowed them to remain in power, so long as they paid extortionate taxes and provided him with military power. Under the leadership of Genghis Khan, the Mongols rapidly conquered an enormous region of Asia. The empire they eventually carved out took in the whole of Central Aisa from China to Persia and stretched as far west as the Mediterranean.

GENGHIS KHAN AND THE SILK ROAD

The Silk Road (or Silk Route) is one of the oldest routes of international trade in the world and was an important path for communication between different parts of the empire. Realising the importance of this major trading route, Genghis Khan advanced to his south in an effort to secure his borders. He made an alliance with the Uighurs, who were closer than the Mongols were to the Silk Road and its subsequent wealth. To advance his progress even further, Genghis Khan arranged for his daughter to be married to the Uighur Khan. The Uighurs were far wealthier than the Mongols, who only had leather, fur and felt to trade. When the Uighur Khan arrived at the wedding with a caravan full of gold, silver, pearls and fancy silks and satins, it gave Genghis Khan the much needed booty to pay his troops.

In 1209, Genghis Khan moved against the Tanguts, who were farmers and herders in north-west China. Like the Uighurs, they were rich in goods and Genghis Khan needed their wealth to improve his status. Because the Mongols were outnumbered by two to one they had to learn new ways of warfare. By depriving them of supplies and water, they managed to overcome the fortified cities, something that they had not encountered in earlier battles.

The Ruzhen Jin occupied northern China and had a firm control of goods along the Silk Road. The leader of the Ruzhen Jin met with Genghis Khan and demanded that the Mongols submit to his army and become vassals. Genghis Khan knew that if he defied this barbarian enemy, he would lose access to vital goods and he made the decision to go to war. In 1211, the Mongols attacked. The Ruzhen Jin had a large and effective army, but they were also under attack from the Chinese south of the Yangzi River. They managed to force the Chinese to retreat and Genghis used this to his advantage. Taking advantage of newly-acquired Chinese siege machines, the Mongols surged forward and ravaged the countryside as they went. They swept from city to city, a savage force which their opponents were totally unprepared for. In the name of conquest, they hacked, burned, slashed and obliterated anything in their path. They inflicted terror and bloodshed on the Ruzhen subjects and gained vital information and booty from each conquest. Revered as a god among his warriors, no name inspired more terror than that of Genghis Khan.

By 1214, Genghis Khan had taken control of the majority of China north of the Yellow River. The Ruzhen emperor was forced to recognize the Mongol leader's authority and relented to paying him the taxes he demanded.

EXPANSION

After five years of fighting the Mongols returned to their native Mongolia, taking with them many engineers who had now become a regular part of the army. They had also taken captive musicians, translators, doctors and learned scribes, along with wagons of goods, including silk, rope, cushions, blankets, robes, rugs, porcelain, perfumes, jewellery, wine, honey, medicines, bronze, gold, silver and many other valuable items. The Mongols were pleased to be home and settled into their new prosperous lifestyle with ease. However, it wasn't long before Genghis Khan yearned more wealth and supplies for his nation.

In 1218, an event took place that would change Ghenghis Khan's realm into a mighty empire. A Mongol caravan travelling from Mongolia to the Persian Empire was stopped by the governor of a Persian frontier province in modern-day Uzbekistan. The governor suspected, and probably rightly, that the caravan included several spies and he ordered the caravan to be attacked and its good seized. He had the chief of the envoys killed and the beards of the others burned, and sent them back to Genghis Khan. This violation of the safe-conduct of caravans was unforgivable, and Genghis sent ambassadors to the Shah of Persia, demanding that the offending governor be turned over to him. The shah, who laughed in the faces of the ambassadors, decided to have them all killed for their impudence. As for Genghis Khan, this was another unforgivable offence and he declared war.

Although the Mongols had already conquered a large area with considerable bloodshed, they had barely made any impact on the frontiers of the vast Persian Empire. Once again Genghis Khan used his intelligence and information that he had gathered from previous battles. He knew that the shah's empire was rather fragmented by different ethnic and religious groups, who were only kept under control by force. What happened next was a very bold act on behalf of Genghis Khan. He ordered two of his generals to hunt down the shah within his own empire and kill anyone who interfered. Word soon spread that anyone who fought against the warring Mongols faced certain death, and the shah fled for his life towards the Caspian Sea, leaving his subjects to be raped and slaughtered.

As Genghis Khan worked his way through his new territory, he left behind him a bloody trail, as one city after another was captured by the Mongols.

Women were raped, inhabitants were tied up and shot with arrows, while others were decapitated. Rich inhabitants were tortured until they revealed where they had hidden their wealth.

As the remorseless army made its way across Armenia and Georgia, Europe became aware of the power of the Mongols and their leader for the first time. Unlike the cumbersome armies of Europe, the Mongols travelled light and were consequently more mobile. They were able to outwit and tire any pursuers, often spending days at a time in the saddle. The Mongols' ability to travel up to 160 km (100 miles) per day, was unheard of by armies of that time.

Although the Mongols were totally ruthless in battle, they always displayed extraordinary military discipline. Originally of nomadic origin, they were very quick to adapt to new siege tactics and they were soon an army with a fearful reputation.

THE DEATH OF A GREAT LEADER

Genghis Khan returned to Mongolia in 1225, having enjoyed great military success. He now ruled everything between the Caspian Sea and Beijing and had control of trade through his empire. For the first time, numerous European envoys, merchants and craftsmen could travel in relative safety throughout Central Asia as far as China.

Genghis Khan went to war one final time when he believed that the Tangut people were not living up to his required standards. Even at the age of sixty-five, Genghis Khan still led his army into battle, and it was in 1227, in his fight against the Tanguts, that he allegedly fell of his horse and died.

In terms of area, Genghis Khan was the greatest conqueror of all time. Although he ultimately paved the way for peace and security, it was at the expense of great destruction in the terms of life and property. He was an organizational and strategic genius and even after his death, the Mongol armies continued to dominate the battlefields. Vengeance was Genghis Khan's usual reason to go to war and he slaughtered people without giving it a second thought. Terror was his principle weapon of war and he is reputed to have said:

> *The greatest joy a man can know is to conquer his enemies and drive them before him. To ride their horses and take away their possessions. To see the faces of those who were dear to them bedewed with tears, and to clasp their wives and daughters in his arms.*

CALIGULA

Gaius Caesar Augustus Germanicus was born in AD 12 and has gone down in history as a coarse and cruel tyrant. He was given the nickname 'Caligula' when he was between two and four years old, from the miniature version of military sandals (*caligae*) that he wore when he lived on the Rhine with his father's legions. Caligula was a tall, rather thin man, who lost his hair at an early age. This was a rather touchy subject. In fact it affected him so much that it was a capital crime for anyone to look down from a high place as Caligula walked by. By contrast, his body was covered with hair, another sensitive topic, and his subjects made sure they made no mention of him being 'hirsute' within his earshot. He was a man with an incredible amount of energy and a sick passion for sadism, which led to many cruel and reckless schemes.

THE YOUNG CALIGULA

Caligula was the third son of Germanicus – who was the nephew of Emperor Tiberius – and Agrippina the elder. His childhood was far from happy, often accompanying his parents on military campaigns dressed in miniature versions of the Roman army's uniform. He lived in a constant atmosphere of paranoia, suspicion and even murder, and a series of personal tragedies had a great effect on his later life. His father died under suspicious circumstances on October 10, AD 19, which caused a major rift between his mother and his grand-uncle, the emperor Tiberius, amid accusations of murder and conspiracy. Because of this Caligula was sent to live with his great-grandmother and Tiberius' mother, Livia. Following her death, two years later, he was moved once again and this time he went to live with his grandmother, Antonia. During this period of his adolescence, Caligula had little contact with people other than his three sisters, Agrippina the Younger, Drusilla and Julia Livilla. It has been suggested that he formed a close relationship with Drusilla and may have even had an incestuous relationship with her.

After the death of his brother in AD 33, Caligula was next in succession for the position of emperor, along with Gemellus, who was the grandson of Tiberius. At this time, Caligula was living with Tiberius on the island of Capri and it is believed that Tiberius perverted and changed Caligula, who was hardly out of his boyhood.

Back in Rome, Tiberius' Praetorian Prefect, Sejanus, was proving to be an exceptionally powerful man. He started to form his own affiliations against Tiberius and his possible successors, in the hope of one day becoming emperor himself. This meant that not only was Tiberius in danger but also Caligula and the rest of his family. Sejanus was a real threat as, in all but name, he had control of Rome as Tiberius was now in semi-retirement.

Sejanus denounced Caligula's mother and two of his brothers, Nero and Drusus – his other two brothers, Gaius Julius and Tiberius had died in childhood. Agrippina was banished to the tiny island of Pandataria in the Tyrrhenian Sea, where she starved herself to death. Nero and Drusus were exiled to the island of Ponza, where they both died. Drusus' body was found locked in a dungeon with the stuffing out of his mattress filling his mouth, which he had eaten to try and stave off the hunger pangs. Nero most likely died due to some violent act, but there is no record of exactly what happened to him.

Tiberius summoned Caligula and told him about the deaths, which must have had a huge impact on the young man. At the time, Caligula appeared to be indifferent to the deaths of his mother and two brothers, but later in his life he admitted this was a ploy to keep himself alive.

CALIGULA, THE EMPEROR

In AD 33, Tiberius appointed Caligula as quaestor, which meant he was responsible for the treasury and financial affairs relating to the empire. He held this post until Tiberius' death in March 37, when Caligula and his cousin, Tiberius Gemellus, became joint heirs of the empire. Caligula was not prepared to share the title and, with the help of the new prefect of the Praetorian Guard, Naevius Sutorius Macro, declared Tiberius' will null and void on the grounds of insanity, leaving Caligula as the sole emperor.

Caligula entered Rome on March 28 and was greeted warmly by the crowds, who hailed him as 'our baby' and 'our star'. Caligula has been described as the first truly popular emperor of Rome, who was admired by everyone. The population of the vast empire felt that the new emperor was the beginning of a new age, and Caligula was certainly very different to the previous emperor in the early years of his reign. He gave cash bonuses to members of the Praetorian Guard, declared that treason trials were now a thing of the past and gave amnesty to political prisoners and their families that Tiberius had denounced. Caligula also arranged for his mother's remains to be sent to Rome so that he could give her a proper burial. He became famous for his lavish spectacles, devising extravagant games for the Romans to enjoy, such as gladiator contests. He revived free elections for the populace and abolished sales tax. Because of his earlier travels with the troops on their campaigns, Caligula had their loyalty and everyone believed that he would take them back to the good times experienced before the reign of Tiberius. On top of this he was a blood relative of Augustus, which meant he was related to the infamous Julius Caesar and the great-grandson of Mark Antony.

A TOUCH OF INSANITY

However, despite this auspicious start, Caligula's short reign was to end in tragedy. It wasn't long before Caligula started to behave oddly. He not only became an egomaniac but also started showing disrespect to others and, by this behaviour, he quickly alienated himself from those who were once loyal to him. As emperor he was automatically head of the religious office, and his blasphemous actions soon proved to be an embarrassment to the Roman Empire. It soon became obvious that an attempt would be made on Caligula's life.

Some people say that Caligula was born insane, while others feel that his insanity was a direct result of a mysterious illness that he developed in October AD 37. Caligula was taken ill just six months after becoming emperor, and although it is unsure of the nature of the sickness, it was possibly a virus that he contracted from all his excesses of drinking, sexual activities and superfluous bathing.

The empire was overcome with sadness and sympathy when they heard their new emperor had fallen sick. The whole empire rejoiced when he made a full recovery, but this rejoicing was to be short-lived because Caligula emerged from his sickness as a monster of lust and unbelievable cruelty.

At the beginning of AD 38, Caligula forced Gemellus and his father-in-law, Gaius Silanus, to commit suicide. He accused them both of treason, something that he had earlier abolished. Later the same year he arranged for the murder of the Praetorian Guard, Macro, the man who had helped him become emperor. Caligula became paranoid that Macro was becoming too powerful in his own right and sent him to Egypt on the pretext of becoming a guard. As soon as Macro set foot in the country he was imprisoned and executed.

One of his first acts of madness was to build a temporary floating bridge using ships as pontoons. This stretched for 3 km (2 miles) from the resort of Baiae to the neighbouring port of Puteoli. It is thought the bridge was meant to be a rival to that built by the Persian King Xerxes, which crossed the Hellespont. After completion, Caligula rode his favourite horse, Incitatus, across the bridge, wearing the breastplate of Alexander the Great. This was an act of defiance, because Tiberius' soothsayer had predicted that 'he had no more chance of becoming emperor than of riding a horse across the Gulf of Baiae'.

Caligula loved dressing up and wore costumes made from the best silk adorned with precious stones.

He was also irresistibly attracted to pretty women and would frequently send for them to be used at his pleasure. He would abuse them and then leave them just like fruit he had tasted and abandoned. It was also reported that Caligula had sexual relationships with men, for example a young and handsome pantomime actor by the name of Mnester.

Caligula's favourite sister, Drusilla, and rumoured lover, died in AD 38 and he had her declared a goddess. Craving adolatry himself, Caligula ordered an altar to be built in his honour, and asked for a statue to be brought to the temple in Judaea so that he could be worshipped there as well. The inhabitants of Rome felt that this was going too far, and when he declared that he was going to make his horse, Incitatus, his consul, people started to realise that perhaps their emperor was going 'mad'.

Caligula loved to spend money and spared no expense on lavish games, ceremonies and elaborate parades. In fact he was such a spendthrift that by AD 39, the imperial treasury was virtually bankrupt. In an attempt to try and refill the imperial coffers, Caligula reintroduced Tiberius' treason trials so that he could purloin the property and money of his enemies. He also auctioned public property in an effort to produce much needed funds.

Other activities by Caligula gained even greater attention – for example, his behaviour on the military front. His military activities were nothing short of ludicrous, with accounts of Gauls dressed up as Germans and Roman troops ordered to pick up seashells as 'spoils of the sea' indicative of his triumph over Neptune. Although Caligula considered expanding his empire into the lands of Germany and Britain, as his father had attempted to do, he never went ahead with these plans. At one point he did take his sisters and Drusilla's widower, Aemilus Lepidus, with him to visit the German provinces. The subsequent events are somewhat shrouded in uncertainty, but it is known that on arrival he had Lepidus and a member of his guard, Gaetulicus, put to death. He also had his sisters' property confiscated and put them into exile for involvement in an alleged conspiracy.

Many of Caligula's actions were seen as paranoia, but as it turned out he had reason to be concerned about his own safety.

CALIGULA'S DEMISE

At the age of twenty-nine in the year AD 41, Caligula was assassinated by members of his own Praetorian Guard. They had both personal and political reasons for wanting him dead, and found support among members of the senate. His continuing obsessive and deranged behaviour alarmed members of the senate, and they were in no doubt that the emperor of their enormous empire was nothing more than a dangerous madman. The three main conspirators were Caligula's own brother-in-law, Marcus Vinicius, Julia Livilla's husband and a high-ranking senator.

On January 24, AD 41, Cassius Chaerea and other guardsmen, attacked Caligula as he was attending the Palatine Games being held for Augustus. Cassius Chaerea was thought to bear a personal grudge against Caligula because as a young man he had been injured in his genitalia and as a result of this he had a high-pitched voice that sounded effeminate. Caligula constantly mocked Chaerea for this, whenever he was on duty, taunting him with watch-words for that particular day, such as *priapus* (Latin for erection) or *Venus* (Roman slang for eunoch). He was the constant butt of Caligula's jokes and to embarrass him further, Caligula used to extend his hand to be kissed, at the same time making an obscene gesture.

Chaerea was anxious to carry out the assassination as soon as possible and had to be restrained on more than one occasion. The conspirators decided to carry out their deed during the Palatine Games because there would be plenty of distractions to give them cover. A temporary wooden theatre had been built in front of the imperial residence. It was quite a small area that would soon be packed with thousands of spectators. Caligula's German bodyguard, who was noted for his strength and brutality, would be hampered by the crowds in coming to his rescue.

There were many omens of Caligula's forth-coming death, most notable of which was a dream that Caligula had. In this dream, he was standing next to the throne of Jupiter when God literally kicked him out of heaven.

On the day of his assassination, a farce was being performed called *The Laureolus*, in which the main character falls during an escape and dies with blood pouring from his mouth. This was quite apt and, coincidentally, was the same play performed on the day that Philip of Macedon had been assassinated.

Caligula entered the small theatre in the morning, when it was already full of people. The festivities started with the sacrifice of a flamingo, after which the emperor took his seat and started eating and drinking with his companions. Caligula was in the habit of leaving the games around mid-day, when he would bathe and take lunch before returning for the afternoon's performance. The conspirators were aware of this routine and planned to attack Caligula as he walked down one of the narrow passageways that led from the theatre into the palace. However, on this particular occasion Caligula showed no signs of wanting to leave. Vinicius panicked and decided to get up and speak to Chaerea about changing their plans. As he rose to leave, Caligula pulled on his toga and asked him where he was going, which meant the senator had no choice but to return to his seat.

Eventually, Caligula was persuaded to take a break by Asprenas and the imperial party left the theatre with Caligula's uncle Claudius, Marcus Vinicius and Valerius Asiaticus taking the lead. They held the crowd back, ostensibly to show respect to the emperor, but in reality they were making space for the conspirators to get through. At the last minute Caligula decided to take the shorter route to the baths, which happened to be the only way that had been left unguarded. As he passed down the narrow passageway, Caligula stopped to speak to a small group of performers, giving his conspirators enough time to get in position for the attack.

The assault started with Chaerea asking Caligula for his watchword of the day. As Caligula gave his usual mocking reply, Chaerea slashed the emperor between his neck and shoulders. Caligula was badly wounded and as he turned in agony to make his escape Sabinus struck him again. Then a crowd of conspirators surrounded Caligula and stabbed him repeatedly, leaving around thirty wounds to various parts of his body. As Caligula dropped to the floor the conspirators jeered and spat in his face.

Some of Caligula's personal bodyguards rushed to his aid, but they were too late. Several Praetorians then swept through the palace seeking to kill any of his remaining relatives. Caligula's fourth wife, Caesonia, was stabbed to death, and his baby daughter's skull was smashed against a wall.

Caligula's bodyguards were so enraged that they started to kill people indisciminately. Most of the conspirators had managed to get away, but those who remained were simply killed along with many innocent people. The bodyguards blocked the exits to the theatre while others entered the area bearing the heads of their victims, which they proceeded to place on an altar. The remaining crowd were subdued and uncertain as to what exactly had happened. No one was sure whether Caligula was dead or just wounded, but the situation was diffused when Arruntius Evarestus, an auctioneer by trade, came into the theatre wearing mourning apparel. In a powerful voice, he announced that Caligula had been assassinated.

As evening fell, Agrippa arranged to have Caligula's body taken to the Gardens of Lamii, which was an imperial property on the Hill of Esquiline, just outside the city limits. His body was given a quick cremation and buried in a temporary grave.

Caligula is best remembered, not as a famous emperor, but as a man who had a weird, depraved love of extremes. His name is synonymous with hedonism, insanity and cruelty, which was merely strengthened by his absolute power as emperor of Rome.

VLAD THE IMPALER

Vlad Tepes, better known as Vlad the Impaler, is probably best remembered as being the character on whom Bram Stoker based his character, Dracula. However, the fictional character of Dracula is nowhere near as evil as the real-life Vlad the Impaler, who killed for the sheer pleasure of watching his victims writhe in pain. He was a tyrant of the worst possible kind and his story can still send shivers down the spine. He is remembered in history for his cruelty and particularly for his favoured form of torture and execution – impalement – from which he received the nickname Vlad the Impaler.

A BRIEF HISTORY

Vlad the Impaler, otherwise known as Vlad III, Dracula, Drakulya, or Tepes, was born in late 1431 in the town of Sighisoara, Transylvania. He was the second son of Vlad II, or Dracul, who was the military governor of the principality of Wallachia. Vlad Dracul was also a knight in the Order of the Dragon, which was a secret fraternity created in

1387 by the emperor. The Order was a group of Slavic rulers and warlords who were sworn to uphold the Christian faith by defending their empire against the Turks of the Ottoman Empire.

Vlad Dracul was not happy to simply serve as the governor of Wallachia and started to gather supporters in 1431 with the aim of taking over control from Alexandru I, the residing Danesti prince. Five years later, Vlad Dracul succeeded with his plan and killed Alexandru and became Prince Vlad II. He took up residence in the palace of Tirgoviste, which is where the young Vlad Tepes had his first taste of the luxurious lifestyle that he grew to love.

After two years of his reign, Vlad II betrayed the Order of the Dragon by forming an alliance with the Turks. His next move probably had a devastating effect on his sons, as he offered Vlad Tepes and his younger brother, Radu, as security that he would not attack the Turks. However, in 1447, Vlad II was assassinated by one of his own relatives, John Hunyadi, who had devoted his life to the Order and did not approve of Vlad II's defiance. Despite the fact that Hunyadi tried to persuade Vlad II to join his Christian forces, he continued to remain neutral and sent his eldest son, Mircea, instead. The Christian army was completely destroyed in the Battle of Varna, although Hunyadi managed to escape. Hunyadi felt hostile towards Vlad II and Mircea and arranged for them both to be assassinated.

Although Vlad Tepes was granted his freedom after his father's death, Radu decided to stay on and support the Turks. While Vlad Tepes was still in captivity, he learned that his elder brother, Mircea, was buried alive after his eyes were gouged out by the boyars of Tirgoviste, and he started to plot his own revenge.

A BRIEF REIGN

The throne of Wallachia, which rightfully belonged to Vlad Tepes, was now occupied by the boyars. With the help of the Turkish cavalry, the now seventeen-year-old Vlad Tepes, managed to briefly seize the Wallachian throne, and became Vlad III. His reign was to be very short, because within two months, Hunyadi forced Vlad III to relinquish his throne and he fled to his cousin, the Prince of Moldavia. Hunyadi appointed Vladislov II to the post, but he unexpectedly set in motion a pro-Turkish policy, which Hunyadi could not accept. Vlad III turned to Hunyadi, despite the fact that he was his father's old enemy, and forged an allegiance with him to try and retake the throne by force.

In 1453, the Christian world suffered when Constantinople fell to the Turks. Hunyadi built up his strength and prepared for battle, but the attack on Turkish Serbia did not take place until 1456. While Hunyadi attacked the Turks, Vlad III invaded

Wallachia, defeating Vladislav II, to reclaim his throne. Hunyadi was killed at the Battle of Belgrade and his army defeated, news of which pleased the new ruler. Little did the citizens of Wallachia realise that this was to be the start of Vlad III's reign of blood and terror.

VLAD THE IMPALER

As soon as Vlad III was back on the throne, he set about getting his revenge, not only for his father's and brother's deaths, but also on those who usurped his power. He started by building himself a lavish home, Poenari Castle on the Arges River. The building of the castle was strenuous work and many of the slaves – the boyers responsible for kiling his father and brother – died in the process. Condemned to a life of slavery, their health suffered and many were forced to work naked as their clothes literally fell to pieces. Vlad III, did not see the slaves as human beings and treated them worse than animals. He hated weakness of any kind and he devised methods of torture to punish any insubordinatation.

Vlad III established his capital at Tirgoviste and one day he decided he wanted to cleanse his empire of those people who he considered to be lazy, unproductive, sick, handicapped or simply because they were born into poverty. He sent out a procla-mation stating that no one should go hungry in his empire and invited all his poor and unfortunate subjects to a banquet in the great hall at Tirgoviste. There was much excitement as the guests gathered in the hall, completely unaware that this was just Vlad's way of eliminating anyone who he considered tainted his ideal concept of what society should be. There was much joviality as the guests filled themselves with food and drink enjoying the luxuries provided to them by their generous prince. When everyone had taken their fill and were feeling complacent, Vlad made his appearance and stood in front of the crowd. The crowd cheered and raised their glasses in thanks. Vlad then asked them if they would enjoy never having to feel the pain of hunger ever again and if they would like to be free of any further worries. Of course, the crowd were enthusiastic, imagining a future life of constant luxury.

Vlad ordered his soldiers to board up the hall with all of his subjects still inside and then set it ablaze – not one person escaped. As if his treatment of his subjects wasn't bad enough, the atrocities he carried out against his enemies and anyone who disobeyed him, were far worse. He created an extremely harsh code of conduct for the citizens of Wallachia and anyone who broke the code was impaled and left in view as a warning. On St. Bartholomew's Day, he had impaled as many as 30,000 merchants who he said had disobeyed his trade laws. Their bodies were left to rot outside the city walls as a reminder of what would happen if anyone else dared to flout his rules.

Vlad soon became infamous for his inhumane cruelty and rumours spread about his empire that he ate the flesh and drank the blood of his victims. Vlad was very proud of his work and liked to arrange his victims in geometric patterns, using the length of the stake to determine their rank. Because he loved to see his victim's suffer, Vlad used impalement as his preferred method of torture as it was one of the most gruesome and painful ways to die. He carried out his torture in various ways, but he usually had a horse attached to each of the victim's legs and then a sharpened stake was gradually forced into the body. Vlad made sure that the end of the stake was not too sharp so that his victim would die slowly, and it was forced up the anus until it came out of the mouth. The impaled would then be hoisted up so that their own weight literally dragged them down onto the thick stakes.

Other hapless victims had their eyes gouged out, were decapitated, skinned alive, boiled, burned, dismembered, eviscerated and even simply disfigured just for Vlad's own entertainment. Turkish ambassadors who refused to remove their turbans in his presence were asked why they insulted the prince in such a manner. When they told him that it was their custom to leave their hats on, he repaid them by having them nailed permanently to their heads. Vlad watched in delight as the men writhed in agony as large nails were driven into their skulls.

Vlad was obsessed with a moral code and was particularly concerned with female chastity. Women who lost their chastity or were unfaithful to their husbands, were subjected to Vlad's cruelty. He went as far as having his own mistress disembowelled in public because she lied about bearing his child. In fact. Vlad loved to torture women, it gave him some sort of sadistic pleasure. He often had their breasts and sexual organs mutilated and it was rumoured that he forced mothers to eat their own babies.

It wasn't long before Vlad's tyranny was such that no one dared to oppose his laws. In fact his subjects were so scared that he flaunted his authority by leaving a gold cup on permanent display in the middle of the central square of Tirgoviste. The cup remained untouched as everyone was fully aware of what the consequences would be.

Many historians have tried to justify Vlad's actions on the basis of political necessity, although in reality it was probably his desire for revenge and a lust for overwhelming power. Throughout his reign Vlad continued his efforts to eradicate the old boyar classes out of Wallachia, determined to introduce his more modern approach and to gain a firm and respected footing in his empire. As he got rid of the boyars he replaced them with new, middle-class men – men he knew would be loyal to him.

BEATEN BY THE TURKS

For the most part, Wallachia had been free from attack from the Turks during the reign of Vlad III. However, a new sultan came to power in 1461 and the Ottoman Empire once again turned their attentions to Wallachia. Vlad was informed of the approaching Turkish army, and knowing that his army would be greatly outnumbered, he planned a daring venture. He waited until it was the middle of the night before leading a small elite force into the Turkish camp. His aim was to catch the sultan off guard and kill him in the hope of demoralising his troops. Due to the element of surprise and Vlad's knowledge of the rough terrain around the camp, his mission was almost successful, although they only managed to wound the sultan.

His attack on their camp only succeeded in making the Turks more determined and Vlad prepared to flee from Targoviste. His wife, who believed that escape from the Turks was impossible, committed suicide by jumping into a river from one of the battlement towers. Vlad managed to escape through a secret passage, with a few guards and his infant son, and fled across the mountains. Not wishing to leave anything for the sultan and his army, he ordered for his kingdom to be completely destroyed. Village after village was razed to the ground and the wells were poisoned.

When the Turks arrived at Targoviste they were shocked to find thousands of dead Turkish prisoners impaled on stakes outside the ruined city's walls. The stench of the decomposing bodies filled the air, which nauseated the sultan's army.

As Vlad and his party escaped through the forest on horseback, he was hit by tragedy for the second time. The servant who was carrying his young son dropped him by mistake, but the Turks were too hot on their heels for them to stop and pick him up. They were forced to leave him behind which meant that Vlad had lost two members of his family in one day. Seeking refuge, Vlad turned to King Matthias Corvinus of Hungary for help. King Matthias was fully aware of Vlad's evil reputation and as soon as he arrived he was thrown into prison in Visegrad, the Hungarian capital.

YEARS OF CONFINEMENT

Although it is uncertain exactly how long Vlad III was held in confinement, it has been indicated that he was a prisoner from 1462 until 1474. It is rumoured that Vlad continued his lust for blood during his years of internment, finding small animals such as rats, cats, birds and insects to impale on sticks just for the fun of it.

Over time Vlad was gradually able to win back favour with King Matthias. He also caught the eye of the king's sister, Ilona, who used her influence on her brother to allow Vlad to have his freedom. Although the king allowed them to marry, he told Vlad he had to remain within the constraints of the city. He was given his own rooms within the palace, which was a far cry from the musty dungeon he was used to. Vlad's new wife bore him a son and slowly, he managed to gain the confidence of the king until he was eventually granted full freedom.

RETURN TO THE THRONE

During his years of confinement, Vlad's brother Radu had occupied the throne of Wallachia. Radu was not very popular with the people of Wallachia and had made an enemy of King Matthias through his treachery to the Order of the Dragons. Surprisingly, Vlad still had supporters among some of his former subjects because, despite his cruelty, he had managed to create an orderly society that was totally free of crime. Vlad decided it was time to reclaim the throne and joined forces with King Matthias and Prince Stefan Bathory of Transylvania.

Vlad and his 5,000-strong Christian army were successful in defeating the sultan, but he never had the satisfaction of dethroning his brother, who had died of syphilis two years earlier. Radu had been succeeded by Prince Basarab the Old, a member of the Danesti clan. When Basarab heard of Vlad's approaching army, he fled along with his cohorts, leaving Vlad to take the throne of Wallachia for the third and final time. Although Vlad was back in power, things would never be the same again. Shortly after taking the throne, Prince Bathory and the majority of Vlad's forces returned to Transylvania, which left Vlad in a vulnerable position. Before he was able to build up a new army, a large Turkish army marched its way into Wallachia. Vlad, who had less than 4,000 men, was forced to march and meet the Turks.

Vlad, the ever fearless warrior, fought against all odds, refusing to accept defeat. Vlad died in this final battle against the Turks, although there is much speculation as to how he lost his life. Some reports say that he was assassinated by disloyal Wallachian boyars, while others have him falling in defeat. Another report claims that he was killed by one of his own men in error, as he was mistaken for a Turk while disguised in one of their uniforms. The one undisputed fact is that his body was ultimately decapitated by the Turks and his head sent to Constantinople. The sultan had it displayed on the top of a stake as proof that the vile Vlad the Impaler had finally met his death.

GILLES DE RAIS

Gilles de Rais is a fascinating historical figure with a Jeckyl and Hyde character. He was a brave and skilful soldier who, as France's military chief was a celebrated wartime companion of Joan of Arc, and yet this same energy and drive compelled him to commit sinister acts. It is hard to believe that the man who had helped save France from utter defeat during the Hundred Years War, kidnapped, tortured and murdered hundreds of peasant children – mostly young boys – in search of sexual thrills. His quest for more wealth to maintain him in his extravagant lifestyle would ultimately lead to his downfall.

GROWING UP

Guy de Rais married Marie d'Craon purely for political and financial reasons, and there is little evidence that they ever loved each other. Nine months after they were married, Marie bore two sons, Gilles (in 1404) and two years later Rene. The early years of Gilles life were relatively uneventful being raised among the gentry in the château of

Machécoul on the borders of Brittany. As the son of one of the wealthiest men in France, he was brought up by nursemaids and expected to behave like a miniature adult. He rarely saw either of his parents and it wasn't until he reached the age of seven – which is the age reason in French society – that he started his training to become a nobleman. He was trained in the classic arts and learned to read and write Latin and Greek. In addition, he was trained in military arts and the ways of the royal court. Gilles excelled at his military training, but when it came to his political skills, he was a little rough around the edges.

Marie de Rais died in 1415 and a short while later Guy de Rais was killed whilst out hunting boar in the woods near one of the family's large estates. Before Guy died, he had left a will giving instructions that his sons were to be raised by a cousin, Jean Tournemine de la Junaudaye. He left strict instructions that they were not to be raised by his father-in-law, Jean d'Craon, who was renowned for his bad temper. However, the terms of his will were ignored and the two boys were sent to live with their grandfather. Jean d'Craon's own son had been killed at the battle of Agincourt in 1415, which meant that Gilles became sole heir to the vast family fortune.

Jean d'Craon was a powerful lord with no ethics and was a poor influence on the two de Rais boys.

Where once they had been closely supervised and educated in morals, ethics and religion, in their new home at Champtoce castle, Gilles and Rene were allowed to run free. Once lesson that Gilles did learn from his grandfather, and one that was to have a great influence on his later life, was the fact that as heir to one of the largest fortunes in France, he was above the law. It was these years in Champtoce that the young Gilles developed the demons that were to haunt him in his adult life.

Jean d'Craon had no scruples about using Gilles to increase his own fortune, and when he was just thirteen years old, his grandfather negotiated a marriage between Gilles and Jeanne Peynel, the daughter of Lord de Hambye of Normandy. This unison would have made the d'Craons the most powerful family in France, but the French parliament forbade the marriage until Jeanne Peynel reached the legal age.

Ten months later, d'Craon tried to arrange a marriage between Gilles and Beatrice de Rohan, who was the niece of the Duke of Brittany, but again he met with no success.

When Gilles was sixteen, the subject of marriage was raised again and this time, with the help of his grandfather, he abducted his cousin, Catherine de Thouars. They were married in 1420, which meant that the de Rais fortune was now greatly increased.

GILLES THE SOLDIER

For the sake of brevity, Gilles' military career has been shortened to a few paragraphs. The insanity of Charles VI, and the power struggle which ensued, was the root of French problems. In 1420, Charles VI (controlled by his wife) disinherited his son, the Dauphin Charles VII, allowing a peace treaty with England that named Henry V as heir to the French throne. However, this was an unpopular decision. Many people in France considered the Dauphin to be the rightful heir to the throne, due to his father's insanity. Among the Dauphin's supporters were Jean d'Craon and Gilles de Rais. Gilles was Prince Regent at Chinon at the time and benefitted from the support of the Dauphin.

In 1429, a seventeen-year-old peasant girl called at Chinon demanding to see the Dauphin. She was a strange girl who claimed to have heard the voices of saints telling her she must go and relieve the besieged city of Orleans and deliver the throne to Charles. This young girl was Joan of Arc. Despite the fact that Charles thought she was mad, he decided it was worth a try and gave her an army. Charles told Gilles to accompany Joan on her mission, possibly because he noticed that Gilles seemed infatuated by the girl's boyish figure.

Gilles fought by Joan of Arc's side at Orleans and again at Patay, both times defeating the English army. By the time Gilles was twenty-four he had become a national hero.

At the coronation of Charles VII, Gilles was bestowed with the honour of collecting the holy oil with which the new king would be anointed. Gilles was appointed Marshal of France and was permitted to wear the *fleur-de-lys* in his coat of arms, in theory making him France's highest-ranking soldier. Little did anyone realise that just two years later Gilles' life of bloodlust and perversion would rear its ugly head.

GILLES THE MONSTER

After the coronation of Charles VII, Gilles retired to look after his estates, but after the life of glory in the army, it appears he found the life incredibly dull. It is thought that his first sexual murder occurred in 1431, and from then on his thirst for blood could not be quenched. Jean d'Craon, who seems to have suspected what was going on, died in 1432, which left Gilles with a completely free rein to do exactly as he wished. Gilles de Rais turned into a monster. He would lure young boys to his castle on some false pretext and then take them down to his 'chamber'. Here he would hang them from a ceiling on a rope or chain until they were barely conscious. Then he would take them down, assuring them that he meant no harm, and then Gilles would strip and rape them. After the sexual act, Gilles would cut their throat and decapitate them with a special sword called a *braquemard*. Unable to satisfy his sexual appetite, Gilles would then further abuse the dead body until he finally obtained satisfaction. After he had an orgasm, Gilles would collapse into a faint and had to be carried off to bed by one of his servants, where he would remain unconscious for several hours. While he slept, his accomplices would dispose of the body.

One of the youths that was brought to the castle was a young lad called Poitou. He was raped, but as Gilles prepared to cut his throat one of his servants pointed out that Poitou was such a handsome boy it would be worth saving his life and keeping him as a servant. Gilles agreed and so the life of Poitou was saved and he became one of his most trusted pages.

Gilles seemed to be transfixed by the act of dying, and with a macabre fascination he would watch the blood trickle down a child's neck until he became aroused. This type of depravity continued unabated for years, taking the lives of countless innocent children, until he was on the verge of ruin.

BLACK MAGIC

On top of his depravity, Gilles de Rais was also an uncontrollable spendthrift. He loved to hold lavish banquets lording over the proceedings like a Roman emperor. In a period of three years, he had spent what would be the equivalent of millions of pounds, which meant he had to start selling off some of his more valuable estates to fund his excessive lifestyle. Rene became extremely worried about his brother's behaviour and went to the king asking him to issue an edict to forbid the sale of any further land. Out of financial desperation, Gilles de Rais turned to black magic and alchemy in an attempt to reverse his fortune. Many years earlier, Gilles had borrowed a book on alchemy from an Angevin knight who had been imprisoned for heresy. Alchemy was outlawed in the fifteenth century, but Gilles thought he could see a way of making money.

Gilles wasn't solely interested in alchemy to increase his wealth. He also felt it would be a good way of giving him more power, something that he desperately craved. He felt that if he could harness a demon, it would make him the most powerful man in the whole of France. He asked a priest by the name of Eustache Blanchet to help him find a reliable magician.

Unfortunately, Gilles was so desperate for money he became gullible and was taken in by several con men. The first man claimed to be a goldsmith who said he had worked out how to convert silver into gold. Gilles met the man at a local tavern where he gave him a silver coin and left him alone to practise his trade. However, when Gilles returned, the man had spent his coin on a flagon of wine and was asleep in the corner of the tavern.

The second alleged magician, Jean de la Riviere, cost Gilles even more money. He took Gilles into the local woods and told him to wait in a clearing while he went off to summon the devil. When Riviere ran out of the trees with an ashen face saying that he had seen the devil, Gilles was completely taken in. The magician told Gilles that he needed supplies to continue, but of course after he had his hands on the money he was never seen in those parts again.

Finally, Blanchet introduced Gilles to a man named Fontanelle, who claimed he could conjure up a demon called Barron. Gilles, who despite his sadistic behaviour, had always remained a good Christian, so it must have been hard for him to have to participate in Devil worsip. Aware that he would need the Devil's help if he were to restore his wealth, he agreed to take part in a black magic ceremony.

Together with his cousin, Gilles de Sille and Fontanelle, they locked themselves in the dungeon of his castle at Tiffauges. Fontanelle warned them against making the sign of the cross or their lives would be in great danger. Sille, who was dubious about the whole thing, decided to stay by the window so that he could make a quick escape. Gilles, nervously entered the magic circle and watched the magician start to conjure up his demon. Allegedly, the three men were blown clear of the dungeon before the roof collapsed.

Still desperate for money, Gilles was not prepared to give up on his search for a genuine magician. In 1439, he asked Blanchet to go to Italy to find someone who was more skilled in the arts of black magic. This time he returned with a man called François Prelati. He was a handsome twenty-two-year-old homosexual, who soon charmed Gilles into believing he was a skilled magician. Gilles was completely taken in by his confidence and charm and could not see that Prelati was simply playing him for a fool. He told Gilles that to please the Devil they would need to offer a child's blood and parts of its body as a sacrifice. Gilles, who seemed to trust him completely, told him that he didn't have any trouble with that and soon found him a young boy. Gilles, who was still refusing to sell his soul to the Devil, was subsequently banned from taking part in any further ceremonies and so he left Prelati to his own devices.

Gilles was conned again and Prelati did nothing to improve his financial position. Gilles realised that supernatural beings were not going to get him out of financial trouble, and with predators hanging around waiting to pounce, his days were numbered.

During all this time, Gilles had continued to abduct and murder children, unable to give up on his perverse addiction. However, as more and more children went missing, the peasants from the neighbouring villages were starting to get suspicious. They accused Gilles of abduction, as many of the children had gone to his castle to beg for food but had never been seen again. During his years of murder, Gilles had come close to being discovered on several occasions. In 1437, his family seized his castle at Champtoce, when they heard he had threatened to sell it. Gilles was terrified because he had left the mutilated bodies of many children there. Luckily for him the bodies were not discovered, and he was able to remove them before his other lifestyle became public knowledge.

THE FATAL MISTAKE

His fatal mistake came in July 1440, after he had sold Mermorte Castle to Geoffrey de Ferron, treasurer to the Duke of Brittany. For some reason Gilles tried to repossess the castle and flew into a rage when he was denied access to what he considered was still his property. They keys were held by Geoffrey de Ferron's brother, who was a priest, and this was where Gilles made his big mistake. Instead of waiting until the priest was in his home, Gilles went into the church of St Etienne de Mermorte, grabbed the priest and took him outside, where he was violently beaten.

This meant at last the authorities had something with which Gilles de Rais could be charged. They had suspected that the nobleman had been leading a secret life for a long time, but up until that time there was simply no proof and nothing they could do about it. Bishop Malestroit seized the chance to bring charges against Gilles and on September 13, 1440, he was summoned before the court. He was charged with being a heretic, an apostate, a conjurer of demons and numerous violations against human nature, including sodomy, sacrilege and murder – in fact the indictment was forty-nine paragraphs long.

When the trial started Gilles de Rais was arrogant and defiant, intially repudiating the charges brought against him. He taunted his accusers, stating that he had been pardoned of any crimes because he had made a full confession to the Father Superior of the Carmelites.

However, as the trial continued his terrified servants finally surrendered their loyalty and spilled the beans. They gave details of the part they had to play in the slaughter of hundreds of young boys, which caused Gilles to change his tune. His once faithful servants described every gory detail of how their master loved to bathe in his victims' blood, decapitating them himself so that he could cover his face with the gore. They talked of obscene torture and sexual acts, details of which sickened members of the court to their stomach. However, the crime of murder, albeit multiple, was not as serious as heresy. If the judges could be convinced that he committed these crimes as a sacrifice to Satan, then he could be punished by death.

The following day Gilles de Rais arrived at the court wearing white to indicate his repentence. He stood up in the dock, showing no sign of the former arrogance, he confessed to a long list of crimes, which were so horrific they were almost beyond belief. Bearing his guilt, Gilles turned to the families of his victims and said:

> *You who are present – you, above all, whose children I have slain – I am your brother in Christ. By Our Lord's Passion, I implore you, pray for me. Forgive me with all your hearts the evil I have done you, as you yourselves hope for God's mercy and pardon.*

Gilles' plea of contrition had the desired effect, because when he was executed on October 26, 1440, the judges, the victims' families and hundreds of spectators could not hold back the tears. He was the first one to be put to death, but his associates followed soon after. As Gilles stood under the gibbet he sang *De Profundis* in a loud voice so that everyone could hear. He asked his henchmen to join him in prayer, and as he got down on his knees and bent his head, the hundreds of spectators prayed with him.

CONTROVERSY

Religion played an important part in the life of Gilles de Rais and evidence of his obvious piety is in direct conflict with the secret life to which he later confessed. This had led many people to doubt the validity behind his grisly reputation. There is no doubt that there were many people who would have stood to gain a tremendous fortune by declaring Gilles a heretic, as he was an exceptionally wealthy nobleman. In fact the Duke of Brittany was so certain of the outcome of the trial, that he disposed of his own share of Gilles lands just fifteen days before the trial started. There was also a good reason for the Church to fabricate a case against Gilles de Rais, because he was a serious challenge to their power over the king and court. If he was found guilty, it meant that the Church stood to gain his lands. There is also evidence that his servants were tortured into providing damning evidence against their master. Of course, the truth about Gilles de Rais will never be known and his reputation as a sadistic killer will probably always outweigh that of the heroic knight.

MARQUIS DE SADE

The flamboyant character of the Marquis de Sade secured literary immortality with his erotic writings, which in turn gave rise to the word *sadism*. Although the Marquis de Sade was never convicted of any crime, he spent much of his life incarcerated in various prisons and an asylum for the insane. It was during this period that he did most of his writing, elaborating on his unrestrained view of freedom, power, evil and desire and his radical defiance of pre-Revolutionary French morality.

THE YOUNG ARISTOCRAT

Donatien Alphonse François de Sade was born on June 2, 1740 in Paris, France, to a privileged aristocratic family. His father was Jean-Baptiste de Sade and his mother, Marie-Eléonore de Maillé, who was a distant cousin of the Prince de Conde. His father was a diplomat and a notorious, bisexual playboy. His mother was a distant woman, who showed her son little affection, and at the age of five, Donatien was sent off to live with his uncle, the

Abbé de Sade. His life with his uncle had a profound effect on the young boy, who learned the true meaning of hypocrisy. Although the Abbé was a man who regularly went to church, he also kept a mistress and, it has been alleged, ran a brothel. The young Donatien soon learned to despise the Church and its morality and to enjoy the pleasures of the flesh.

His experience at the Jesuit school, Louis Le Grand, where the pupils were regularly beaten, together with joining the army at the age of fourteen, possibly sowed the initial seeds for his love of violence. Until he was twenty-six, de Sade was in active military service, taking part in the Seven Years War. He found it hard to communicate with the other soldiers and remained a somewhat solitary character. Despite this, he managed to achieve the rank of captain by virtue of his bloodline.

THE HIGH LIFE

After the war, de Sade slipped easily into the aristocratic life in Paris, developing a love of the theatre and the arts. Despite the fact that he had a mistress, La Beauvoisin, de Sade regularly frequented brothels and often invited the prostitutes back to his house.

In May 1763, according to the wishes of his family, de Sade married a rich young aristocrat by the name of Renée-Pelagie de Montreuil. Despite the fact that he was an unfaithful husband, his wife proved to be surprisingly devoted to de Sade, even when the marriage vows did nothing to stem his debaucheries with the working women on the Paris streets. However, his love of orgies, blasphemy and subversion soon got him into trouble.

In October 1763, de Sade was arrested for his 'excesses' and sentenced to the first of what would be many periods in prison. His indiscretions were such that he wrote to the prison governor begging him not to disclose the reasons for his incarceration, explaining that his reputation would be completely ruined if the truth ever came out. After serving several months in prison, de Sade was released and exiled to live outside Paris, under the watchful eye of the French authorities. However, jail did little to dampen his lust and de Sade returned to his life of debauchery, despite the fact that a Paris police inspector asked the brothel madams not to release any of their girls for de Sade's pleasure.

The Marquis de Sade found it hard to settle back into Parisian life following the scandal of 1763. On his release he begged to see his wife, apologising profusely for having offended her. De Sade eventually retreated to live in his chateau at La Coste, accompanied for a short while by his mistress, La Beauvoisin. She played the role of his wife, even going as far as entertaining the Provençal nobility, but this was all to come to an unhappy end in 1768.

It was Easter Sunday when de Sade met a young widow called Rose Keller on the streets and, finding her attractive, he offered her a job as a maid. Keller went with de Sade to his small house in Arcueil where, according to the widow, he threatened to kill her before tying her to a bedpost and whipping her with a birch branch. Then he made gashes in her buttocks and poured molten wax into the wounds. Keller managed to escape by tying sheets together and climbing out of a bedroom window. She ran straight to the police and told them about her ordeal.

When the authorities questioned de Sade about what had taken place, he told them that Keller was a willing partner who agreed to be paid for sex and 'extras', but he categorically denied having made any cuts to her buttocks. When she was examined by a doctor, it showed that she had been whipped but there were no signs of any other injuries. Once again de Sade paid for his indiscretion and received two rather short prison sentences.

His wife stood by him, and when he was released they went to live in exile in Provence. For about three years de Sade managed to rein his passions and they played happy families. They had three children and de Sade, who seemed happy to be lord of his manor, produced several plays in his theatre. However, if his wife thought that he was going to play the dutiful husband and father for very long, she was under a serious misconception.

LIFE OF EXCESS

In 1771, the Marquis de Sade saw the inside of a prison once again, but this time it was over payment of a debt. It appears that when he was released, he went back to his old way of life and started off by upsetting his mother-in-law. He seduced her younger daughter, Anne-Prospre, who was not only a virgin and a canoness, but of course the sister of his wife.

In 1772, de Sade received the penalty of death for accidentally poisoning several prostitutes with Spanish fly. This was a drug, which he used for purposes of seduction, but it was dangerous as the amount required was minuscule and the difference between the effective dose and the harmful dose was very narrow. De Sade managed to escape to Italy, accompanied by his loyal servant, Latour, and Anne-Prospre. While in Italy, de Sade and Latour were both sentenced to death *in absentia*, and Anne-Prospre decided to take refuge in a French convent, where she stayed for the remainder of her life.

De Sade was caught and imprisoned in the chateau of Miolans, but he was able to make an escape thanks to his ever-faithful wife who, for some unknown reason, still supported him during his life on the run. They returned to live in his chateau La Coste and, with the help of his wife, de Sade hired several handsome valets, an illiterate but attractive secretary, a beautiful cook and several young prostitutes to work as maids. De Sade was in his element and spent the season at his country estate forcing the girls into various acts of humiliation and sexual indignity. However, his activities were soon to come to an abrupt halt as the cook became pregnant, the secretary was taken away by his parents and the girls, whose worried families had contacted the authorities, were dispatched to various convents and safe houses.

The Marquis de Sade was once again arrested on February 13, 1777, this time due to the contrivance of his mother-in-law, who had never forgiven him for seducing her daughter. He was imprisoned in the chateau at Vincennes before being moved to Aix to face the courts. However, he managed to escape while under guard and hid once again at La Coste. Having learned nothing from his previous experiences, de Sade immediately slipped back into his old ways. He enlisted the help of a local priest to bring in a new group of girls for his orgies, but this soon backfired on him. An outraged father tracked his daughter down to the chateau and attempted to shoot de Sade at close range. Luckily for de Sade, the gun misfired, but it was enough for him to re-evaluate his situation. He made the mistake of returning to Paris, where he was immediately arrested by the authorities on September 7, 1778.

A LIFE BEHIND BARS

In 1778, de Sade began an eleven-year term in prison, first at Vincennes, and then later at the notorious Bastille in Paris. Denied the decadent lifestyle and pleasures that he was used to, de Sade started to write down his fantasies, living out his dreams in the form of words. His works became more and more disturbing, describing severe sexual mutilation, rape, murder and incest.

It was during this period that he produced his famous works – *Dialgoue between a Priest and a Dying Man*, *The 120 Days of Sodom*, *The Misfortunes of Virtue*, *Aline and Valcour* and the first drafts of *Justine* and *Juliette*. Keeping his writing secret from his jailers, de Sade let his imagination run away with him, his mind matching the filthy prison cells where he was forced to spend his time. The contents of these works, along with other plays and numerous short stories, were so disturbing that they were secreted out of the prison and published anonymously.

The Marquis de Sade's philosphy was simple:

> *Lust is to the other passions what the nervous fluid is to life; it supports them all, lends strength to them all . . . ambition, cruelty, avarice, revenge, are all founded on lust.*

His most famous work, *Justine*, has been descibed

as 'fit for corrupting the devil' and goes into graphic detail about the sexual encounters of a young peasant girl.

FREEDOM

On Good Friday, July 14, 1789, following the outbreak of the French Revolution, the prisoners of the Bastille were freed by a revolutionary mob. This became known as Bastille Day, and the Marquis de Sade, with his new-found freedom, started to get involved in French politics.

His wife, who no longer wanted anything to do with her husband, asked for a separation. His children, who he had hardly ever seen, were strangers to him and de Sade was now free from the constraints of family life. With Paris in the heat of a revolution and enormous changes taking place throughout France, the petty crimes of the Marquis de Sade were no longer of importance. He became politically active, writing political pamphlets, and was voted as the President of the Piques section in Paris. As part of his duties, he presided as Grand Juror over many trials, including, ironically, that of his mother-in-law. Given that she had been instrumental in his imprisonment, de Sade could have exacted his revenge, but he did for her what he did for most of the prisoners, he dismissed the case. He was loath to apply the death penalty to anyone.

However, with the revolution came issues that de Sade was unable to accept. He started to advocate, somewhat hypocritically, for total socialism and the complete abolition of property, despite the fact that he insisted on keeping his own estates. The Reign of Terror, which took place between 1793 and 1994, saw thousands of public executions, something that made de Sade recoil in horror. Though he had committed far worse tortures to satisfy his own passions, he was unable to stand the sight of these indiscriminate deaths.

Now grossly overweight and no longer technically a marquis, de Sade was still unrepentant for his previous life. He still lusted after the pleasures of the flesh and, even as he penned his revolutionary documents, he continued to write his novels of sexual depravity. Unable to get financial backing, de Sade decided to sell off some of his family holdings, which enabled him to continue to write.

He resigned his post in 1793, but he didn't remain a free man for much longer. He found himself in prison once again, this time at the hands of the Emperor Napoleon's government, accused of writing damning literature. He served a 375-day sentence and wrote:

> *My government imprisonment, with the guillotine before my eyes, did me more harm than all the Bastilles imaginable.*

On his release, it appears that much of the old drive and cravings had gone. Once again he found himself in financial difficulties and was forced to sell La Coste, making himself a very small profit. The money didn't last long and he was forced to stay with a local farmer, far removed from his earlier luxurious lifestyle. He took a job as an actor in Versailles, which earned him about 40 sous a day, playing the part of Fabrice in his own play *Oxtiern*.

LIFE IN AN ASYLUM

In the early part of 1800, de Sade was forced to go into hospital, suffering from cold and starvation, and the thought of facing debtor's prison once again affected his nerves. On April 5, 1801, he was imprisoned in Sainte-Pelagie, but with his sanity now in doubt, he was moved to Charenton, an asylum for the mentally insane. Madame Quesnet, a woman who had taken pity on the now pathetic figure, pretended to be his daughter and managed to get a room next to de Sade's. Quesnet was a loyal friend and stayed by his side for the remainder of his life.

In the security of an institution, de Sade settled and once again started his writings. From inside the asylum he was able to publish *Philosophy in the Bedroom* and completed a modified version of *Justine* and *Juliette*.

He also started work on an immense ten-volume document called *Les Journées de Forbelle*, but, like his personal journals and memoirs, this work did not survive. Although de Sade continued writing, he became more and more paranoid and despite the fact that he was encouraged to stage plays with other inmates, their content was such that they often had to be stopped because they caused too much excitement.

The Marquis de Sade died peacefully in his sleep on December 2, 1814, at the age of seventy-four. To this day the word 'sadism' is synonymous with cruelty and bloodshed, and will always be connected with his name. Although there is no doubt he was as an incredibly disturbed man, possibly even a freak, who wrote extreme erotica, it must be remembered that he was also a product of nineteenth century France. The motto of the upper classes during this period was *plaisir a tout prix* – pleasure at any price – something that de Sade lived up to in every respect. It was a period of unrestrained indulgence, which even the clergy were not exempt from. Parisian police records show that many hundreds of monks, curates and other religious workers were caught in acts of indencency. Prostitution increased to an estimated 30,000 during the French Revolution and regulations were abandoned as it was felt that it would be an affront to personal freedom.

De Sade's family, who were embarrassed by his writing, attempted to have all of his works burned after his death, but many survived to be published a century later. His grave was desecrated many years on, in order to take phrenological measurements of his skull for the purpose of medical investigations.

His masterpiece, *The 120 Days of Sodom*, which was feared lost, was discovered in 1904, rolled up in a bedpost in one of his cells. It was published, despite earlier restrictions imposed by the Catholic Church, and the Marquis de Sade was declared as being a man who was 'ahead of his time'.

PART TWO

FEMALE
FIENDS

COUNTESS BATHORY

Erzsébet (Elizabeth) Bathory was a Hungarian countess who was purported to be a witch, a vampire, a werewolf and supposedly bathed in the blood of young virgins to maintain her youthful appearance. She is certainly one of the first women ever recorded to be motivated by bloodlust and is believed to have murdered as many as 600 young women in an effort to maintain her failing grasp on youthfulness.

TRAINING IN SORCERY

Elizabeth Bathory was born in 1560 in Hungary, approximately 100 years after Vlad the Impaler. In fact one of her ancestors, Prince Steven Bathory, was a commanding officer in Vlad's army. Her parents George and Anna Bathory, stemmed from one of the oldest and wealthiest families in the country. Elizabeth's cousin was the Hungarian prime minister, another relative was a cardinal, while her uncle Stephen became king of Poland. However, despite being rich and famous, the

Bathory family had a dark and sinister side. Inter-marriage within the family led to some major problems including psychoses, evil geniuses and an uncle who was a known devil-worshipper. Insanity and perversion ran in the Bathory blood, and Elizabeth was no exception.

Elizabeth was a fit and active child raised as Magyar royalty. She was a beautiful girl with delicate features, a creamy complexion and a slender build, but her nature did not match her appearance. From a young age she started to experience seizures and she had an uncontrollable temper revealing a vindictive side to her nature.

At the age of eleven, Elizabeth was betrothed to Count Ferencz Nadasdy, and in the spring of 1575 they married when he was twenty-five and she was still only fifteen. This was not an uncommon prac-tice in the sixteenth century, as the life expectancy then was only thirty-five to forty years. The wed-ding ceremony was a lavish affair, which joined together two Protestant families, and was held at Varanno Castle. Although Nadasdy added Eliza-beth's name to his, she defiantly chose to keep the name Bathory, claiming that her family name was older and therefore more illustrious than his own.

After the ceremony the couple went to live in the Count's remote, mountain-top Csejthe Castle, which overlooked the village of Csejthe in Transylvania. Count Nadasdy was a sadistic man with a love of the occult. Elizabeth shared his passion and was a willing pupil in her husband's lessons on how to 'discipline' the servants. He showed her how to beat them to within an inch of their life, or to cover their bodies with honey and leave them tied up outside to the mercy of the bugs.

However, Elizabeth was to experience much loneliness as her husband thrived on conflict and war, preferring the battlefield to his life of domesticity in the castle. Her home was deep within the Carpathian Mountains and deprived of any urban activity, life in the gloomy, dank castle became dull. While her husband was away fulfilling his passion, Elizabeth started to find ways of amusing herself.

She started to take young peasant men into her castle as lovers and sat for many hours in front of the mirror admiring her own beauty. She carried the disciplining of her servants so far that today it would be classed as sadism. According to accounts, she beat her servants with a heavy club, inflicted pain by sticking pins under their nails, and her harshest, and most favoured punishment was to drag girls out into the snow, pour cold water on them and leave them to freeze to death.

For the first ten years of their marriage, Elizabeth bore no children, which was hardly surprising as her husband rarely returned to the castle. Then around 1585, his visits became more frequent and she bore him a girl named Anna. Over the period of the next nine years she gave birth to two more girls, Ursula and Katherine and, in 1598, had her first son, Paul. Despite her appalling treatment of her servants, there is evidence that she was both a loving wife and mother.

Another thing Elizabeth did to occupy her time during her husband's absence, was to make frequent visits to her aunt Klara. She was an open bisexual who always had plenty of young, beautiful girls around her. During these visits Elizabeth would participate in orgies with women and it was then she realised her passion for hurting young girls.

THE TORTURE CHAMBER

It was also around this time that Elizabeth started to develop a serious interest in the occult. With the help of an elderly maid by the name of Dorothea Szentes, also known as Dorka, who claimed to be a real witch, Elizabeth was instructed in the art of witchcraft and black magic. As she experimented more and more in depravity, she enlisted the help of her old nurse Iloona Joo, her manservant Johannes Ujvary and a maid named Anna Darvula, who was allegedly Elizabeth's lover. With the aid of her new clan, they set up an underground room in the castle, which became known as 'her Lady's torture chamber'. It was here that she subjected young girls to the worst possible tortures that she could devise.

The more her victims screamed, the more excited Elizabeth became. The more copious the blood, the more her excitement heightened, watching in glee as their faces contorted in pain and horror. Before long, Elizabeth started to crave the taste of flesh and she started biting chunks of flesh from her victims' necks, cheeks and shoulders. Soon her obsession with blood and her own beauty drove her to new depths of perversion.

BATHS OF BLOOD

Count Nadasdy died in 1600, which meant that Elizabeth was left completely unsupervised to carry on her perverse activities. As Elizabeth aged, her beauty began to wane and, despite the fact that she tried desperately to conceal it with cosmetics and expensive clothes, there was nothing she could do to stop the ever-spreading wrinkles. Then one fateful day, a young servant girl who was attending to Elizabeth, accidentally pulled her hair while she was combing her long, almost black locks. Elizabeth was fuming and slapped the girl's face so hard, that spots of blood splashed onto her own hand. As the blood touched her, Elizabeth immediately thought that her own skin took on a new youthfulness, like that of the young servant girl. She asked Dorka and Johannes Ujvary to undress the girl and to hold her over a large bath while she cut her arteries. When the girl was drained of all her blood, Elizabeth stepped into the bath and soaked in the warm liquid, sure that she had now discovered the secret of eternal youth.

Believing that she would take on the qualities of her victims, Elizabeth asked her trusted accomplices to capture beautiful young virgins and bring them back to the castle. Young peasant girls were procured from the local villages on the pretext of being hired as maids. Every now and then a particularly beautiful girl would be brought down to the chamber and, as a special treat, Elizabeth would drink the child's blood from a special golden goblet.

After a period of a few years, Elizabeth started to realise that the blood of simple peasant girls, was having little effect on her fading beauty. She believed that if she wanted to regain her former youth and radiance she would need a better quality of blood. Following the advice of an old sorceress, Erzsi Majorova, Elizabeth arranged for girls of noble birth to be brought to the castle. In 1609, she established an academy, offering to take twenty-five girls at a time to finish off their educations. However, she didn't just *finish off* their educations – she brought them to an *abrupt halt.* These hapless students were consumed and killed in the same fashion as the peasant girls, culminating in a warm bath accompanied by witchcraft rites.

However, as more and more girls of noble birth disappeared, Elizabeth started to become careless and suspicions were aroused. During one particular frenzy of lust, her accomplices threw four blood-drained bodies from the castle turrets. Added to this, a Lutheran pastor of Csejthe named Reverand Andras Berthoni had been commanded by Elizabeth to bury the bloodless corpses in secret graves. However, just before he died he left a note regarding his suspicions about the countess. Local villagers who had seen the bodies of the girls outside the castle, took their bodies for identification and started adding two and two together. Countess Bathory's secret was out.

THE GRIM DISCOVERY

As the rumours became more and more widespread it wasn't long before they reached the ears of the Hungarian emperor. When he heard of the atrocities that had been taking place at Csejthe Castle, he ordered Elizabeth's own cousin, Count Cuyorgy Thurzo, who was governor of the province, to organise a raid of the castle.

On December 30, 1610, a group of soldiers, led by Count Thurzo, raided the castle at night. Nothing could have prepared them for the sights they encountered when they went entered the sinister Csejthe Castle. Lying in the main hall was a body of a young girl who had been completely drained of her blood. In another room they found a girl who was still alive, but had been pierced through the abdomen. As they went down into the dungeon, they heard the cries of young girls who were imprisoned, some of whom had been unbelievably mutilated and tortured. When they came across Elizabeth's torture chamber, not only did they find the countess herself but also the bodies of some fifty girls.

A FITTING END

Elizabeth Bathory never attended her own trial in 1611, partly due to political reasons, but mainly due to her nobility. The trail was mainly for show, and to make it even more official, a transcript was made of the whole proceedings, which still survives in Hungary today. All of Elizabeth's four accomplices were made to stand trial and a register of over 650 victims written in Elizabeth's own handwriting was produced as evidence. As the accounts of her tortures were revealed, even the judges blanched at the macabre and sadistic behaviour of a once beautiful woman.

While Elizabeth remained confined to her castle, her four cohorts were charged with vampirism, witchcraft and performing pagan rituals, and were sentenced to death. Two of the torturers were beheaded while Iloona Joo and Dorothea Szentes had their fingers pulled off before being buried alive. The Countess Elizabeth Bathory, who was found to be criminally insane, received her own form of fitting punishment. The emperor condemned her to lifelong imprisonment in her own castle, and ordered that stonemasons wall up the windows and doors of her bedchamber with Elizabeth still inside. The only light that permeated the room was a small opening through which her guards passed her food. As her sentence was read out, Count Thurzo stood up and said of Elizabeth:

> *You, Elizabeth, are like a wild animal . . .*
> *You do not deserve to breathe the air on earth,*
> *nor to see the light of the Lord. You shall*
> *disappear from this world and shall never*
> *reappear in it again. The shadows will*
> *envelop you and you will find time to repent*
> *your bestial life. I condemn you, Lady of*
> *Csejthe, to lifelong imprisonment in your*
> *own castle.*

In 1614, four years after her room was sealed up, one of her guards discovered that Elizabeth hadn't touched her food. When he peered through the small hatch, he noticed a haggard looking Elizabeth Bathory lying face down on the floor. The famous 'Countess of Blood' was dead at the age of fifty-four. During her years of confinement, Elizabeth Bathory never uttered one single word of remorse.

LUCRETIA BORGIA

Lucretia Borgia was probably Italy's most notorious female Renaissance villain with a passion for incest, murder and corruption. She was born in April 18, 1480, the illegitimate child of Cardinal Rodrigo Borgia and his mistress Vanozza Catanei. The Borgias were a family of Spanish descent, which relocated to Italy at the end of the Renaissance period. Cardinal Borgia, who later became Pope Alexander IV through bribery, behaved in a very unsaintly manner, having a string of mistresses, fathering many illigetimate children and holding wild orgies in his papal residence. Lucretia and her brother, Cesare, often took part in their father's debauched antics, and it was no secret that Lucretia had carnal relations with both men on more than one occasion.

Vanozza Catanei came from a poor background and had been the cardinal's mistress since 1473, an affair which spanned over ten years. She was a beautiful woman and loved the lavish lifestyle the cardinal provided for her and their four children – Cesare, Juan, Lucretia and Jofre.

Lucretia was a beautiful baby with blue eyes and blonde hair, who completely captured her father's heart. For the first three years of her life she lived with her mother, with regular visits from her adoring father. Vanozza was a widow at the time, but the cardinal arranged a marriage for his mistress to keep up appearances. Once she was remarried, the cardinal took all four children away and placed them under the care of his cousin, Adriana de Mila.

Lucretia's lifestyle changed dramatically during the next few years. Raised in the Spanish way by the Borgia family she learned a new kind of family loyalty. The young Lucretia came into frequent contact with important and influential people within the Roman society and she soon learned the art of socialising.

When Lucretia was nine she met a young lady who would have a great influence on her. Adriana's son, Orsino Orsini, married a fifteen-year-old girl by the name of Giulia Farnese. She was stunningly beautiful with a nature to match, and the two girls became very close friends. Lucretia looked upon Giulia as an elder sister, and the pair would spend hours dressing up and admiring themselves in the mirror. Her charmed life was to change when her father became Pope Alexander VI in 1492. Suddenly the family were in the limelight and things started to change. Adriana, Lucretia and Giulia (who by this time had been abandoned by her husband), were sent to live in a newly-built palace, Maria del Portico. The palace had a secret passage that led directly into St Peters, which meant Lucretia's father could visit his daughter whenever he pleased. However, it also gave him access to his latest mistress – Guilia. Soon rumours were spreading throughout Rome about the Pope and his concubine, and suddenly the Borgia family obtained an unsavoury reputation.

ARRANGED MARRIAGE

Despite everything that was going on around them, the three women remained close friends. Lucretia's father started to investigate possible beneficial marriage alliances and before Lucretia's thirteenth birthday, he had arranged and cancelled two betrothals to Spanish noblemen. Finally, when Lucretia was thirteen, he found what he considered to be the perfect match, Giovannia Sforza, Count of Pesare. The couple were married on June 12, 1493, with an arranged dowry of 31,000 ducats. Unfortunately, Lucretia's father and brother decided they had sold her in haste and felt she could be the perfect bait to get them a foothold in the house of Aragon. Sforza was declared as being impotent and the marriage was annulled due to non consummation. Sforza felt humiliated and outraged at the blatant lies and swore revenge against the Borgia family. Despite the fact that Lucretia was genuinely in love with her husband, she dare not go against the wishes of her father and brother, but this was to be a major turning point in the reputation of Lucretia Borgia.

The fact that Sforza had sired several illegitimate children and his first wife had died in childbirth, disputed the paper that he was forced to sign stating that he was impotent. After considerable pressure, Sforza was forced to accept the annulment, but he was so filled with bitterness and damaged pride that he hit back at the Borgia family with an accusation that would haunt them for the rest of their lives. Sforza spread the news that his marriage to Lucretia had been annulled because Pope Alexander VI wanted her for himself!

SCANDAL

When Lucretia found out that her father had planned the divorce, she fled to the convent of San Sisto in Rome. Lucretia felt that divorce was a humiliating affair and she left the palace without informing any other members of her family. Her father was furious and attempted to have Lucretia removed from the convent, however, the strong will of the Mother Superior forbade it. She told the pope that his daughter needed the peace and tranquillity that the convent could provide and for once in their life father and daughter were at a stalemate.

In February 1498, there were rumours circulating that Lucretia was pregnant. It was believed that the father was a handsome young Spaniard by the name of Pedro Calderon, who had been visiting the convent as a messenger for Lucretia's father. Cesare Borgia was furious when he heard the news and had the young man thrown into prison. Several days later his body was found floating, face down, in the river.

The baby from this liaison was born in secret. He was named Giovanni and was always referred to as Lucretia's 'little brother'. Lucretia's father claimed the child was a product of an affair between Cesare and his mistress, but all this subterfuge did was to lead people to believe it was a child of incest. Giovanni never inherited the Borgia title and spent his life as a minor functionary in the courts of Rome. He died half a century later in relative obscurity.

While still living in the convent, Lucretia received the devastating news that her brother, Juan, had been viciously murdered and his corpse thrown into the Tiber. The whole affair was covered up because Lucretia's father believed it was the work of his son, Cesare, over jealousy of his sister.

MARRIAGE NUMBER TWO

In 1498, Lucretia's father succeeded in forging an alliance with the House of Aragon and by the end of the year she was married to the seventeen-year-old nephew of the King of Naples, Alfonso, Duke of Bisceglie. The marriage was arranged in an effort to move Cesare one rung closer to his goal of marrying the King of Naples daughter, Carlotta.

Lucretia's second marriage turned out to be a genuine love match, but the Borgia family soon put pay to her happiness. Cesare had become jealous of his sister's obvious affection for her husband and, on top of that political changes had meant that her marriage served no useful purpose to the Borgia family. Alfonso was attacked on the steps of St Peters on the night of July 15, 1500. He was on the brink of death, when Lucretia, with a band of trusted guards, rescued him and took him to the Borgia tower in the Vatican. She nursed him and stayed by his side for the next month, but her efforts proved to be in vain. Although Alfonso was healing well from his wounds, Lucretia was eventually tricked by Cesare into leaving his bedside, giving him a chance to have Alfonso strangled.

Despite the fact that Lucretia was heartbroken, she once again remained loyal to her family. She left Rome, accompanied by the son she had with Alfonso. Meanwhile, Lucretia's father and brother left her to mourn while they arranged a more profitable marriage.

MARRIAGE NUMBER THREE

The next major event in Lucretia's life was an arranged marriage with Alfonso d'Este. The Este family were one of the most noble and respected families in Italy and ruled over Ferrara. They were horrified at the prospect of this union as Lucretia had a dreadful reputation, and they flatly turned down the proposal. After the constant pressure from the pope and a offer of a dowry of over 200,000 ducats, which they found hard to refuse, Alfonso finally relented to the marriage.

Although the marriage seemed doomed from the start, it survived longer than people expected. Lucretia bore Alfonso four children, but she carried on numerous affairs behind her husband's back. One of these affairs ended in a messy scandal, when a young poet by the name of Ercole Strozzi was found gruesomely murdered. Whether Lucretia arranged for his murder, or whether it was just another fit of jealous rage by her brother, no one is really certain.

In 1505, Lucretia became the Duchess of Ferrara after the death of her father-in-law, Duke Ercole. She quickly became the centre of court life and entertained many of the greatest poets of the time. Lucretia developed a close relationship with a humanist poet by the name of Pietro Bembo, flattered by the romantic poems be wrote about her.

HER LAST FEW YEARS

In August 1503, Cesare was preparing for an expedition when, in the middle of the preparations, both he and his father were taken ill with fever. It has been suggested that Cesare inadvertently poisoned his father and himself with wine laced with white arsenic that he probably intended to use on someone else. Rodrigo died as a result, at the age of seventy-seven, but Cesare, despite being desperately ill, recovered and returned to his life of ruthlessness and political intrigue.

Lucretia died in childbirth on June 24, 1519, possibly worn out having given birth to eleven children. She was only thirty-eight years old. Her husband, despite his early indifference, had grown to love her over the years. He was so upset by her death that he fainted at her funeral and had to be carried out.

Many feel that Lucretia Borgia's reputation as a licentious, bloodthirsty and power-hungry woman has been grossly exaggerated by historians over the years, and that she was not nearly as black as she has been painted. Although she certainly had a love of carnal excess, whether she was ever involved in murder is questionable. It is possible that Lucretia Borgia was just a victim of her father's and brother's ruthless repuations.

BELLE GUNNESS

In the early hours of the morning on April 28, 1908, Joe Maxon, a hired hand in the employ of Mrs Belle Gunness, woke to find his second-floor room full of smoke. He covered his mouth and opened the bedroom door, only to find the landing was engulfed in flames. He screamed out Belle's name and those of her three children – Myrtle aged eleven, Lucy aged nine and Phillip aged five – but got no response. He quickly shut his door again and then, only wearing his underwear, he leapt out of the window. He survived the fall and managed to run into town to get help. However, by the time the old-fashioned hook and ladder arrived at the farmhouse on the outskirts of La Porte, Indiana, it had already been reduced to a pile of smouldering ruins.

When investigators managed to get close enough to carry out a search, they found all the floors had collapsed and that there were four bodies in the cellar. One of the bodies was that of an adult woman, but it could not immediately be identified as Belle's, because the head was missing and, in fact, was never found. The other three corpses were all children, who were lying next the woman's body. Covering the bodies, was Belle's pride and joy, her grand piano.

The county sheriff, Albert Smutzer, who had been given the job of investigating the fire, realised that this was no ordinary case. It would not have been possible for the piano to be on top of the bodies if they had been asleep on the second floor at the time the fire broke out. It soon became evident that the four victims had been killed and their bodies placed in the cellar before the fire had even started, and that the fire had most probably been set to cover up the crime.

During his investigations, Smutzer discovered that Belle had gone into town the day before to see her lawyer. She had asked him to make out a will for her, leaving everything to her children. She also told her lawyer that she had been receiving threats from her ex-handyman, Ray Lamphere, who apparently had fallen in love with Belle. He became extremely jealous if a man called at the house to court Belle and would make a scene and threaten her. Belle became frightened and fired him on February 3, 1908. Belle told her lawyer that, 'I'm afraid he's going to kill me and burn the house.'

Smutzer wasted no time in arresting Lamphere, who asked 'Did widow Gunness and the kids get out all right?' even before the sheriff had mentioned that there had been a fire. Lamphere vehemently denied having anything to do with the fire and claimed that he wasn't even in the vicinity at the time. However, the sheriff had a witness. A young man by the name of John Solyem, who said he had been near the Gunness farm on that morning and he had seen Lamphere running down the road just before the building burst into flames. Solyem went on to say that Lamphere had found him hiding in the bushes and that he had threatened to kill him if he didn't leave. Lamphere was arrested and charged with four counts of arson and murder.

Smutzer organised a thorough search of the ruins to see if they could come up with some conclusive evidence. The missing head was giving him some concern and he decided to enlist the help of some of Belle's neighbours to see if they could identify the charred remains of the body. Two farmers and some close friends and neighbours all studied the corpse, and they were unanimous that it was definitely not the body of Belle Gunness. Detailed measurements of the corpse were compared with those on file in several dressmakers in La Porte where Belle had her clothes made, which further proved it could not possibly have been the widow who had died in the fire. When a biopsy was carried out on the internal organs of the corpse, it was found that the woman had been dead before the fire started and that the cause of death was strychnine poisoning.

A TWIST IN THE TALE

On May 2, a man called Asle Helgelein showed up in La Porte, looking for his brother Andrew. Asle believed that his brother had met with foul play after he answered an advertisement placed in a Norwegian newspaper by Belle Gunness. Andrew had communicated with Belle for several months, after which time Belle invited him to come and stay with her in La Porte. Andrew had apparently sold his property, takeng out all his savings and arrived in La Porte with assets of approximately $3,000.

When Asle heard nothing from his brother for several months, he became concerned and contacted Belle. She told Asle that his brother had left La Porte as the relationship had not worked out and that, as far as she knew, he had gone to Norway. Asle did not believe her story, as he knew his brother would have let him know his whereabouts, and so he decided to come to La Porte himself.

He went to see Sheriff Smutzer on May 4, and explained the situation to him and that he suspected his brother had been killed by Belle Gunness. He asked permission from the sheriff to dig through the remains of the Gunness farm. At first the sheriff dismissed Asle's accusations and denied his request. However, Joe Maxon came forward with a piece of information that the sheriff simply couldn't ignore. He told the sheriff that Belle had asked him to bring wheelbarrows full of dirt to an area where she kept her pigs. Maxon said that he noticed several large indentations in the ground that had recently been covered by dirt. Belle told him that it was where she buried her household waste and asked him to level the ground with the extra dirt.

On May 5, Sheriff Smutzer took a dozen men back to the farm and started to dig in the area pointed out by Maxon. About 120 cm (4 ft) below ground level, the sheriff's men discovered the first body. Unfortunately for Asle, it turned out to be that of his brother Andrew. The more they dug, the more bodies and body parts they uncovered, until they eventually made the gruesome discovery of over forty men and children buried in shallow graves all around Belle's property.

The sheriff still had the problem of identifying the body of the woman found in the fire. He decided to enlist the help of Ira Norton, Belle's dentist. He said that if they could find the teeth of the headless corpse, he would have no difficulty in ascertaining whether they belonged to Belle. They hired a former miner, Louis Schultz, to build a sluice and to start sifting through all the debris. This proved to be successful, and on May 19, Schultz uncovered a piece of bridgework that contained two human teeth, some porcelain teeth and a portion of gold crown. Norton soon identified it as being a bridge that he had made for Belle Gunness, and the female body discovered in the ashes was deemed to be that of the famous widow.

THE TRIAL

Ray Lamphere was brought to trial in November 1908. He pleaded guilty to arson but denied murder. Lamphere's defence was hinged on the fact that the body did not belong to Belle Gunness, and his lawyer cleverly introduced evidence that contradicted that of the dentist, Norton. He bought a local jeweller to court to testify that the gold crown on the bridge would have melted had it been in the fire, as the fierce heat had melted the gold on several watches and items of jewellery found in the cinders. Two doctors replicated the conditions of the fire by attaching a similar piece of bridgework to a human jawbone and placing it in a blacksmith's forge. The real teeth disintegrated, the porcelain teeth came out pitted and blackened, while the gold crown did in fact melt. Joe Moxon and another man testified that they had both seen Schultz take the bridgework out of his pocket and plant it shortly before he claimed to have discovered it.

On this evidence, Lamphere was found guilty of arson but was cleared of murder, and he was sentenced to twenty years in prison. He grew ill while in detention and died of consumption on December 30, 1909.

BELLE'S BACKGROUND

At this stage in the story of Belle Gunness, it will probably be helpful to give some detail about her background. Belle Paulson was born on November 22, 1859, in the small village of Selbu in Norway. Her family were extremely poor and from a very young age, Belle had to work as a farmhand. As she grew older and tired of the hard work and long hours, she grew jealous of her employers' lifestyles. She started to yearn for money and a different way of life and, in 1884, she married a man by the name of Max Sorenson, a detective for a local department store.

In 1896, the couple moved to Chicago and opened a sweet shop. Unfortunately, the business did not make any money and within a year it had been burned to the ground. When investigators looked into the fire, Belle told them that it had been started by a kerosene lamp that had accidentally exploded. However, when they searched the remains, no such lamp was ever found.

With the money from the insurance, Belle and Max bought their first house in the suburb of Austin. This house was also destroyed by fire in 1898, and once again they used the insurance money to buy a bigger and better home.

The Sorensons had four children – Caroline, Axel, Myrtle and Lucy. Caroline and Axel both died in infancy of acute colitis, the symptoms of which matched with those of poisoning. Both the children were insured and the insurance companies paid out to the grieving parents.

Max himself died on July 30, 1900, which happened to be the only day that two concurrent life insurance policies overlapped. Although the symptoms were those of strychnine poisoning, the Sorenson's doctor had previously been treating Max for an enlarged heart, and so no autopsy was deemed to be necessary. This was when Belle experienced her first real wealth; the insurance companies paid out $8,500, which was an exceptionally large sum of money in the nineteenth century. She used this money to buy the farm at La Porte, and moved in with her two daughters and a young ward by the name of Jennie Olsen.

Belle got married for a second time on April 1, 1902, to a man named Peter Gunness. Just one week after the wedding, Peter's infant daughter died while she was in the care of Belle. Peter also died in December 1902. Belle told the coroner that a piece of a sausage grinder had fallen off a shelf and hit her husband on the head. However, one of Belle's daughters told a friend that, 'Momma brained Papa with a meat cleaver'. No one took the accusation seriously and the authories ruled that Peter's death was accidental, which netted Belle a further $3,000 insurance money.

Belle continued to run the farm with the help of hired hands, one of whom was Ray Lamphere, who started to work for her in 1906.

Following the death of her second husband, Belle started to place lonely hearts advertisements in Scandinavian newspapers, in search of husband number three.

WANTED

A woman who owns a beautifully located and valuable farm in first-class condition, wants a good and reliable man as partner in the same. Some little cash is required for which will be furnished first-class security.

Neighbours later reported that they remember seeing several middle-aged men arriving with cases, but no one ever saw them leave. Jennie Olsen disappeared in late 1906, and when friends enquired as to her whereabouts, Belle told them that she had been sent to a Lutheran college in California. Olsen's was the second body that investigators discovered when they started excavations at the farm. As more and more people went missing, Belle got more and more visitors who had come in search of their loved ones and friends. Ray Lamphere, who was allegedly madly in love with Belle, became insanely jealous of her male visitors, which caused Belle to fire him.

The only person who is believed to have known the full story about the murders was Belle's closest friend, Liz Smith. She came to live in La Porte shortly after the Civil War ended and is believed to have had several prominent lovers in the area. Liz promised to tell Wirt Worden, Lamphere's lawyer, the whole story, but unfortunately she was taken ill and died, and consequently her secrets died with her.

DEATHBED CONFESSION

Ray Lamphere, however, gave a detailed confession on his deathbed, which shed light on exactly what had happened to Belle Gunness. The mystery of the headless corpse was finally revealed and she turned out to be a housekeeper that Belle had hired just days before the fire.

As more and more evidence was mounting up against Belle, she decided to make plans for the perfect escape. Belle, according to Lamphere, had drugged the housekeeper, then hit her over the head before decapitating her. She then took the head and dumped it in a local swamp, after first tying weights to it to ensure it did not come to the surface. Lamphere then claimed that she doped her own children with chloroform before smothering them to death and then dragged their bodies and that of the headless corpse to the cellar. She dressed the corpse in her own clothes and then removed her false teeth and placed them next to the body, so that people would think that it was her own body that had burned in the fire.

With the help of Lamphere she then set fire to the house and fled. Her savings accounts, which amounted to vast sums, had been cleared, and so it would appear Belle Gunness got away with all her ill-gotten gains.

In the years after the fire, there were many reported sightings of Belle Gunness, but it will probably never be known what really happened on the night of April 28, 1908. Some say she was a criminal mastermind, who carefully planned her escape, while others are still convinced that she perished that night in the fire.

NANNIE DOSS

Nancy Hazle Doss was born in 1905 in the Blue Mountain region of Alabama in the USA. She later became known as Nannie and also 'the black widow', because she not only killed off her husbands but members of her family as well. When she was eventually arrested, Nannie found the entire police interrogation highly amusing and became famous for her girlish giggle, which resulted in the police giving her the nickname 'The Giggling Granny'. Nannie Doss never showed any remorse and many believe that she never even realised she had done anything wrong.

THE YOUNG NANNIE

Twentieth-century records show that Nannie Doss was born out of wedlock and that her mother, Louisa, married James Hazel some time later. James Hazel had a bad temper and if he didn't get his own way, he made his feelings known by taking it out on his terrified wife and daughter. Nannie's school attendance was erratic; farm work always came first, and if she was needed to help out her schoolwork had to come second.

Nannie's method of escape from the daily torment was in reading her mother's romance magazines, which gave her an insight into how she believed life should be. She also developed a penchant for prunes in her early years, something that she used to her advantage in her later life.

Her mental instability was blamed on an accident when she was travelling by train to Alabama to visit a relative. The train had to make an emergency stop and Nannie hit her head on the seat in front of her. After this she suffered from blackouts, mood swings and severe headaches for the rest of her life. As she got older, Nannie became more and more obsessed with her mother's magazines and scanned the lonely hearts adverts, dreaming of the day she would be allowed to go courting. Her father did not allow her to date as he considered her time was far too precious to waste it on socialising, and he found more and more jobs for her to do around the farm. As each day went by, Nannie grew more and more unhappy. She was forbidden from wearing pretty clothes or makeup, as her father said it would only make her look like a whore. He told her that when it was time for her to marry, he would choose her a suitable husband.

THE ONE THAT GOT AWAY

Just as her father had promised, in 1921, he forced Nannie to marry Charley Braggs. Nannie worked with Charley at the Linen Thread Company and had only known him a few months before her father arranged the wedding. Instead of giving Nannie the life she dreamed of, marriage tied her down even more. The only family Charley had was his unmarried mother, who was a very dominant figure who made Nannie's life a misery. Charley and Nannie had four daughters, the eldest, Melvina born in 1923 and the youngest, Florine, who was born in 1927. To try and drown her sorrows, Nannie took to drinking and smoking, and over the years the couple spent less and less time in each other's company.

In 1927, Nannie's two middle daughters died from 'accidental' food poisoning. Charley, who was suspicious of his wife, decided to leave and took their eldest daughter with him. Florine had only just been born and was still dependent on her mother, so Charley decided to leave her behind. Charley had told his mother that he had become frightened of his own wife, who would never eat anything that she had cooked, especially if she was in one of her 'bad' moods. Nannie's mother, to the contrary, believed that her daughter was a loving and happy mother and that she would do nothing to harm her own children.

HUSBAND NUMBER TWO

To support herself and her baby, Nannie was forced to take employment at a cotton mill and went back to live with her parents. Once again, she returned to reading her favourite lonely hearts advertisements, but this time it went further than just dreaming. Nannie decided to write to the men that took her fancy, and when a 23-year-old factory worker by the name of Frank Harrelson wrote her a romantic poem, she was delighted. Nannie not only wrote back in a flirtatious manner, but she also went to the trouble of baking him a cake in the hope of luring him to Blue Mountain.

Frank was flattered and very taken with the picture of a very pretty, young lady. When he arrived on Nannie's doorstep, he told her that her picture had not done her justice and that he was captivated by what he called 'the fire in her eyes'.

Frank and Nannie married in 1929 and for a while they were truly happy. Nannie's happiness, however, was to be short-lived as just a couple of months later she discovered her new husband was an alcoholic. Several times the police had to knock on Nannie's door to tell her that her husband was drunk and had been brawling at the local tavern. Nannie was not amused and her moods became darker and darker.

Surprisingly, Nannie put up with Frank's drinking

for several years, and even when he started to beat her, she stayed put. Although she was desperately unhappy, the marriage lasted for sixteen years – perhaps Nannie had not yet perfected the art of getting rid of her husbands.

THE LOVING GRANDMA!

Nannie's two surviving daughters, Melvina and Florine, were now grown up and married. In 1943 Melvina had a son, Robert, and in 1945 she was pregnant again. The labour was a difficult one and, frightened that she might die, she asked for her mother to be at her bedside. Nannie was the dutiful mother and stayed with her daughter throughout the night, attempting to comfort her. Just before dawn, Melvina, Nannie and her son-in-law, Mosie, celebrated the birth of a lovely baby girl.

Only one hour later, when Mosie was asleep beside his wife in a chair and Melvina still dopey from the ether, the baby mysteriously died. Melvina was puzzled because the child had been born healthy, but she thought she remembered in her hazy state, seeing her mother poke something in the side of the baby's head. At the time she dismissed the matter, not believing that her mother would wish to harm her granddaughter. However, her husband confirmed her suspicions when he said he had seen Nannie turning a hatpin around in her fingers earlier that evening.

Melvina's other child, Robert, also died six months later, while being looked after by Nannie. Melvina had gone to stay with her father, Charley Braggs, following an argument with her husband, and had asked Nannie to look after Robert. His death was a mystery, and doctors recorded it as asphyxiation from unknown causes. Nannie played the grieving grandma and wept and wailed when they lowered the tiny coffin into the ground. What her daughter didn't know, was that Nannie had collected a $500 insurance policy, which she had taken out on Robert shortly after his birth.

Nannie, having perfected the art of murder, decided that now was the time to do something about her husband, Frank Harrelson. All she had to do now was wait for the right opportunity.

GOODBYE NUMBER TWO

On the night of September 15, 1945, Frank Harrelson had spent his usual evening down the local tavern. He returned home much the worse for wear and demanded his conjugal rights. Rather than suffer a severe beating, Nannie lay back on her bed and stared blankly at the ceiling, vowing that she would get her revenge.

The next morning, Nannie was tending her beloved garden when she hit something hard with her spade. What she uncovered was her husband's corn liquor jar, which he thought he had so carefully hidden. This gave Nannie an idea, and she took the jar to her shed, tipped out some of the liquor and replaced it with rat poison. She hid the jar back in the garden and continued to tend her roses.

Frank died the same evening of excruciating stomach pains and as he lay dying, Nannie could be seen at her kitchen sink washing out the empty corn jar with soap.

HUSBAND NUMBER THREE

Determined not to be on her own for too long, Nannie started scouring the adverts once again. Husband number three was a man called Arlie Lanning. Nannie had moved several times since the death of Frank, and when she met Arlie, she was living in Lexington, North Carolina. The couple were married within days of meeting, but he turned out to be little better than husband number one or two. Arlie had a reputation for being a drunkard and a womaniser, whereas Nannie was thought to be a brave and caring martyr. In fact, his drinking was so bad that he hardly noticed if his wife went missing for days on end. Nannie often took off to escape, sometimes going to visit her sister who was suffering from cancer or to visit Arlie's elderly mother.

When Nannie was at home she played the perfect housewife and her neighbours often remarked on how beautifully she kept her home. She became an active member of the Church and made close friends with the ministers and their families. Everyone sympathised with Nannie, and her friends did all they could to shelter her from the shocking behaviour of her husband.

The more Arlie drank, the more his health deteriorated until one day he was unable to get out of bed, suffering from excruciating pain. He only lasted a couple of days and died in February 1950. The doctor who examined him shortly after he died said that there was no necessity for an autopsy due to the fact that he considered his body just couldn't take any more alcohol abuse.

The whole town turned out for Arlie's funeral, not because they liked the man, but because they wanted to support his grieving widow. Nannie explained to her friends that the last thing her husband had taken had been a cup of coffee and a bowl of prunes, and that he became exceptionally ill and died just two days later. Ironically, the last words Arlie said to his wife was, 'It must have been the coffee!'

Arlie had left a will leaving everything to his sister, but oddly the house burned to the ground two months after he died, destroying any evidence. The only thing to survive the fire was Nannie's beloved television, which she had taken to be repaired just the day before. Nannie went to stay with Arlie's elderly mother while the insurance company carried out their checks. The insurance company eventually mailed a cheque to 'Arlie Lanning, deceased', which Nannie rapidly cashed. Nannie was forced to leave North Carolina shortly afterwards when Mrs Lanning died suddenly in her sleep.

Nannie then turned up at her sister Dovie's house in Gadsden, Alabama, where she nursed her until her condition worsened. She died in her sleep on June 30, 1950.

HUSBAND NUMBER FOUR

Nannie was now forty-seven, and her looks were certainly starting to fade. Her once lithe figure had widened considerably, and a double chin and glasses changed the appearance of what was once a very pretty face. Knowing that she no longer turned heads as she walked down the streets, rather than using her traditional method of reading the lonely hearts advertisements, Nannie decided to join the Diamond Circle Club. For a meagre $15 per annum, the correspondence club sent out a monthly news-letter giving details of its latest members. Nannie decided that she needed to attract a more mature man, rather than the handsome youths she had previously gone for, and a retired businessman by the name of Richard L. Morton of Emporia, Kansas, caught her eye.

Richard was smitten by Nannie and he immediately wrote to the Diamond Circle Club requesting that their names be removed from their availability list. He even wrote to the club thanking them for introducing him to the 'sweetest and most wonderful woman I have ever met'. Richard and Nannie decided not to waste any time, and they married in October 1952.

Despite being a middle-aged man, Richard had kept his good looks. He was tall, dark and half American Indian. Unlike her previous husbands, he showered her with expensive gifts and life in the plains of Kansas was, for a while anyway, quite blissful for Nannie. Within months, however, the marriage turned sour, as Richard ran out of money. Not only was he in debt up to his ears, but Nannie soon found out that he also had a mistress, which he told her in no uncertain terms, 'he had no intention of dropping'.

Richard's visits into town became more and more prolific and each time he stayed longer and longer. Little did he realise at that time that he had messed with the wrong woman!

His life was probably spared temporarily by the fact that Nannie's father died and her mother, Louisa, asked if she could come and stay with the couple. However, after just a couple of days with her daughter and son-in-law, Louisa complained of violent stomach cramps and suddenly died. Just three months later, Richard was also buried, having died of similar symptoms.

Despite the number of deaths that surrounded Nannie, no one seemed to question her. Once again it seems she got away with murder.

SAM DOSS

Sam Doss was a highway inspector for the state of Oklahoma. Despite being fifty-nine, he looked far younger and had retained his good looks. He was a home-loving man who took great care of his money, unlike the previous men that Nannie had been associated with. Nannie was delighted when Sam proposed to her in June 1953, but she soon tired of his boring ways.

Not only did he stop her from watching her beloved television, but he also denied her the pleasure of reading her favourite romance magazines. He told her that, 'Christian women don't need a television or romance magazines to be happy,' adding that they were the route to all evil. Bedtime in the Doss household was strictly at 9.30 p.m. and sex was very limited. The boring life soon became too much for Nannie, and she packed her bags and headed back to Alabama. Sam was soon hot on her heels, writing letters saying that he was prepared to change his ways. To show how much he loved her, Sam said that he was prepared to open up a bank account in her own name, so that she could spend money when she liked. However, when she continued to ignore his advances, Sam made the final sacrifice and took out two life insurance policies, naming Nannie as the sole beneficiary. This turned out to be a very big mistake – in effect signing his own death warrant.

Nannie returned to Oklahoma and for a month life seemed to be going well. However, one evening in September 1953, Sam sat down to a dinner prepared by his loving wife. After the main course, Sam pushed his plate aside and cut himself a piece of Nannie's famous prune cake. By the evening, like his predecessors, Sam was writhing in agony. Over the next couple of days he lost a lot of weight and eventually he had to be admitted to hospital. He stayed there for twenty-three days and was diagnosed with having a severe digestional tract infection.

Sam was released on October 5 and Nannie, who was disgusted that he should have survived her first attempt, went right back to where she had started. She had prepared him a special welcome-home dinner promising him that it would soon 'have him back on his feet'. She had cooked him a delicious roast pork dinner, which was in fact quite harmless. It was the coffee that followed that was laced with arsenic. By midnight, Sam Doss was dead.

Nannie's big mistake on this occasion was, in her hurry to kill husband number four, she hadn't waited long enough. Doctor Schwelbein, who was very upset by the death of his patient, decided to order an autopsy. He knew that Sam was healthy when he left hospital and to him it didn't make any sense. His suspicions were justified, Sam Doss had not died of natural causes. In the intestines and stomach, the doctor found enough arsenic to kill several horses. Nannie, who was unable to give an explanation about the poison, was immediately arrested.

THE GIGGLING GRANNY

During the hours of interrogation, Nannie behaved like a giggling schoolgirl. She kept maintaining that she was innocent and spent all the time thumbing through the pages of her beloved magazines, saying that she was convinced that she would find her ultimate mate. The investigator assigned to the case, special agent Ray Page, was getting extremely frustrated and told Nannie to put the magazine down and to pay attention to what he was saying. It was hard for him to get angry with a woman who appeared to be a sweet grey-haired, old grandmother.

Eventually, after various phone calls, Page learned that Nannie's previous three husbands had all died under similar circumstances. When the agent confronted her, Nannie replied, 'Are you saying, young man, that I killed all my husbands?' and broke into a fit of giggles.

Finally, Page could stand it no more and tore the magazine out of Nannie's hands, telling her that he was aware that many other people who Nannie had associated with had dropped dead.

Without her magazine to keep her amused, Nannie seemed to lose spirit, and eventually said, 'All right, all right.' She confessed to having murdered Sam Doss, saying that he had been a miser and hadn't allowed her the pleasures of television or her magazines.

'OK, there you have it. Can I have my magazine back now?' Nannie asked, seemingly unrepentant.

Agent Page said she could have it back as soon as they had talked about her other husbands. Nannie paused for a moment and thought, and then asked if they would return her magazine if she told them everything. Page promised and Nannie shrugged and winked at the agent saying, 'It's a deal'. Page could hardly believe what he was hearing. She told him that all she had ever wanted was a man to love her and take care of her, but she had always ended up with a 'baddun'. The confessions followed one after another and Page, who just shook his head in disbelief, simply handed Nannie back her copy of *Romantic Hearts*.

The following day agent Page and other detectives flew from Alabama to Kansas and North Carolina, and arranged for the bodies of Nannie's husbands, her sister Dovie, mother Louisa, grandson Robert and Arlie Lanning's mother to be exhumed. Investigators found arsenic in the bodies of all her husbands and Nannie's own mother. The remaining members of her family had most probably been smothered in their sleep. When Page requested that the bodies of Nannie's two daughters be exhumed, the request was denied as the government felt they already had enough evidence to put the granny away for the rest of her life.

Although Nannie was wanted in other states, she was only tried in Oklahoma. Nannie was declared fit to stand trial and the date was set for June 2, 1955 in the criminal court of Tula. However, her lawyers advised her to plead guilty to avoid going to trial, and she was subsequently given life imprisonment. She was spared the death penalty because she was a woman, but Nannie spent the remainder of her days in the Oklahoma State Penitentiary dreaming of eternal love. Nannie Doss died of leukaemia on the prison's hospital ward in 1965.

PHOOLAN DEVI

Phoolan Devi was one of India's best-known women, who was literally adored by thousands of lower-caste Hindus. Her career in crime started out as a quest for revenge against the traitorous Ram brothers, Sri Ram Singh and Lala Ram Singh. Sri Ram was the leader of a notorious gang of dacoits who incurred the wrath of Phoolan by murdering her lover, Vikram Mallah, while he slept at her side.

HER EARLY LIFE

Phoolan Devi was born on August 10, 1963, in the village of Gorha Ka Purwa, Uttar Pradesh, in India. Her family were sub-caste boatmen called *mallah* and she was the second child in a family of four sisters and one younger brother. Even though the *mallah* were poor, Phoolan learned pride from a very early age. Her father, Devidin, was a meek man with little backbone, who owned about an acre of land and a valuable Neem tree that grew on it. Phoolan and her sisters were constantly raped and beaten by their uncle, Bihari, who had made sure that the family inheritance belonged to him.

When Bihari died, he bequeathed the estate to his eldest son, Mayadin, and even as a young child Phoolan distrusted her cousin. She was right to distrust him, because it wasn't long before Mayadin showed his darker side. One night, while Phoolan's parents were away, Mayadin sent some men to cut down Devidin's Neem tree. He intended to sell the valuable wood and take the proceeds for himself.

When her father returned and saw that the tree had been felled, he said nothing, knowing that it would be futile to fight back. Phoolan was appalled by her father's lack of mettle and decided to take matters into her own hands. She was fearless and headstrong and confronted her cousin, demanding compensation for the Neem tree. Mayadin totally ignored her, but when she taunted him in public, he finally lost his patience and threw a brick at her head, knocking Phoolin unconscious.

Despite the beating, Phoolin was not prepared to give up and continued to jeer at her cousin, making him a public spectacle. Mayadin decided that he would silence Phoolin once and for all, and he arranged for her to be married to a man called Putti Lal who lived some distance away from her village. At the time Phoolin was eleven, while Putti Lal was a man in his thirties. As a young girl, Phoolin had no idea what was expected of her in a marriage, and she was soon subjected to more rape and abuse. When she saw the sight of his penis, or 'snake' as she called it, she was so frightened she cried and pleaded with him not to come near her. Fed up with fighting with his feisty young wife, Putti Lal, who already had another wife, decided to give Phoolin menial duties around the house. She was so miserable that she ran away from her husband and managed to walk all the way home, despite the fact that it was an exceptionally long way.

When she arrived back at her village, her family were horrified, a woman didn't simply leave her husband – it was unheard of in their culture. Her mother was so ashamed of her daughter, that she told her to jump in the well and kill herself. Phoolan ignored her mother's rantings, annoyed that anyone should decide her fate for her, and she decided to stay put and accept her family's condemnations. She never let up on Mayadin, even going as far as taking him to court for seizing property that belonged to her father. In court she would shout and cause a scene, resulting in her having to be physically removed.

Mayadin retaliated and accused Phoolin of stealing from his house. Phoolin adamantly denied the accusation, but was arrested anyway and received abuse at the hands of the police. After being beaten and raped she was thrown face-down into a cell full of rats and left there to die. She knew that her cousin was behind this injustice and, despite the fact that her body was greatly weakened, her mind and will became stronger and stronger. It was while lying in that cell that Phoolin developed a strong hatred for the way the majority of men treated women.

THE DACOITS

In July 1979, a gang of dacoits (or armed robbers), led by their notorious leader Babu Gujar Singh, set up camp on the edge of Phoolin's village. The villagers felt threatened by their presence and Phoolin, now freed from her cell, told the people of Gorha Ka Purwa to stand up for themselves. Babu Gujar, who learned of Phoolin's impertinence, sent her a note saying that if she continued in that manner he would kidnap her and cut off her nose. This was a traditional punishment for women who stepped out of line.

The next chain of events is only supposition, because Phoolin herself gave conflicting stories of what exactly happened. Apparently Phoolin was abducted from her village and taken to the dacoit camp, which was deep in the jungle, a trek which took several days. In the dacoit gang there were two factions – the thakurs, led by Babu Gujar Singh, and the mallahs, led by Vickram Mallah. Vickram had been impressed by Phoolin the first time he saw her, and realised she had a strength beyond most mallah women. When Babu Gujar attempted to rape Phoolin time and time again, Vickram tried to defend her, much to the annoyance of Babu Gujar.

He asked Vikram why Phoolan was so special, when they had raped so many girls before.

Vickram replied, 'I told you not to touch her. She belongs to my community . . . If you touch her, I'll shoot you.'

Babu Gujar ignored Vickram and continued to abuse Phoolan, which resulted in Vickram killing him and taking over as leader of the dacoits. Phoolan had great respect for Vickram and it wasn't long before they became lovers. He became her mentor and taught Phoolin how to use a rifle, and before long she took part in all the gang's activities. For once in her life her bold and fearless nature was respected, and she saw their raids as a way of oppressing the upper-castes and redistributing their wealth.

Phoolan and Vickram enjoyed a life of romance and adventure, similar to that of Bonnie and Clyde. Vickram was the first person to show Phoolan that life could be good and he treated her well. However, just like Bonnie and Clyde, the good times were soon to run out.

THE RIVAL

Sri Ram was a member of the thakur caste, who had spent time in prison with Vikram. In prison Sri Ram became Vikram's 'guru' and taught him many lessons on the ways of gang life. When Vikram was released from prison, he managed to raise 80,000 rupees to bail out Sri Ram and his brother Lala Ram. On his release, Vikram told Sri Ram that due to his seniority and experience he should take over as leader of the dacoit gang, but this met with a lot of opposition from other members as they were distrustful of Sri Ram. Phoolan was also doubtful about Vikram's decision and made her feelings known. Gradually the gang divided into two separate factions – Vikram's men and Sri Ram's men.

Phoolan and Vikram had been invited to a wedding in a neighbouring village, and as they prepared to leave with some of their gang members, the two Ram brothers approached them and told them they would like to come as well. They set off down the road just after it turned dark, carrying torches to light their way. After a couple of hours they stopped along the road to buy some melon, but as Vikram went to take his first bite, two shots rang out from a field close by. Vikram immediately collapsed on the floor and when Phoolan rushed over to him, she found he had been shot twice in the back.

She looked around and noticed that Sri Ram was missing. Due to the rivalry between him and Vikram, she had no doubt that he had been the one that had fired the shots. To try and stem the flow of blood coming from Vikram's wounds, Phoolan tied cloth around his torso and managed to get him carried to a doctor. After being examined, the doctor said it would be too dangerous to remove the bullet as it was lodged too close to his spine. Vikram was expected to die, but despite the doctor's prognosis, several weeks later he was able to get out of bed and walk.

As Vikram became stronger, he gathered his gang members around him and soon they were back to their old ways of raiding and looting. However, tension within the gang was rife and Phoolan could not rest easy at night. She would sit outside his tent with her rifle poised. One evening she let her guard drop and decided to spend the night with her lover, but she was woken in the middle of the night by the sound of gunfire. As her eyes started to focus in the dark she could clearly see the outline of Sri Ram holding a gun as Vikram whispered, 'Phoolan. It's him. The bastard shot me . . .'

Sri Ram dragged Phoolan from the tent and when she struggled he hit her over the head with the butt of his rifle. She was carried to the river and forced onto a boat. As the boat was pushed away from the shore she turned to Sri Ram and asked him why he hadn't killed her as well.

'Oh, you can still be a great deal of use,' Sri Ram replied with a grotesque smirk on his face.

TORTURE AND HUMILIATION

When the boat pulled into the bank, Phoolan, who had been dragged naked from her tent, had to put up with further humiliation as she was led into a village. She was made to stand in the centre of the village while Sri Ram publicly declared that she had just killed her lover, Vikram. This news incited the men of the village and they demanded that she should be punished. Sri Ram was the first to rape her and then she was literally passed from man to man. Added to this she was beaten and cursed and called a '*mallah* whore'. Phoolan had to endure this type of torture for over three weeks. She was bruised and filthy from being dragged around on the end of a leash like a dog, but all the time she resolved to keep her strength so that she could one day get her revenge.

When Phoolan felt she could take no more she was finally rescued by an elderly Brahmin. Her face was barely recognizable, it was so swollen and covered with blood. Her rescuer managed to sneak into the camp where the dacoits were holding Phoolin, and he took her away on the back on a cart drawn by an ox. He took her deep into the jungle where she was nursed back to health by one of the villager's wives. Although most of her wounds had healed, there was one that would never recover, and that was her hatred of Sri Ram.

PHOOLAN'S OWN GANG

As soon as Phoolan was well enough to leave the jungle, she started building up her own band of dacoits. She arranged for the kidnap of two wealthy merchants, for which she earned 50,000 rupees in ransom and she approached another dacoit leader, Baba Muskatim, who she knew sympathised with her plight. Muskatim gave her ten of his own men to start her gang. One of the men she chose was a tall, bearded man with long black hair, called Man Singh. He told Phoolan to wear a red cloth tied round her head to symbolise her mission to get revenge. With Singh's help, Phoolan's hunt for Sri Ram began in earnest.

She went from village to village and became famous as an avenger for women rights. As soon as she heard of a rape or any abuse against a woman, she took it into her own hands to punish the man concerned. Phoolan interrogated villagers to try and glean information about the whereabouts of Sri Ram. Eventually, her thoroughness paid off and she found out that Sri Ram and his gang were in hiding in Behmai, a thakur village close to where she had been tortured. She led her gang to a village close to Behmai, but decided to lay low until she had perfected a plan of ambush. She was determined that she was not going to let Sri Ram get away.

When they finally attacked the village on

February 14, 1981, Phoolan divided her men into separate groups so that they approached from all sides. However, they did not have the result they had hoped for as Sri Ram and his brother were nowhere to be found. Phoolan was angry and was convinced that the villagers were hiding the Ram brothers. She told her men to round up all the young thakur men and bring them to her in the town square. Here she told the thakurs to line up and threatened them with death if they didn't tell her where the Ram brothers were hiding. The thakurs pleaded ignorance, but Phoolan still didn't believe them and started to hit them in the groin with the butt of her rifle. When they still denied knowledge of the men's hideout, Phoolan became even more enraged and ordered her men to start shooting at them. When her fury was spent, twenty-two of the thirty young men were dead.

THE BANDIT QUEEN

After the massacre at Behmai, the police began an intensive hunt to find Phoolan Devi. By this time her reputation had spread far and wide, and she had been given the name of 'Bandit Queen'. Dolls of Phoolan Devi, dressed as the Hindu goddess, Durga, were being sold in the markets of Uttar Pradesh and she was being glorified by the Indian media.

After two years of searching, the police came no

closer to arresting Phoolan, and Indira Gandhi decided to try and negotiate a surrender. In 1983, Phoolan was in poor health and many members of her gang members were dead. In February, no longer having the strength to fight, Phoolan agreed to a surrender to the authorities. Phoolan dictated the terms of the surrender as she said she didn't trust the police of Uttar Pradesh. She stated that she would only lay down her arms in front of Mahatma Gandhi and the Goddess Durga and not the police. She also made a list of conditions:

- She should not get the death penalty
- Her gang remaining members should not get more than eight years in prison
- Her brother should be given permanent employment
- Her father should be given his own plot of land
- Her whole family should be escorted to the surrender ceremony

Eventually, the government feigned to agree to her terms and an unarmed police officer arranged to meet Phoolan at Chambal. They walked to Bhind, where she laid her rifle before pictures of Gandhi and Durga watched by over 10,000 people and 300 police. Phoolan was charged with forty-eight crimes, including murder, banditry and kidnapping, but her trial was delayed for eleven years, during which time she remained in custody. The remainder of her terms were totally ignored.

Phoolin Devin was finally released on parole in 1994. She married Umed Singh, her sister's husband, and joined the regional Samajwadi Party, which represented the Hindu lower-castes. She became famous for her feisty, blunt-spoken public speaking and always managed to draw large crowds. Although she was elected as a Member of Parliament in 1966 for the Samajwadi Party, she proved to be rather ineffective and was defeated in the 1998 elections. During her election campaigns, which she ran with the same ruthlessness and passion that she used to run her gang, she was frequently criticised by the widows of the men she had killed in Behmai. Her supporters, on the other hand, hailed her as a larger-than-life heroine who fought for the rights of downtrodden women.

MURDER

Phoolan Devi did not trust anyone – her gang members, her lawyers, not even her husband – and told her friends that she had had a premonition about her death. She said that the thakurs of Behmai refused to leave her alone, and that she was living in constant fear, always having to watch her back.

On July 25, 2001, three assassins gunned down Phoolan Devi in broad daylight as she was about to enter her house in the Indian capital of Delhi. She had just walked home from a morning session in parliament, and was going to have some lunch. The leader of the assassins was a man named Sher Singh Rana, who admitted he had killed Phoolan as retribution for the Behmai massacre. However, there were also rumours that her husband, Umed Singh, wanted her dead because she had threatened to cut him out of her will.

However, when her husband was eventually questioned by the police, he was adamant that the murder of his wife had been part of a complex conspiracy. Umed Singh said he was convinced the key suspect in the murder, Sher Singh Rana, was just small fry and there was a much larger organisation behind the killing of his wife.

'This was no ordinary murder. There is a deep conspiracy behind it. The real killers have not been exposed by the police,' Singh said. 'She was my wife, but the whole world was her family. She was an MP and she was killed with such ease. It is no joke. I cannot take it lying down any more.'

On February 17, 2004, Sher Singh Rana, the prime suspect in the Phoolan Devi murder case, made a daring escape from the high-security Tihar jail. Despite the efforts of the police force's elite departments, the crime branch and special cell, they failed to track down Rana. Although special cell claimed to have cracked the case with the arrest of

Rana's brother, they still failed to lay their hands on the mastermind until 2006. He was eventually re-arrested in April by a special cell of the Delhi police at Dharamtalla in Kolkata. He was tracked down and picked up from his hotel room, carrying a passport that bore his picture but which had been issued in the name of Sanjay Gupta. The case is still ongoing which means that over six years later the Phoolan Devi story is still not over.

As for her arch rival, Sri Ram, who mercilessly tortured Phoolan, she had the satisfaction of receiving a note from his brother Lala, shortly before she surrendered in 1983. Lala told her that her enemy was now dead. Lala had killed his own brother when they had quarrelled over a woman.

MARIA LICCIARDI

Although the Mafia is by tradition a masculine-dominated organisation, some of the most feared operators in the modern Mafia are the *Madrinas*, or Godmothers. Over the past century, Mafia woman have been portrayed as the loyal, loving wife and mother, while their gun-toting husbands carried out their Cosa Nostra business. However, across Italy today, times are changing and women are penetrating the male world and are taking an increasingly high-profile role in Mafia activities. The first arrest of a woman suspected to be involved with the Mafia came in 1990, but by 1995 this had escalated to eighty-nine such indictments.

In an effort to keep the Mafia line 'in the family' after their husbands are either killed or incarcerated, it appears that women all over Italy have taken command of organised crime. Far from being a far gentler Mafia, these women are taking matters into their own hands, negotiating syndicate structures, clinching drug deals and ordering executions. For example, Concetta Scalisi was arrested in April 1999 on a charge of triple murder. She took over the reins, so to speak, when her father Mafia chief Antonio Scalisi, was murdered by rival mobsters in an ambush in 1982. His position was automatically passed down to his son, Salvatore, but he too was killed due to inter-clan feuding, just five years later. Concetta successfully showed herself equal to the task when she ordered the murder of three men who were seen to be a threat to the Scalisi family.

CAPPO DI TUTTI CAPPO

Maria Licciardi was considered to be the *Cappo di Tutti Cappo* (the boss of bosses) of the Camorra family based in Naples, Italy. Among Camorra women, she was respectfully known as 'the Princess' and has been described as a born leader with exceptional intelligence. Maria was born on March 24, 1951 in Napoli, or Naples, which is home to the Camorra family. The Camorra are thought to have got a hold on the city shortly after World War II, when they took control of the weapon and cigarette smuggling operations. Since then they have expanded into the drug trade and also control much of the real estate in the area.

Maria knew exactly what the Camorra represented. She had grown up in a world of violence with her brothers all taking an active role. Her elder brother, Gennaro 'the monkey' Licciardi, had been appointed the Camorra boss and earned a considerable amount of respect. Even her husband, Antonio Teghemié, was an active member, so Maria had never known any other way of life.

In the role of a mobster's wife, Maria had been taught to be loyal and tight-lipped, while she looked after her husband and raised their children. However, as the Italian government closed in on the Mafia bosses and put more and more members behind bars, the role of the women started to change. With most of their men either, dead, behind bars or simply not old enough to take over from their fathers, the women had to step in to fill the vacancies in the organisation. One of the first women to take a major role was Rosetta 'Ice Eyes' Cutolo. She assumed leadership when her brother Raffaele was put in prison.

Maria, however, had a much longer wait before she took control. She had to wait behind her two brothers Pietro and Vincenzo as well as her husband. It wasn't until they were all either incarcerated or killed that she got to play a major role. Her first major hurdle was proving to other members of the Camorra that she was worthy of the role, and she did this by setting up meetings with rival Camorra gangs. She boldly told the clans that the fighting and rivalry over territory had to stop, because it was of no advantage and it meant that everyone was out of pocket. Maria advised that the clans worked together in an effort to expand their smuggling, drug dealing and racketeering and in that way they could all make a profit. The leaders of the rival gangs agreed that what she said made sense and Maria realised that she had overcome the first hurdle.

Maria took full control of her family and made one of her first jobs to bring the Camorra into the prostitution business. Until she took over, the family had avoided the trade because of a code of honour, but under Maria that code was broken. They purchased girls from branches of the Albanian Mafia and put them on the streets, taking a high percentage of their earnings. Soon the money was rolling in. To stop the girls from trying to run away or becoming informants, Maria made sure they became addicted to narcotics so they would keep returning to feed their habit. When the girls became too old to become useful, the Camorra simply had them killed off.

Another business that turned profitable under Maria's leadership, was drug trafficking. The Camorra employed young dealers to sell heroine and cocaine on the streets, making sure they regularly changed their locations. Under the control of Maria Licciardi, the Camorra soon reached new heights, becoming even more violent and tight-lipped. The police found it hard to penetrate their organisation, as many people protected them and worked with them against the authorities.

OVERSTEPPED THE MARK

Everything was going exceptionally well for Maria Licciardi until one of her Camorra clan was not prepared to accept one of her orders. The disagreement was over a large shipment of pure, unrefined heroine, which Maria felt was too dangerous and would bring law enforcement officers flocking. She ordered that the shipment wasn't to be sold, but the Lo Russo clan went behind her back. They prepared the drug to be sold on the streets, but their disloyalty soon backfired on them. After just a few days heroine addicts, who had bought the forbidden substance, were found dead on the streets. It was not only the law enforcement officers that clamped down on the Camorra clan, but the public as well, demanding that something was done and fast. The peace that Maria had worked so hard at achieving started to crumble around her feet, as wars between the rival clans erupted once more. As soon as a member of the Licciardi clan was attacked, Maria declared war. It is estimated that as many as 100 mobsters were killed during this period.

Law enforcement officers started closing in and before long Maria Licciardi was on the 'thirty most wanted Italians' list. She decided it would be safer for her to go into hiding, but even from her retreat she still managed to control her family. As soon as Maria felt that prosecutor Luigi Bobbio and his men were getting too close, she decided to take appropriate action. In January 2001, she sent Bobbio a warning by bombing his office building. It didn't have the desired effect – in fact it had the reverse reaction – and Bobbio increased his forces and gradually started to break through the Licciardi wall. Bobbio arrested seventy Licciardi men, who all maintained a code of silence, accepting a term of imprisonment instead. Maria herself seemed untouchable and, apart from one photograph, the police really had no idea what she looked like. Bobbio felt sure that she would have changed her appearance while in hiding and they really were unsure of what to look for. However, he kept up the pressure and eventually Bobbio discovered the whereabouts of her hideout.

On June 14, 2001, the police raided a house and found Maria Licciardi looking exactly the same as the photograph they had recently distributed. Maria, who was now fifty years old, decided it was hopeless to try and resist arrest and she was taken into custody. Maria Licciardi's reign as the Camorra boss was now officially over.

ERMINIA GIULIANO

Another Camorra woman to take over the lead of a clan, was Erminia Giuliano. She took over the role as boss of the syndicate when her brothers Guglielmo

Carmine 'the Lion' and 'Little Liugi' Guglielmo were both arrested. She was nicknamed the 'Queen of the Clan' and showed the qualities of a true leader usually associated with crime godfathers. At the age of forty-five, the matriarch reorganised the syndicate's structure and daily operations and she eventually became one of the most dangerous criminals wanted by the Italian police.

When law enforcement agents got too close for comfort, Erminia went into hiding in her daughter's flat in the Forcella quarter of Naples, which was the heartland of the Giuliano clan. She managed to avoid arrest for ten months, but eventually the police managed to track down her hideout. They stormed the house just after midnight, destroying the front door as they charged into the flat. The flat had been used as a base to build a drugs, counterfeiting, extortion and gambling empire. Erminia was discovered hiding in a secret room, which was concealed behind a kitchen cupboard and a sliding wall panel. She was no wilting wallflower, and as the officers placed handcuffs on her wrists, Erminia told her daughter, 'I am counting on you now . . . I have taught you all the true values in life.'

Ironically, before she would leave the flat, Erminia told the officers she wanted a beautician to come and attend to her hair and makeup. She eventually walked out looking immaculate in her leopard-print coat and stiletto heels.

It took a while for Italians to realise the danger that women posed within the Mafia. However, they are now only too aware that women have become entrenched in mafia values just like their male counterparts. They have proved to be just as ferocious and ruthless as men – if not even more.

PART THREE

ORGANISED
CRIME

THE MAFIA

The Mafia, a secret criminal society, developed in Sicily in the second half of the nineteenth century, and later became prevalent on the East Coast of the USA after Sicilian immigrants settled there. The term 'Mafia' was first coined in 1863, in a play called *I Mafiusi di la Vicaria,* by Guiseppe Rizzotto and Gaetano Mosca, about the criminal gangs that were operating in the prison at Palermo. At the time, these gangs were a new phenomenon in Sicilian society, so the name was used to describe this new social group. Although its members were violent men engaged in organised crime, the Mafia were distinguished from common criminals by the importance they were given in Sicilian society. These men were the heads of large, often wealthy families, and as such held an important position: they often had connections with leading figures in the world of business, politics and local authority administration, and they saw themselves as patriarchs. They took it upon themselves to protect the weak in society, given that very little protection was forthcoming from the state, and liked to see themselves as benefactors of the community. Family values were held in high regard, and their members were governed by a vow of silence known as 'omerta'. Anyone, even a rival gang, found breaking the vow – ie. reporting criminal activities to the police, or collaborating in any way with the forces of justice – would be dealt with in the most brutal way, often tortured and murdered.

CODE OF HONOUR

Thus, although their business interests of drug running, prostitution, gambling and so on were much the same as those of any other common criminals, the Mafia were governed by a code of honour that they regarded as elevating them above the level of the ordinary crook. As the Sicilian ethnographer, Giuseppe Pitrè, put it:

> *Mafia is the consciousness of one's own worth, the exaggerated concept of individual force as the sole arbiter of every conflict, of every clash of interests or ideas.*

However, as became clear during the twentieth century and into the new millennium, the Mafia contained the seeds of its own destruction. The constant warring between the different families over territory led to a high rate of murder, with many of the leading figures in the Mafia being killed. While the members valued blood ties, they were not able in many cases to protect their families, even their children, who were often killed in revenge attacks. In addition, the corruption the Mafia introduced into the state bureaucracy, whether at central or local authority level, was not sustainable. Not only were there numerous clashes of interest, but in Sicily many high-ranking government officials were killed, and public services deteriorated to the point of chaos. Thus, the lawless reign of the Mafia in Sicily, and to a lesser degree on the East Coast of the USA, was unworkable, even within its own terms, causing the deaths of its own leaders and their families, as well as making life intolerable for those in the communities they professed to serve.

Another name for the Mafia – regarded by many of its members as the real name – is the Cosa Nostra, meaning 'our thing'. The name signifies adherence to a set of beliefs, traditions and values. Like many other secret societies, rituals are practised to initiate new members into it. In one such ritual, the young man is brought to meet three elders of the family. The oldest of the three tells him that he must protect the weak against the strong, and pricks his finger, spilling the blood onto the image of a saint. The image is then lit, and the initiate must hold it in his hands until it burns up, withstanding the pain as best he can, and swearing to uphold the principles of the Cosa Nostra.

THE BOSS OF ALL BOSSES

In order to regulate its business interests, the Cosa Nostra has a chain of command known as 'The Honoured Society', which imitates the corporate structure of a modern business empire. At the top of the command is the 'Capo di Tutti Capi' (the 'Boss of all Bosses'). Next in importance is the 'Capo di Capi Re' (the 'King Boss of Bosses'), who is usually a retired member. The 'Capo Crimine', known as the Don, and his right-hand man the 'Capo Bastone', lead the crime families and are involved in the day-to-day administration of illegal business dealings. The 'Consigliere' is the advisor, while the 'Caporegime' commands a group of 'Sgarrista', foot soldiers. At the bottom is the 'Picciotto', or 'little man', who is an enforcer, and the 'Giovane D'Onore', a person who is not of Italian origin but is associated with the organisation.

The history of the Mafia is a complex one, but essentially it arose out of the disruption caused by revolutions in Italy during the nineteenth century, and was initially concerned with cattle rustling, protection rackets and bribery of state officials. In addition, the Mafia styled itself as a Catholic organisation, in contrast to the secular state, gaining some adherents among the peasantry of Sicily. During the twentieth century, the Fascist regime began to prosecute Mafia members, so many fled to the USA and set up business there. In the wake of the war, Mafia leader 'Lucky' Luciano, who had been imprisoned in the USA, helped the US military to invade Italy by providing intelligence information, and helped to build up the organisation in Italy as a bulwark against the state. An additional benefit, as the USA saw it, was that many of the Mafia's members were violently anticommunist.

It has been alleged that, in exchange for his help, the US authorities allowed Luciano to run his Mafia interests in the USA, and later in Italy, where he was deported to after the war. Luciano set up major heroin trafficking networks between Italy, Corsica and France, with supplies from Turkey, establishing the so-called 'French Connection'. Later, in the wake of the Vietnam War, he expanded his operations to South-east Asia, establishing the 'Golden Triangle' and importing enormous amounts of heroine into the USA, Australia and other countries through the US military.

THE MAFIA TODAY

Today, the Mafia in the USA is a separate organisation from the Sicilian Mafia. It is thought to be the largest organised crime group in the USA, despite the fact that it was the subject of a major FBI investigation in the late 1990s. The Cosa Nostra is strongest in New York, Philadelphia, Detroit and Chicago. It also operates international organised crime networks across the world. Its activities include extortion, drug running, corruption of government officials, gambling, loan sharking, prostitution, pornography, tax fraud schemes and labour racketeering. Murder, torture and kidnapping are common ways of enforcing deals within the organisation. In recent years, Mafia members have become involved in more white-collar crime, such as stock manipulation scams and other nefarious financial activities. Some commentators have argued that in the twenty-first century, the FBI's preoccupation with tracking down terrorists, and the consequent lack of attention paid to organised crime, has led to a rise in Mafia activity in all areas of organised crime.

In Sicily, the criminal activities of the Mafia are still a major issue, and they constitute a serious threat to law and order in the region. During the 1980s and 1990s, rival gang wars took out many leading Mafia figures, to the degree that the organisation's power was seriously undermined. For that reason, the Sicilian Mafia, like their US counterparts, have begun to infiltrate the white-collar business world, recognising that large profits are to be made from underhand dealing on the stock exchange, which is a safer, less violent way to make money than racketeering, drug running and the like.

There have been a series of attempts on the part of government officials in the police and judiciary to prosecute Mafia members for their criminal activities, but many of these courageous individuals have been murdered by the organisation. For example, two magistrates, Giovanni Falcone and Paolo Borsellino, both from a poor area of Palermo, dedicated their lives to prosecuting members of the Mafia to improve conditions of life for their people. Falcone helped to set up the Maxi Trial, charging over 400 Mafiosi with crimes, over 100 of them in absentia. He gained the trust of Tommaso Buscetta, the first Sicilian member of the Mafia ever to inform on the organisation. He also cooperated with US Attorney Rudolph Guiliani (later Mayor of New York) to prosecute members of the Gambino and Inzerillo families there. However, both Falcone and Borsellino were killed in bomb attacks in 1992, which took place less than two months apart.

Today, there is some evidence to show that law enforcement is beginning to prevail in Sicily, and that the code of 'Omerta' is finally breaking down. However, other developments are that women are beginning to take control of the Mafia there, since so many of the male members of the organisation are now in jail.

TRIADS

The Triads are a complex group of underground criminal societies currently based in Hong Kong, whose network stretches across mainland China, Macau, Taiwan, Singapore and Malaysia. The Triads also operate in the Chinatown areas of many major cities across the world, from North America, Europe, Australia and New Zealand to South Africa. Like the Mafia, the main business interests of the Triads include drug trafficking, gambling, prostitution, money laundering, theft and many other forms of crime. In recent years, the Triads have become involved in piracy and counterfeiting of CDs, DVDs, computer software and other products. The gangs' speed in understanding and adapting fast-changing technology to their own ends has resulted in substantial profits for their members, and it has become more and more difficult for police to track them down.

VIOLENCE AND EXTORTION

Triads have a long history, beginning in the late eighteenth century, when a society called the Tian

Di Hui was set up in China. The members of Tian Di Hui, which means Heaven and Earth Society, were dedicated to the overthrow of the Qing Dynasty, and wanted to install a Han Chinese ruler in place of the Manchu emperor that led the dynasty. The society soon became popular and spread to many regions in China, spawning new societies, many of which used the symbol of the triangle to illustrate their names. These names often consisted of three parts (for example, the Three Harmonies Society, whose three elements were heaven, the earth and human beings). Eventually, the existence of these societies became known to the British government in Hong Kong, who called them 'Triads', referring to the use of triangle in their imagery.

The Triads slowly developed from a political group, with moral beliefs and aims, to an underground criminal organisation. This development took place over centuries, and at first the change was imperceptible. During this time, the Qing Dynasty was overthrown in China, which was in some ways a victory for the societies, but from 1911, some members, particularly those of the Hung Clan, found themselves without a political purpose. Having lived for years as outlaws, many of them were unable to adapt to ordinary life as citizens, and therefore began to form underground groups with a criminal, rather than political purpose. This was because they no longer received donations from the general public, but had to fund the organisations themselves. Instead, they began to extort money from ordinary people through violence and intimidation. Little was done to ban their activities, since the general population were so afraid of them.

CRACKDOWN ON CRIME

This bullying reached a peak in the early part of the twentieth century. However, in 1949, the Communist Party of China took control, and there was a crackdown on organised crime across the entire country. The Triads found it difficult to operate within their usual territories in China and were forced to move to Hong Kong, which was ruled by the British at that time. Here, they began to prosper, dividing the different areas of Hong Kong between the various ethnic groups, and operating a system whereby each area was controlled by its own branch. There were initially eight main groups: the Luen, the Yee On, the Fuk Yee King, the Sing, the Chuen, the Tung, the Rung and the Wo. This setup persisted into the 1950s, and the Triads became more powerful than ever in the 1960s and 1970s. During this time, the Hong Kong police began to collude with the Triads, leaving it to the thugs to control their regions as they thought fit, in return for a quiet life and, in some cases, a share of the profits. However, in 1974, after years of criticism, an independent commission was set up to stamp out police corruption, which did a great deal to limit the Triads' activities, especially in big business. The gangs were forced to take control of other areas of the economy, and began to operate in secret, conducting nefarious business dealings in areas such as entertainment, especially cinema.

Today, it is estimated that there are over fifty Triad groups in Hong Kong, including the Sun Yee On, the Wo Shing Wo and 14K. In general, they operate on a small scale, wielding power over small areas such as a street, a building, a market or park. Their organisation is complex, and in many cases there is no one overall leader, a situation that often helps them evade prosecution by the police. In some areas, small groups are formed as subsidiaries of larger groups (for example, the King Yee is a subsidiary group of the Sun Yee On), but these small groups do not necessarily take orders from the central group. A great deal of violence takes place among Triad members of different groups, but unlike the Sicilian and American Mafia, it is comparatively rare for Triads to involve outsiders, or the general public, in their gang warfare.

HANGING THE BLUE LANTERN

In modern times, few Triad gangsters earn their entire living from their illegal business activities as part of the clan, so the structure of the groups has become quite flexible. A Triad leader, or 'Red Pole', will have a small group of around fifteen men at his command, but most of these will be working in different fields as well as conducting Triad business. There is a traditional structure within the Triad group, consisting of the Mountain Master at the top; under him, the Vanguard, The Deputy, The Ceremony or Incense Master and, under them, the Advisor, or 'White Paper Fan', the Fighter or 'Red Pole', and the Liaison Officer, or 'Straw Sandal'. At the bottom are the Ordinary Members and the Temporary Members. However, in many cases, this structure is modified, and in some cases, ignored altogether, to prevent the police finding the kingpin of the operation. In a further effort to make the activities of the organisation impenetrable to outside observers, a series of coded numbers are used to identify ranks within the Triad structure: for example, the code 49 denotes an Ordinary Member of the group, whereas the code 489 denotes the Mountain Master. Some of the codes are now well known, having been used in the press and in films, so much so that the code 25, used to denote the 'spy', or undercover member of the group, has come into common parlance in Hong Kong, and is used to signify a traitor.

The once complex ceremonies and procedures used to initiate new Triad members have also been simplified in recent years. Today, the most common one is 'Hanging the Blue Lantern', in which the initiate gives an informal verbal promise to obey the leader. Also, the notion of moral duty and responsibility has changed within the Triad underworld; whereas in the past, a Triad member was expected to demonstrate his commitment to the group, whether or not it was in his personal interests to do so, today there is less onus on him to do so. In many cases, Triad members change their allegiances to suit their own ends; and this has resulted in an overall decline of the individual organisations, which can no longer rely on the loyalty of their members.

THE TRIADS TODAY

Currently, Triad groups are thought to exist in the Chinatowns of New York City, Chicago, San Francisco, Boston, Los Angeles, New Orleans, Seattle, Toronto and among other cities in North America. New Triad groups are also said to be moving into Amsterdam, London, Manchester, Dublin and Belfast, where much of their activity centres on the smuggling of East Asian illegal immigrants into Canada, the USA and the UK.

Today, the Triads are still powerful in Hong Kong. There have been several initiatives by the Organised Crime and Triad Bureau (OCTB) to try to combat the problem. Together with the Criminal Intelligence

Bureau, Narcotics Bureau, Commercial Crime Bureau, Customs and Excise Department and Immigration Department, the OCTB work to identify the leaders of the gangs and the territories they cover, to limit the expansion of the criminal network.

Since the police have not been given adequate authority to investigate matters under the law, a series of special Ordinances have been issued that are directly aimed at the Triads. It has now become a crime to manage a Triad organisation, with a punishment of up to fifteen years' imprisonment and a fine of one million Hong Kong dollars. Membership of a Triad group carries a penalty of three to seven years' imprisonment, and there are also fines for this, ranging from 100,000 to 250,000 Hong Kong dollars. In addition, a Witness Protection Unit has been formed to encourage the public to report serious criminal activities by Triad gangs. In recent years, there have been a number of scandals regarding high-level police corruption among officers working with Triad groups in Hong Kong. However, from the late 1990s to the present day, the proportion of Triad crimes in the city – at around three per cent of all crime – has remained fairly steady.

LUCKY LUCIANO

Lucky Luciano is a pivotal figure in the history of organised crime. As one of the most powerful Mafia bosses of the twentieth century, he almost single-handedly transformed the 'Cosa Nostra' into a massive underground criminal network, and at the same time masterminded the expansion of the drug trade, particularly heroin. By the end of his career, the Mafia had evolved from a few rival Italian families who were constantly in violent conflict with one another, to an international empire with a large number of ethnic groups connected to it, involved in all kinds of criminal activities from prostitution to drug trafficking to white-collar crime. Like his colleague Al Capone, Luciano was a ruthless, violent man who had absolutely no qualms about killing – viciously and repeatedly – to get whatever he wanted. And also like Capone, he was more than a common thug: he was a sharp-witted businessman, able to seize opportunities to make money whenever they arose, with a powerful personality which enabled him to rule those around him with a rod of iron. Not only this, Luciano was a patriotic American who ended up helping the American government during and after World War II, while serving a prison sentence for his crimes. The contradictions of his life were many, such that in later life he was deported from the USA, the country he regarded as home; and only when he died was he finally allowed to resume his place as a US citizen – as a corpse buried in a graveyard.

PIMPING AND PROTECTION RACKETS

Charles 'Lucky' Luciano was born Salvatore Lucania on November 24, 1897 in a town called Lercara Friddi, known for its sulphur mines, near Corleone in Sicily. In 1907, when he was ten years old, he moved with his family to the USA, in search of a better life. The family settled in New York, where the young Salvatore, or 'Charles', as he now became known, began his career of crime.

The year he arrived, he was arrested for shoplifting. He also set up a protection racket on the rough streets around his home, demanding that the younger children playing on the streets paid him a cent a day to protect them from older ones. The children who would or could not pay were given a beating. One of those who refused to be intimidated by Luciano was the young Meyer Lansky, who gave as good as he got when Luciano began to fight with him. In later years, Luciano and Lansky became firm friends, and both became leading Mafia bosses.

By the time he was eighteen, Luciano was involved in the drug trade and was sentenced to six months in a reformatory for selling heroine and morphine on the streets. When he was released, he was anything but reformed, and straight away he joined a team of criminals known as the Five Points Gang, headed by local gangster John Torrio. At one time, the members of the gang also included Al Capone, who was a close associate of Torrio's. The gang was a thorn in the side of the New York police, and were suspected of being involved in many serious crimes, including murder. Following his childhood interests, Luciano's special area of responsibility was the protection rackets; he also organised pimping and prostitution rings, and dealt heroine on the streets.

AMAZING SURVIVAL

Luciano's tireless commitment to the expansion of crime on the streets of New York soon attracted the attention of powerful local Mafia bosses, including Frank Costello and Vito Genovese. Luciano was promoted to work for them, and began to carve out a career for himself under the tutelage of the most influential Mafia families in the country, the

Masserias. Here, he built up an empire of bootlegging and drug trafficking activities, as well as running numerous prostitution businesses. However, his increasing profile as one of Joe 'The Boss' Masseria's right-hand men made him a target for a rival family, the Maranzanos. By the end of the 1920s, the Masserias and the Maranzanos were at loggerheads as they battled for control of the same turf, and it was Luciano who almost lost his life as a result.

Maranzano's men were sent to take out Luciano, and captured him as he stood on the dockside, waiting to receive an illegal shipment of drugs. The thugs bundled him into a car, taped his mouth shut, and took him out to the beaches of New York Bay, where they beat him, stabbed him and cut his throat. Assuming that he was dead, or about to die, they left him in a ditch. However, by some extra-ordinary chance, he managed to survive the ordeal. He was left with a large scar on his face and a drooping eye. Some believe that this incident was how he acquired the nickname 'Lucky'; others point to his skill at gambling as the origin of the name, since he was known for his ability to pick winning horses at the races.

RUTHLESS AMBITION

Unlike many Mafia men, Luciano had very little time for the traditional Italian way of doing business and had few family loyalties. He was a ruthlessly ambitious man, who would stop at nothing to achieve his ends and amass his fortune. Thus, he was happy to do business with ethnic groups outside the narrow world of the Italian Mafia, and indeed anyone who would advance his cause. In the same way, he had few qualms about getting anyone out of the way who tried to stop him. Thus, he joined forces with Jewish gangsters such as his old friend Meyer Lansky; he also did business with Bugsy Siegel. Together, the three went on to form the so-called National Crime Syndicate, with Luciano as the boss, Siegel as the brawn and Lansky as the brains.

Luciano's boss, Masseria, opposed this innovation of working with other ethnic groups. Masseria was also losing ground in the turf wars with his rival Maranzano. Realising that he was backing a loser, Luciano switched sides, and arranged for Masseria to be taken out. Six months later, he decided it was time to dispatch his new boss, Maranzano. Now, with all obstacles out of his way, he became leader of a large criminal network, which he went on to restructure. Instead of allowing the warring families to continue fighting over their territories, he gave each of them a separate responsibility for a different area of crime, and he also allowed non-Italian families to take part. His own role was to act as an arbiter of any disputes that arose, and to make sure that the entire network was running smoothly. What he had realised, in contrast to the Mafia bosses before him, was that everyone involved in the crime world would be more successful, and make a lot more money, if the different parties involved worked together instead of against each other – and if old feuds, as well as old loyalties, were swept away.

BROUGHT TO JUSTICE

For many years, Luciano's organisation, the National Crime Syndicate, ruled the criminal underworld. Working on a corporate model, Luciano formed a commission with a board of directors, whose task it was to discipline and regulate Mafia bosses. These included Frank Costello, Joe Adonis, Dutch Schultz, Louis Lepke and others. In addition, the National Crime Syndicate offered various services and perks to their members, including a hit man service, known as Murder Inc. As a result of such innovations, New York's criminal underworld, for the first time, merited the title of 'organised' crime, and it was Luciano who was largely responsible.

Since the Mafia had become so powerful, tightly-knit and well run, it was extremely difficult for the forces of justice to penetrate Luciano's defences. It took years of hard work and commitment for the US Attorney of New York, Thomas E. Dewey, to nail Luciano, who ruled over the underworld like a lord. However, eventually, Dewey was able to get enough evidence to charge Luciano with running a huge chain of prostitution businesses, and he was tried, convicted and given a long prison sentence.

While in jail, the US government asked him to help them with their military plans for the invasion of Sicily at the end of World War II. Luciano duly called on his contacts in the world of crime there, who aided the Allies in their manoeuvres. His reward was to be released from jail on parole, provided that he return to Italy.

On his release, Luciano went to Cuba to organise a crime syndicate, but he was soon found out and was forced to go back to his homeland. There, he continued to involve himself in the New York Mafia, handing out instructions from his base in Sicily. During this time, he became the subject of a murder plot, and also plotted several murders himself. In 1962, he was taken ill at the airport in Naples and died of a heart attack. A court ruled that, since he was now a corpse, he was no longer a deportee and could be buried in the USA. Thus, after his death, his body was flown to New York and buried at St John's Cemetery in Queens, in the country he always regarded as his true home.

AL CAPONE

Al Capone, known as 'Scarface', is one of the most famous gangsters of all time. Operating in the 1920s and 1930s, his career was based on the illegal trafficking of alcohol during the period of Prohibition in the USA, which gave rise to an enormous amount of organised crime and created millionaire bootleggers and gangsters in the process. Not only this, but the black-market trade also involved tremendous violence in which many people, not only gangsters but the general public, lost their lives.

Today, Capone is remembered for the St Valentine's Day massacre in 1929, in which seven men were machine-gunned down in cold blood as a warning to an enemy, Bugs Moran, who controlled rival gangs on the North Side of Chicago. He is also remembered as the gangster who combined vicious, bloodthirsty violence with a talent for business, in a mixture of calculation and brutality that fascinated both his friends and enemies. He was just as capable of conscientious bookkeeping as he was of beating a man to death with a baseball bat. His powerful personality intimidated almost all those who came into contact with him, and over much of his career, he ruled gangland Chicago with the tacit agreement of the police. He was placed on the Chicago Crime Commission's list of public enemies, but he was never charged with his violent crimes. Ironically, in the end, he was jailed for tax evasion, rather than for the murder and torture of his many enemies, as well as his numerous racketeering operations.

Alphonse Gabriel Capone was born in Brooklyn, New York, on January 17, 1899, the fourth child of nine. His parents, Gabriele and Teresina Capone, were Italian immigrants; his father came from Castellammare di Stabia, a village near Naples, and his mother from Angri, a town in the province of Salerno. Only five years before the birth of Alphonse, the Capones had left their home country and settled in the Navy Yard area of downtown Brooklyn. From there, they moved to the more salubrious area of Carroll Gardens, Brooklyn, where Alphonse grew up. It was here that he met his future wife, Mae Josephine Coughlin, and gangster Anthony Espitia, both of whom were to be important figures in his life.

A LIFE OF CRIME

The Capone parents worked hard to earn their living, and although by no means wealthy, they were better off than many of their recently arrived countrymen. Gabriel was a barber by trade and was able to read and write. His first job in the city was as a grocer, and after saving some money, he was able to open his own barbershop. In this way, he moved his family out of the immigrant area in which they had first set up home to a more prosperous part of the city, in which there were many different ethnic communities. As a result, Alphonse, or 'Al' as he now became, was unusual among his peers for his lack of ethnic, or even racial, prejudice, and later in his career, unlike many other Italian mob leaders, he did not restrict his social and business milieu to the Italian community.

Up to the age of fourteen, Capone stayed in school and did reasonably well, but as he entered his teenage years it became clear that, unlike his hard-working, law-abiding parents, he was headed for a life of crime. He joined two local gangs, the Brooklyn Rippers and the Forty Thieves Juniors, and became more and more unruly at school, until the situation reached breaking point. As a result of his disruptive behaviour, he got into a fight with a teacher: she struck him, and he responded by punching her. Not surprisingly, he was expelled from school, and after that date, he worked at odd jobs around the city, at one point selling sweets in a sweet shop, and at another, working in a bowling alley.

Capone's early career in the junior gangs gave him a good deal of credibility among more serious local gangsters, and he soon got to know Joseph Torrio, boss of The James Street Gang. From here, he went on to join the notorious Five Points Gang, along with Charles 'Lucky' Luciano, a childhood friend. Thus it was that two of the most famous gangsters in the USA began their careers at the same time, both of them ruthless men who would stop at nothing to achieve their ends and who became the godfathers of modern organised crime, building up a powerful network of illegal activities including bootlegging, drug trafficking, prostitution, gambling and protection rackets.

KNIFED ACROSS THE FACE

Capone got his nickname, Scarface, as a result of an incident that took place when Frankie Yale, leader of the Five Points gang, offered him a job working as a bartender in the Harvard Tavern in Coney Island. While at work, Capone got involved in a dispute with a gangster named Frank Gallucio, who knifed him three times across the face. These wounds led to Capone's lifelong nickname: Scarface.

Capone and Torrio then moved operations to Chicago, where the boss at the time was a man named Big Jim Colosimo, whose main business was running brothels. When Prohibition came into force, Torrio wanted to pursue bootlegging, recognising that the real money was in illicit liquor. However,

Colosimo wasn't interested in pursuing this line of business. Displaying the ruthlessness that was to become their trademark in the future, Torrio and Capone arranged alibis for themselves and hired their old friend Frankie Yale from New York to shoot Colosimo down in his own nightclub. The killing took place on May 11, 1920 and heralded the arrival of a new boss on the scene: Joseph Torrio, along with his right-hand man, the notorious Scarface.

As Torrio and Capone had predicted, there were huge profits to be made from bootlegging, and over the next few years, their gang built up a strong undeground crime network, As a result of usurping the territory of many other gangs in Chicago, they also made many enemies, among them Dion O'Banion, leader of the Irish North Side Gang. Thus, it was not long before Torrio and Capone called upon the services of Frankie Yale once gain, and in 1924, O'Banion was dispatched. As a result, the feuding increased, and the following year, Torrio himself was badly wounded in an assassination attempt. He decided to give up the business and passed control on to his protege Al Capone.

ST VALENTINE'S DAY MASSACRE

Although only twenty-five, Capone soon showed himself to be an effective leader, able to cooperate with other gangs thanks to his lack of prejudice against working with Jewish or Irish people. However, Capone brooked no opposition, and those who tried to usurp his turf paid a high price. This became clear when Bugs Moran, the leader of an Irish gang, got in his way. Capone decided to set an ambush for his rival, luring him to a meeting to make a deal for some bootleg whisky. His plan was that fake police would then arrive, disarm the Moran gang and shoot them dead. Everything went well: seven of the Moran gang were tricked by the fake officers, who lined them up against a wall and machine gunned them to death, killing six of them on the spot. The only problem was that Moran himself arrived late to the meet and thus escaped certain death.

On this occasion, Capone was not present at the massacre, although he ordered it. However, when two of his men, John Scalise and Albert Anselmi, were suspected of double-crossing him, Capone personally presided over their execution. The two unfortunate men were invited to a grand dinner in their honour, and at end of the meal. Capone was presented with a gift-wrapped parcel, which proved to contain a baseball bat. While his bodyguards held down the two victims, Capone beat them both to death with the bat.

BROUGHT TO JUSTICE

Capone was by now an extremely powerful figure in Chicago, and he intimidated all and sundry, including the police. In the suburb of Cicero where he lived, his minions were elected into local government positions, and he avoided prosecution for his illegal business activities by paying off police and politicians alike. However the FBI, now under a new director, Elliot Ness, was determined to break his power, and found a new way of doing so: charging him with tax evasion on their ill-gotten gains. Eventually, with the help of an inside informant Frank O'Hare, Ness managed to build up his case against Capone, and after years of hard work, he eventually managed to bring the gangster to justice.

Finally, Capone was convicted on several tax evasion charges, and in 1931, he was sentenced to eleven years in prison. He was incarcerated in Alcatraz and released eight years later, by which time his health had deteriorated. This was largely due to the fact that he had contracted syphilis, and it had remained untreated while he was in jail. After his release, Capone retreated to his Florida mansion, where he spent his declining years before dying on January 25, 1947.

ARNOLD ROTHSTEIN

Arnold Rothstein, nicknamed 'The Brain', was a true criminal mastermind who managed to make millions by bankrolling numerous criminal activities. During his lifetime, he was responsible for overseeing such activities as gambling, prostitution, bootlegging and narcotics smuggling and for transforming the New York criminal underworld into a network of highly efficient crime syndicates.

Today, he is best remembered for his involvement in the 'Black Sox' scandal of 1919, in which it was alleged that he had paid the Chicago baseball team to lose an important match in the World Series, in order to recoup profits from his gambling operations. However, Rothstein's involvement was never proved, and he was never brought to justice. Indeed, by the end of his life, he had never been convicted of breaking any law whatsoever. Nevertheless, there was a kind of justice in the way he eventually met his death: in 1928 he was shot, apparently in a drunken brawl, after failing to pay a gambling debt. Although Rothstein had not personally involved himself in any violent crime, his business dealings had constantly brought him into close contact with many cold-blooded killers, and it was his connections with such men that ultimately brought about his demise.

'THE BRAIN'

Rothstein was born in 1882 in New York, the son of a wealthy Jewish businessman, Abraham Rothstein. His childhood was an unhappy one: he felt that his parents did not care for him, and was very jealous of his older brother Harry, on whom they seemed to lavish affection. The young Arnold was educated at expensive schools, but he never did very well, although his mathematics teachers noted that he was extremely good with figures. By the age of sixteen, he had completely lost interest in his studies and dropped out of school. Initially, he found a job as a travelling salesman, much to his father's consternation. Brother Harry, meanwhile, had delighted his parents by becoming a rabbi. However, the Rothstein family were devastated when Harry became ill with pneumonia and died. Arnold was racked with guilt for his lifelong jealousy of his brother and returned home to try to make amends. He worked in his father's factory and began to observe his religious faith once more, accompanying his parents to synagogue. But the death of the favoured son had been a severe blow to Abraham, and he continued to reject Arnold. Arnold's plan to try to become closer to his father after his brother's death failed, so he now left the family fold for good and began a career in crime.

The first step was to use his mathematical ability in the pursuit of gambling. He started to hang around pool halls in the city and managed to earn himself a living by playing pool, poker and craps for money. By the age of twenty he had set himself up in business, booking bets on horse races, boxing fights, elections and baseball games. In addition, he also made loans to his customers at extremely high interest rates. To impress his colleagues and custo- mers, he began to carry a large stash of money around with him, earning himself the nickname, 'The Big Bankroll'. Carrying so much money on his person also enabled him to immediately finance any deals he made, wherever he was, whenever he needed to. However, he also had to employ a number of bodyguards to be with him at all times, in case anyone should try to steal the money from him.

SHADY DEALINGS

Rothstein soon gained a reputation as a hard-headed businessman who was far more intelligent than most of the criminal element he associated with. He began to make a great deal of money, which at first he invested in legitimate businesses such as shops and car dealerships. He also started a bookmaking business, which is thought to be the way he earned most of his large fortune. Although the bookmaking business was legitimate, it seemed that Rothstein was also involved in a lot of shady dealing behind the scenes, and he gained a reputation as a 'fixer'. He once remarked that he would bet on anything except the weather, because that was the one thing that he couldn't fix.

In 1909, Rothstein fell in love with Carolyn Greene, a young, up-and-coming actress. Legend has it that he impressed her by proposing to her in a restaurant with a large wad of $100 bills sitting on the table in front of him. Whether this story is true or not, Carolyn decided to marry him, and Arnold jubilantly took her home to meet his parents. However, the meeting was not a success. His father Abraham asked Carolyn if she would change her faith to become Jewish but Carolyn answered that she would not. As a result, the Rothstein parents remained implacably opposed to the union and did not attend the couple's wedding. According to some sources, on the day of the wedding, instead of coming to the service, Abraham Rothstein stayed at home and recited the Kaddish, the Jewish prayer of the dead, for his son.

Arnold told his new wife that he would endeavour to keep her in luxury for the rest of her life, and resolved to step up his income to support her. She knew that he was involved in the world of gambling, but later professed to know nothing of the details of her husband's business ventures. True to his word, over the years that followed, Rothstein began to build up a veritable gambling empire, setting up a number of pool halls across New York City. He also himself earned a reputation as one of the best pool players in New York, and he beat many opponents at the table, earning a great deal of money for himself in the process. But it was not only the pool halls that provided Carolyn with a life of luxury; there were numerous other ventures, some legal and some not so legal, that Rothstein presided over. This great network of interests was presided over by Rothstein himself, from his so-called 'office' at Lindy's Restaurant on the corner of Broadway and 49th Street. Here, he would stand on the street, surrounded by bodyguards, to collect money from those who owed it to him, and to conduct his business deals.

MAJOR PLAYER

Little by little, Rothstein became one of the most powerful figures in New York. His good manners and intelligence made him a pivotal figure. On the one hand, he consorted with corrupt politicians, on the other, with ruthless mobsters. He received protection from Tammany Hall boss Charles F. Murphy and his advisor, Tom Foley, and also from Mafia bosses such as Lucky Luciano, Meyer Lansky and Bugsy Siegal. As well as his gambling interests, he ran a real estate enterprise, a bail bond business and a racing stables. With his legal and illegal operations, he amassed a fortune and expanded his interests in and around the New York area. Today, Rothstein, along with Luciano, is credited with transforming the criminal underworld of New York into a series of organised crime syndicates, and being a major player in what later became known as the Mafia.

THE 'BLACK SOX' SCANDAL

As well as betting on horse races and baseball games, Rothstein was also rumoured to be a 'fixer'. The most sensational of these fixes hit the headlines in 1919, during the World Series, when it was claimed that members of the Chicago White Sox team had been bribed to lose the game to the Cincinnati Reds. In 1921, eight of the men were convicted of fraud and were banned from playing baseball again professionally. Rothstein was called to testify in the case, but denied any wrongdoing, shifting the blame onto a former associate, Abe Attell. Eventually, Rothstein was acquitted due to lack of evidence; however, it is believed that

Rothstein had placed bets on the Cincinnati Reds to the tune of $270,000.

After the scandal, Rothstein announced that he was retiring from the gambling business and ceased to have any direct ownership of his gambling houses. Instead, he covertly moved his operations into labour racketeering, drug dealing and bootlegging. In 1928, however, his luck ran out. He became involved in a high-stakes game of poker, which lasted over several days, and ended up losing a total of over $300,000. In the weeks afterwards, he was unable or unwilling to pay off his debts. Eventually, the host of the game, George McManus, called him to a meeting in a hotel room to discuss the issue, and in the fracas that ensued, Rothstein was shot in the stomach. McManus was arrested but later acquitted due to lack of evidence. However, the shot proved fatal, and several days later, Rothstein died. Thus it was that Arnold 'The Brain' Rothstein, one of the most powerful figures in New York society, met his end in a sordid quarrel over a game of cards.

BENJAMIN 'BUGSY' SIEGEL

People who know the history behind Las Vegas in the US state of Nevada, associate the *Flamingo* hotel and casino with a hoodlum by the name of Bugsy Siegel, but few appreciate just how big a criminal he was. By the age of twenty-one it would be hard to mention any crime that he hadn't been involved in. He was guilty of hijacking, bootlegging, narcotics trafficking, white slavery, rape, burglary, robbery, the numbers racket, extortion and numerous murders.

The nickname 'Bugsy' was generally used as a term of endearment among the world of gangsters, and was given to those who showed no fear in the face of danger. However, Benjamin Siegel hated the name with a passion, and anyone who dared to use it to his face risked their own personal safety. Perhaps it is strange, therefore, that the name he is best remembered for should be the one he hated the most. Siegel was not a man to be messed with, and through experience his associates learned to show him respect.

EARLY DAYS

Benjamin Siegel was born in 1906 to Russian immigrant parents. They lived in the deprived area of New York called Hell's Kitchen, where thousands of Irish, Italian and Jewish immigrants struggled against poverty and disease. It was a breeding ground for crime, and this is the world that the young Siegel vowed he would rise above. He learned early on in his life that in his part of the world, crime was the most lucrative occupation.

Siegel had a good childhood friend called Moey Sedway, and together they formed a minor extortion racket against the street vendors. Siegel would approach the vendor begging for some money, but when he was told to push off, Sedway would splash the vendor's wares with kerosene and throw a match onto the stall. The next time the two boys approached the vendor, he was more than willing to pay up. From there they moved up into the protection game, offering vendors on Lafayette Street security in return for money. It was while Siegel was running this racket, that he met another teenager, Meyer Lanksy – a young man with big plans. Together Lansky and Siegel gradually built up a gang of killers, which would eventually become one of the most notorious national crime syndicates in the USA.

Siegel and Langsky were of similar age and backgrounds, and they both had big plans for the future. Siegel was gaining himself a repuation as a fearless fighter, prepared to rush into gun battles without giving a second thought for his own safety.

In 1929, Siegel married his childhood sweetheart, Esta Krakow, who was the sister of a fellow hit man Whitey Krakow.

FIRST TASTE OF MURDER

In 1930, Siegel and Lansky joined forces with Charles 'Lucky' Luciano. Siegel became a boot-legger and carried out operations in New York, New Jersey and Philadelphia. His first taste of murder was in the form of a revenge killing for his associate Luciano. Lansky had close associations with both Jewish and Sicilian mobs, mainly because of his friendship with Luciano. When Luciano was imprisoned on drug charges, both Siegel and Lansky knew it was up to them to settle the debt.

The man responsible for putting Luciano away was an Irish policeman, and when Luciano was released he wanted immediate revenge. Lansky warned against him acting too quickly and told him to leave the matter in the hands of himself and Siegel. One year after his release, Lansky advised Luciano to take a short holiday and, while he was out of the way, Siegel and Lansky took their revenge.

The body of the nineteen-year-old policeman was never found despite a massive manhunt. Just as

Siegel and Lansky felt they were in the clear, a woman came forward saying that she had information regarding the murder. Luciano, Siegel and Lansky had the woman savagely beaten, but were caught in the act by the police. Although they were taken to court, the woman never turned up to give her side of the story, and the three men walked free.

Eight years later the same woman bumped into Siegel in a bar and jeered at him for being a violent thug. Siegel, who was not prepared to let the matter rest, followed the woman home and brutally raped her in a side alley. Siegel was arrested and charged with rape, but after a private word from 'Bugsy' all the charges were dropped.

BUILDING AN EMPIRE

In the years after the murder of the young policeman, Luciano, Siegel and Lansky kept a fairly low profile. They were keen to make money and used this time to carefully build their own criminal empire. They started to look at ways to fund their plans and decided they would overpower a security guard who was taking money to a bank. They were successful in this venture and got away with $8,000.

Although gambling was dominated by much more powerful New York gangs, Siegel and his friends decided they wanted in on the action. Siegel, in his own inimitable fashion, started challenging the bigger gangs and soon made his mark. He sent over twenty men to do battle with a rival gang which numbered over 100 members. Although Siegel was arrested during the affray, he had sent out a clear message that he was not someone who should be taken lightly.

Bugsy Siegel also made a vast profit out of the Prohibition laws that banned the sale of alcohol. He became involved with the illegal distribution of alcohol in New York and opened hundreds of underground drinking bars. As alcohol was smuggled across the USA, rival gangs tried to hijack each other's cargos. While Siegel was taking control of New York, his childhood friend, Al Capone, was busy supplying alcohol in Chicago. The two cleverly built up a network between the two areas that was of mutual benefit, and a great alliance was formed.

Charlie Luciano decided to join a rival gang, the Masseria, but still managed to stay good friends with Lansky and Siegel. The Masserias were at loggerheads with a rival rang, the Maranzanos, because the leader of each gang wanted to become the *capo di tutti capo* or 'the boss of bosses', so that they could take total control.

To try and help their friend, Siegel and Lansky thought up a plan to try and bring Luciano to power. Luciano arranged to meet his *capo* for lunch. While they were sitting at the table, a group of men, led by Siegel, walked straight in and killed Masseria.

Luciano immediately became the head of the Masseria gang. Not satisfied with this position, he also killed the head of the rival gang, Sal Maranzano, so that he eventually gained ultimate power.

RECKLESS BEHAVIOUR

As the reputation of Siegel and Lansky spread, so did their number of enemies, and it wasn't long before there was a contract put on their heads. The Frabrazzo brothers were the first people to take action, by placing a bomb in Siegel's house. Luckily for Siegel, he discovered the bomb just before it exploded and managed to throw it clear of the house. Although Siegel was injured in the blast, he managed to track down two of the Frabrazzo brothers and get his revenge. A third brother, Tony, who was scared for his own life, claimed to have written a book that incriminated Siegel and many of his associates. He said that as long as he stayed alive the book would remain unpublished.

However, Siegel, using his contacts, learned that Tony hadn't even started the chapter that would incriminate him, and so he made plans to take his life. At the time Siegel was in hospital being treated for wounds he received in the blast. He managed to sneak out of the room and meet up with some other gang members, murdering Tony Frabrazzo in front of his elderly parents. Siegel was then driven back to the hospital, where he climbed back through the window before anyone realised that he had gone.

Frabrazzo's murder was a big mistake for Siegel, who was forced to go underground for a while. Siegel, despite being very close friends with Lansky, was fed up with playing second fiddle, and he jumped at the chance when he was offered a new position on the West Coast.

BUGSY AND 'THE FLAMINGO'

Siegel and his family moved to a plush mansion in Hollywood and it didn't take long for him to slip into the glamorous new lifestyle. He got in touch with old contacts and, although Jack Dragna ran the gambling side of things, he reluctantly agreed that Siegel could take control of the unions. Using his union influences he was able to obtain large 'loans' from movie stars, which left him in an exceptionally powerful position.

On his first visit to Las Vegas, Siegel was not impressed, but he was sent there in 1941 by the Chicago Outfit crime syndicate to establish the Trans America race wire service to compete with the Continental Press in Nevada. It took him nearly six years to complete his task, but in the end he was able to eliminate Continental.

Initially Siegel only saw Las Vegas as a hot, arid place in the middle of nowhere, but it did have one major advantage, it was legal to gamble in Nevada. Siegel saw this as an opportunity to make money. He attempted to buy some already established gambling houses, but this wasn't successful until he met a man called Billy Wilkerson. Wilkerson had big ideas and wanted to build the largest and most luxurious hotel that Las Vegas had ever seen. He showed Siegel his drawings with individual air conditioners, tiled bathrooms and two swimming pools. Siegel himself had no experience in building whatsoever, but what he did have was some cash to help finance Wilkerson's dream. When Wilkerson's money finally ran out, Siegel bought the controlling interest and finalised his plans to build an oasis in the middle of the desert where travellers from both the East and West Coast could come for gambling, fine food, luxury accommodation and great entertainment. Siegel decided to call his dream 'The Flamingo', allegedly after his mistress, Virginia Hill.

Siegel encountered difficulties right from the out-set. Construction materials were difficult to get hold of and were extremely expensive, and conditions made it difficult to transport goods across the desert. Siegel talked some of his gangster friends into investing in the project, as well as the mob, and it was this factor that ultimately led to his death.

The project soon spiralled out of control. The initial estimate of $1.2 million had now escalated to $6 million, and Lansky and the other investors started to get worried about Siegel's desert dream. Siegel was a mobster, not a construction engineer, and workers ripped him off left, right and centre. By December 1946, one year after they started on the project, the casino was literally sucking the mob dry.

The organisation were not happy and wanted something done about Siegel, and fast. Meyer Lansky managed to convince them to give his friend one more chance, and that was to wait until Christmas when the casino opened. He said that if it didn't make any money after it opened, then the mob could put a contract out on Siegel's life.

When Christmas arrived, Siegel pulled out all the stops and arranged the most extravagant entertainment money could buy, in an effort to draw in the punters. There were big names on the venue such as Clark Gable, Lana Turner, Joan Crawford, Anne Jeffreys and Caesar Romero. However, despite his efforts, the punters didn't come, which was probably made worst by an appalling spell of bad weather. Added to that Lansky revealed even more disturbing news to the mob, and that was that Siegel had apparently been stealing money from the mob and placing it in numbered Swiss bank accounts.

By now the mob were after Siegel's blood, and once again his friend Lansky stepped in and saved the day. He told the syndicate that he was convinced that Las Vegas would soon become a very profitable resort. He suggested that they should put

The Flamingo into receivership to stop any further losses, and then the mob could buy out the original partners. Once again Bugsy Siegel had a reprieve.

THE LAST CHAPTER

The Flamingo barely limped through the month of January and Siegel decided to close it until the hotel rooms were completed. He felt the problem was, that with nowhere to stay, his customers were taking their money away and spending it elsewhere. Luckily, he still had the backing of Lansky and Luciano, who continued to believe that The Flamingo could make money. Siegel was exhausted. He spent every hour of the day making sure that the Flamingo would be ready for its grand reopening in March. Siegel's determination and hard work paid off. When The Flamingo reopened in March his dream came true. It showed a profit of $250,000 for the first half of 1947, even though the month of January had been a major disaster.

At last Siegel felt as though he could relax and he sent a wire to his mistress, Virginia Hill, and asked her to join him in Vegas. However, before long the couple had one of their famous arguments and Hill reportedly hit one of The Flamingo's female patrons around the face with a bottle. She was very quickly despatched to Zurich.

Despite Siegel's new-found glory, it appears that

the mob never really forgave him for the financial problems he put them through. On the evening of June 20, 1947, Siegel was sitting at home in his bungalow when a burst of gunfire smashed through the living room window. The first bullet hit Siegel in the head, causing his eye to shoot out of its socket. Four more bullets hit his torso, breaking his ribs and tearing holes in his lungs. Bugsy Siegel, at forty-two years of age, was dead.

Even though his death made front page news, not one of his mobster friends made the funeral, not even his most trusted and loyal friend Lansky. The only people to attend were five of his relatives. It is widely suspected that Lansky was under strict mob orders not to attend and, needless to say, no one was ever convicted of his murder.

For many years The Flamingo was definitely the best that Las Vegas had to offer. With more than 3,500 rooms it was one of the largest hotels in the world. Siegel's original Flamingo hotel was pulled down in the 1980s and replaced when the Hilton Corporation bought the site and put up their own version of the Flamingo casino and hotel.

DUTCH SHULTZ

Arthur Simon Flegenheimer, better known as Dutch Shultz, was born on August 6, 1902 in the Bronx area of New York. It was a tough area to grow up in, and to try and afford himself some sort of protection he joined a street gang at an early age. When Schultz was fourteen, his father left home, which seemed to have a traumatic effect on the youth. He told his friends that his father had died tragically of a disease, rather than own up to the embarrassing fact that he had abandoned his family. After his father left, Shultz quit school and took a variety of odd jobs to try and help support his mother. He soon realised that he was not going to get rich by doing an honest day's work, and he started hanging around a nightclub, which he knew was frequented by local mobsters.

Shultz was befriended by a local hood by the name of Marcel Poffo, who had a police record for robbery and extortion. To try and impress his new friend, Shultz started his criminal career by holding up crap games that had refused to pay Poffo a percentage of their winnings. His first brush with the law came at the age of seventeen, when Schultz was arrested for breaking into an apartment in the Bronx. He was sent to a brutal prison which was located in the middle of the East River and later to an even tougher one, Westhampton Farms. He was so miserable he attempted an escape, but he only managed to keep his freedom for a few hours. He was sent back and had a further two months added to his sentence. When he eventually returned to the Bronx, his old friends in the Bergen Gang dubbed him with the name 'Dutch Shultz', which was appropriated from a legendary deceased New York gang member.

By the early 1920s, Shultz had become not only criminally successful but also had useful political connections. He gained control of the numbers racket (which was an illegal form of the Lottery) by using money and violence, and his empire soon spread to take in Harlem and parts of Manhattan.

By 1925, Shutz realised that bootlegging was the way to make serious money, and he became involved in the beer trade. He was a driver for some of the bigger operations such as the legendary Arnold Rothstein and also had close associations with Charles 'Lucky' Luciano.

In early 1928, Shultz was working in a bar owned by a childhood friend called Joey Noe. He gained a reputation for ruthlessness and brutality, which gained him the admiration of Noe, who invited him to be a partner in his business. It wasn't long before the two men were on their way to building a large beer empire in the Bronx. Schultz started to move in on rival speakeasies – a speakeasy was an establishment that was used for selling and drinking alcoholic beverages during the period of the Prohibition (1920–33) – forcing owners to buy his beer or face the consequences. With the profits from the speakeasy business, Noe and Shultz opened more operations and their business expanded outside of the Bronx. They decided if they were going to make it big, they needed to buy their own trucks and for a while Shultz rode shotgun to protect their merchandise from hijack.

The two partners realised they could make far more money if they started selling beer to their rivals. Any speakeasy owners who declined to buy their beer were threatened into submission, with the exception of two brothers Joe and John Rock. They refused to be pushed around and although John, decided to give in, his hotheaded Irish brother refused to play ball with the gangsters. Members of the Noe/Shultz gang kidnapped Joe, took him to one of their warehouses and hung him by the thumbs on a meat hook. While he was suspended, Schultz allegedly smeared a piece of gauze with the discharge from a gonorrhoea infection and had it taped over Joe's eyes. The Rock family paid the gang $35,000 for his release, but not long afterwards Joe reportedly lost his sight.

Their reputation spread, which made it a lot easier for Noe and Schultz to take control of the beer trade in the Bronx. Around this time, Schultz started to hire new muscle for their operation, including a group of toughs called Vincent 'Mad Dog' Coll and his brother Peter, Abe 'Bo' Weinberg and his brother George, Larry Carney, 'Fatty' Walsh and Edward 'Fats' McCarthy. With the extra manpower and strength the Schultz/Noe partnership were ready to move on to bigger things. They started operating in Manhattan, which placed them in direct competition with Schultz's former associate, Jack 'Legs' Diamond.

CLASH WITH THE DIAMOND GANG

It didn't take long before the Diamond gang retaliated to the new opposition on their patch. On the morning of October 15, 1928, at about seven o'clock in the morning, Diamond's hardmen ambushed Joey Noe outside the Chateau Madrid nightclub on Sixth Avenue. Despite the fact that Noe was wearing a bulletproof vest, a garment which had become part of his everyday attire, bullets ripped through his chest. Before Noe collapsed he managed to fire a few shots of his own and witnesses reported seeing a blue Cadillac hit a parked car and then speed away after losing one of its doors. When the police found the car about one hour later, the body of a Diamond gang gunman, Louis Weinberg, was lying dead in the back seat.

Noe was rushed to hospital where, despite efforts to save his life, he died three weeks later on November 21, weighing a mere 40 kg (90 lb). Noe's death hit Shultz hard, and he was bent on revenge.

On November 4, 1928, Arnold Rothstein, who was the financier of the New York underworld, was shot in the foyer of the Park Central Hotel. Although the common belief was that Rothstein was murdered because he had evaded a gambling debt, in the underworld there were rumours that Schultz may have been involved because of Rothstein's friendship with Diamond.

Jack 'Legs' Diamond's enemies finally caught up with him on December 18, 1931. He was shot three times in the back of the head on the day he had been sentenced to four years in jail on kidnapping charges. There has been much speculation as to who was responsible for the murder, including Dutch Shultz, the Oley Brothers (local thugs) and the Albany Police Department.

VINCENT 'MAD DOG' COLL

Shortly after the death of Rothstein, Vincent Coll broke away from the Schultz gang, taking with him about a dozen gangsters, including his own brother Peter. They formed their own gang in the Bronx and Harlem, and Coll's first retaliation against his old boss, Schultz, was to gun down two of his lieutenants, Slats Bologna and Franka Amato. The following day Peter Coll was murdered as revenge.

Vincent Coll continued to ambush Schultz's trucks and killed several more of his men. In his heavy-handed way to get at Schultz, Coll also managed to kill several innocent bystanders, including a five-year-old boy. Because Coll did not have the business acumen to take over the underworld beer industry, he decided to try and make money by kidnapping. At that time kidnapping was not a federal offence, and it was not unknown for gangs to kidnap famous personalities or rival bootleggers to reap large ransoms. Coll was very successful in his kidnapping business and earned himself a lot of money, but eventually Schultz had had enough of his rival and he posted a $50,000 reward for his murder.

Coll was eventually murdered by a member of the Owney 'The Killer' Madden's gang. Madden was a leading Irish gangster in Manhattan during the time of the Prohibition. He also rang the Cotton Club and was a leading boxing promoter in the 1930s. A gunman, using a sub-machine gun, fired at Coll while he made a call from a telephone booth inside a drug store. Eighteen bullets penetrated his body, almost cutting his torso in half. The remainder of Coll's gang were either killed or imprisoned within a period of six months.

INDEPENDENT OPERATOR

With Noe gone, Schultz was now on his own, and with no partner and Diamond out of the way, he was able to move freely in the New York underworld as an independent operator. When Prohibition ended in 1933, Schultz realised that he had to find a new way of earning a living and decided to turn to the numbers racket.

The end of Prohibition did nothing to slow Shultz down. If anything, he tightened his control over the unions and the numbers racket. He also increased his influence at Tammany Hall, which was the Democratic Party political machine that played a major role in controlling the courts, the police, in fact just about everything in New York city. Schultz literally had a free hand at everything, and raids and arrests became a thing of the past.

Eventually, when the local authorities failed to do anything about the immense power that Schultz seemed to have, the Federal Government decided to step in. In 1933, Shultz was indicted for tax evasion, but this did little to curtail his activities. The New York police refused to pursue him and for two years no one made a serious threat at having him arrested.

When J. Edgar Hoover took over as Director of the FBI, he named Schultz as 'Public Enemy Number One'. Rather than face the same fate as John Dillinger – he was shot by two FBI agents – Schultz decided to surrender.

SCHULTZ IS PUSHED OUT

Schultz's trial for tax evasion started in early 1934. Aware that Al Capone and his brother had recently been brought down by the relatively new charge of evasion, Schultz decided to play his trump card. He sent his lawyer to the Inland Revenue with $100,000 in cash as a settlement offer. However, the Inland Revenue refused the money saying that Schultz owed them a far greater amount. After a mistrial, the judge set a second date and Schultz used some of his lesser-known associates to try and influence the jury. They tried to convince the members of the jury that Schultz was really the 'good guy' who was being persecuted by a corrupt government. This ploy seemed to work in Schultz's favour, and one week later the jury returned with a 'not guilty' verdict.

Schultz's business had suffered badly during his absence. Added to this, many other leading New York gang members had begun to muscle in on his rackets. They did their best to keep Schultz out of New York, so he decided to set up a new base in Newark, New Jersey. Along with his three closest associates, Bernard Rosenkrantz, Otto Berman and Abe Landau, Schultz held regular business meetings in a back room at the Palace Chop House on Park Street. Unfortunately, this routine made the men easy targets.

The three men were ambushed on the night of October 23, 1935. The men chosen to carry out the hit were members of the infamous Murder, Inc. – Charles 'Charlie the Bug' Workman and the driver, Emanuel 'Mendy' Weiss. Although there are varying stories on what exactly happened that night, the general consensus was that Workman walked into the Palace Chop House while Weiss provided cover. Workman walked the length of the bar and pushed open the door to the men's room. Inside was a man, who he mistook as one of Schultz's bodyguards. He opened fire and the man immediately dropped to the floor. Workman then went to the backroom where Schultz was holding his meeting and fired at the three men sitting round the table. When he realised that Schultz wasn't among them, it dawned on him that he must have been the one that he shot in the men's room.

All four men were taken to Newark City Hospital. Berman was the first to die, approximately four-and-a-half hours after the shooting. Landau, died next from a severed artery in his neck. Schultz, whose wound caused massive internal bleeding and an infection, died at around 8.30 p.m., at the relatively young age of thirty-three. Rosenkrantz survived the longest, dying at 3.20 a.m. on October 25.

Before Schultz died, he lingered in a state of fevered delirium. As police questioned him about his killers, he rambled incoherently in gangster jargon. Saying things like:

Mother is the best bet and don't let Satan draw you too fast.

Oh, oh; dog biscuit, and when he is happy he doesn't get snappy.

We don't owe a nickel; fold it! Instead, fold it against him. I am a pretty good pretzeler.

The surreal nature of his ramblings inspired a number of writers to devote their works to the famous Dutch Schultz.

As for the killers, they fled. When the police later found the abandoned car, there were too few clues to identify the culprits and they simply moved on to another case. Eventually, in 1941, Workman was identified as Schultz's killer by an informer by the name of Abe Reles. He was found guilty and sentenced to life imprisonment and parolled in 1964.

No one really knows for certain who ordered the killing of Dutch Schultz. It was most probably Lucky Luciano and the syndicate who simply wanted him out of the way. Schultz was becoming a major threat to the underworld because he had approached them with plans to kill his nemesis, the US Attorney, Thomas Dewey. While a few of the mob saw advantages in his proposal, the majority shot him down in flames, fearing that their entire world would collapse around their heads if Schultz got his way. When Schultz left the meeting he was furious, claiming the commission tried to steal his rackets while he was being held in custody and was convinced that they were trying to get him arrested once again. After he left, Murder, Inc. head, Louis Lepke, was asked to handle the situation, which of course is exactly what he did.

MICKEY COHEN

It is fair to say that Mickey Cohen walked in the shadow of Bugsy Siegel. While Siegel comfortably dined with Hollywood's elite, Cohen broke into their houses and robbed them of their wealth. In many ways they were opposite sides of the same coin. Although they shared many of the same likes and dislikes, Siegel could hide his darker side while the violent and less-refined side of Cohen's persona kept breaking the surface. After Siegel was punished by the mob for his Flamingo project, Cohen flourished as a muscle man on the West Coast. He was shot at, bombed, arrested, imprisoned and constantly threatened and yet he still bounced back. Although Mickey Cohen may not be remembered as a top-notch gangster, he was efficient and ruthless at his job and proved himself to be a cunning mastermind in the world of organised crime.

BORN TO CRIME

Cohen was born on July 29, 1914, in Brownville, New York. It was a tough area full of poverty and life among the slums taught the young Cohen to use his fists to survive. When he was six years old, Cohen's family moved to Los Angeles opening a drugstore in Boyle Heights. During the years of the Prohibition, Cohen's older brother ran a small-time gin mill in the back of the drugstore, and Mickey used to be his delivery boy. It was because of this moon-shine operation, that Cohen had his first brush with the law, being arrested when he was just nine years old. However, his brother had connections with the underworld and nothing came of the charge.

Cohen loved the feel of money in his pocket and he soon learned that crime 'does pay'. However, he knew that if he wanted to stay in the world of bootlegging, he would need to know how to look after himself – that was how he first discovered his passion for boxing. Although boxing was illegal in California at the time, he managed to find ways of getting into backroom fights. His success not only earned him cash but also respect, and Cohen decided to pursue a career in boxing. With the blessing of his older brother, but keeping it a secret from his mother, Cohen moved back to the East Coast to become a prize fighter.

Boxing opened up a whole new world for the young teenager when he met some of New York's well known gangsters such as Tommy Dioguardi, Johnny Dio and Owney Madden. Cohen was impressed with the respect given to these men and decided one day he would like to be included in their world of crime. Cohen's career as a boxer ended abruptly when he was knocked senseless by featherweight world champion, Tommy Paul. Aware that he did not have the skill to survive on the professional circuit, Cohen made up his mind to leave the fighting world.

Cohen found himself with few choices with regards to his future. With no education and only gangsters for friends, Cohen resorted to the one job he knew – hustling. What he didn't realise, however, was that the places he was robbing were controlled by the mobs, and he was starting to step on the toes of the big boys. Luckily for him, the gangsters saw a raw talent in the young boy, and he was moved to Chicago to work as an enforcer for an East Coast mob.

Cohen's first taste of being part of the world of organised crime was when he met Al Capone. Capone was impressed by the young man's spunk and offered him a job in his outfit. Under the supervision of Capone's young brother, Mattie, Cohen started running illegal card games and crap tables. However, this taught him an important lesson that playing with the big boys was a dangerous game. After an assassination attempt, Cohen was forced to move to Cleveland, where he worked with Lou Rochkopf, a close friend of Meyer Lansky and Benny Siegel. However, Cohen never really settled in Cleveland as he was used to the action of Chicago, so he was sent to Los Angeles to work with Siegel.

BUILDING AN EMPIRE

It is fair to say that Los Angeles was way behind in terms of organised crime. So the combination of Siegel and Cohen with their bright young minds soon transformed the area with their control over gambling, drugs, unions, racketeering and politics. They turned it into a lucrative operation and Mickey Cohen flourished.

Jack Dragna, who had basically been running things before Cohen and Siegel's intervention, hated playing second fiddle. He had reluctantly accepted Lucky Luciano's admonition that Siegel and Cohen were there to take control, but when Siegel headed off to Nevada to pursue his dream to build The Flamingo, Dragna soon found the courage to feud quite openly with Cohen.

When Siegel was assassinated in 1947, Cohen was primed to take over, and Dragna was furious and decided to take on his rival. Cohen at this time was mixing with the cream of Hollywood. He made friends with politicians, studio bosses and actors including Frank Sinatra and Sammy Davis Jr. However, when he wasn't rubbing shoulders with them, he was exploiting them and often blackmailed the stars who had sordid secrets they would rather not have revealed. Even J. Edgar Hoover of the FBI was aware of Cohen's sideline, which kept him feared and respected by many of Hollywood's film fraternity.

However, his new glamorous associates could do nothing to stop the wrath of his rival Dragna, who made an all-out effort to get rid of Cohen. Whether it was just luck or Dragna's incompetence, Cohen miraculously survived several attempts on his life.

The first time Dragna's men hit was when Cohen was driving towards home. As bullets sprayed his Cadillac, Cohen managed to lie on his side but still steer the car up Wilshire Boulevard without actually hitting anything. He escaped on that occasion with only a few cuts from the flying glass.

Two attempts to blow up his house failed, but a sharpshooter was a little more successful when he succeeded in hitting Cohen in the arm while he ate in a crowded late-night diner. The shot tore away much of the flesh of Cohen's arm, but Neddy Herbert, a lifelong friend, was not so lucky and was killed in the shoot-out.

Another assassin tried to take Cohen's life as he bent down to examine a scratch on his new Cadillac. As he did so a bullet whizzed past his ear, but the gunman didn't hang around long enough for a second shot.

By now the ongoing war between Cohen and Dragna had attracted the attention of the Kefauver

Committee, headed by Estes Kefauver. It was the first committee set up to try and fight and expose organised crime. Cohen was subpoenaed to testify before the committee and was criticised severely by New Hampshire Senator, Charles Tobey. Ironically, the final charge against Cohen was evasion of income tax and he was sentenced to four years in federal prison.

MICKEY AND LANA TURNER

While Cohen was banged up on McNeil Island, a close friend of his, Johnny Stompanato, began dating a famous actress by the name of Lana Turner. Stompanato was a handsome, former marine, while Turner was beautiful and wealthy but exceptionally high maintenance. She was an alcoholic with a reputation for whirlwind romances and had worked her way through several husbands. Johnny and Lana had a tempestuous relationship, attracted to each other like moths to a flame, an attraction which eventually ended in tears.

Cohen had no time for Lana and he wasn't afraid to make his feelings known. One morning the phone rang and he was told that Johnny had been killed by Lana's daughter, Cheryl Crane. Cohen was shocked, but the more he thought about it, the more he disbelieved the story he had been told.

Although the anger between Cohen and Lana

simmered slightly, she still let it be known that she was scared he might seek revenge. Cohen was angry about the bad press his friend Johnny was receiving and got his own back by sending Lana's love letters to the newspapers. Although Cohen was only trying to show the true relationship between Lana and Johnny, his plan backfired when it appeared as if he was trying to blackmail the actress. Cheryl Crane was found not guilty and Cohen was angry that the real killer, probably rival gangsters, had got clean away.

LOCKED AWAY AGAIN

Cohen was found guilty of tax evasion once again in 1961. He spent fifteen years in the infamous Alcatraz prison in San Francisco and then he was transferred to a prison in Atlanta, Georgia. He suffered a vicious attack from a psychotic inmate, after which he was left partially paralysed and spent the remainder of his time in the prison hospital at Springfield, Missouri.

When he was finally released in 1972, the now ageing mobster decided to go into retirement and spent the time travelling around visiting old friends. He hit the headlines again in 1974, when heiress Patricia Hearst was kidnapped by the Symbionese Liberation Army (SLA). The SLA was a group of US terrorists who saw successful capitalists as the enemy. William Randolph Hearst, the newspaper magnate and his family, were considered to be prime targets due to their vast wealth and media empire. Shortly after Patricia was kidnapped, the Hearst family approached Cohen for his help. Cohen used his old underworld connections to try and track Patricia down, but it soon became clear that she wasn't going to return home willingly. When Patricia's parents told Cohen that they didn't think it was such a good idea to bring their daughter home because they feared her past actions would send her to prison, he decided to end his involvement then and there.

After the Hearst interlude, Mickey Cohen stayed out of the limelight, keeping a low profile. Barely mobile and the desire to fight, long gone, he died peacefully in his home in 1976.

JOHN GOTTI

John Gotti became famous as the Godfather of the Gambino family who were, without doubt, the richest and most powerful criminal family in the USA in the twentieth and twenty-first centuries. Towards the middle of the twentieth century, federal law agencies were starting to dismantle organised crime families, but in the middle of their efforts, John Gotti stepped forward and captured the media's attention as he left his mark as a Hollywood-style gangster. Despite his dapper appearance, Gotti somehow lacked the capabilities of his predecessors such as Al Capone, Lucky Luciano, Meyer Lansky and Arnold Rothstein, but he still left behind him a trail of blood.

John Joseph Gotti Jr, was born on October 27, 1940 in a dirt-ridden section of the Bronx. His father worked hard and managed to save enough money to move the family to a tough Italian neighbourhood in Brooklyn. Life on the streets was harsh and the young Gotti learned to survive by using his fists. He regularly saw gangsters standing around on street corners in their smart suits, and he aspired to one day becoming like them. By the time he was twelve years old, Gotti, together with his brothers, Peter and Richard, became part of a local gang that ran errands for the gangsters he so admired.

Although his education on the streets was regular, his attendance at school was erratic. He constantly played truant and because he was considered to be a classroom bully, often disturbing the lessons when he was there, his absence was usually overlooked.

In the summer of 1954, Gotti was injured during a robbery with some local youths. They were in the process of stealing a cement mixer from a building site, when the mixer fell over and crushed Gotti's toes. He spent the remainder of the summer in hospital and then went back on the streets with a limp that stayed with him for the rest of his life.

When Gotti was sixteen, he decided to leave school and joined the Fulton-Rockaway Boys. They mugged, stole cars and fenced stolen goods, and between the years of 1957 and 1961, Gotti was arrested five times. The charges, however, were either dismissed or reduced to a probationary sentence for one reason or another.

GOTTI FINDS LOVE

Gotti fell in love with Victoria DiGiorgio when he was twenty. He was infatuated by her tiny frame and beautiful dark hair and the couple married on

March 6, 1962. Despite the fact they had a stormy relationship, and there were doubts that the marriage would survive, they stayed together and had three children – Angela, Victoria and John A., who became known as 'Junior'.

For a while Gotti tried his hand at doing legitimate work, but he was frustrated at the small financial rewards and decided to devote his entire life to crime, much to the disgust of his wife.

Gotti's first taste of prison life came in 1963, when he was arrested with Angelo Ruggiero's younger brother, Salvatore. They were driving a rental car that had been reported as stolen and for this he was given a twenty-day sentence. He received another short sentence for attempted robbery in 1966. However, 1966 proved to be an important year for our would-be gangster, because for the first time he became an associate member of a Mafia organisation headed by Carmine Fatico and his brother, Daniel, called the Bergin crew. The Faticos were answerable to the powerful Gambino family.

LIFE AS A MAFIA ASSOCIATE

Gotti started his life within the Mafia as a hijacker and, although he wasn't particularly successful he did make enough money to move his family to a better home in Brooklyn. Gotti's fourth child, Frank, was born a short while later.

In November 1967, with the aid of another gang member, Gotti forged the name of a forwarding company agent and managed to drive off with $30,000 worth of merchandise from JFK airport's cargo terminal. Four days later, the FBI, who had Gotti under surveillance, watched as he and Angelo Ruggiero loaded up a lorry, this time at Northwest Airlines cargo bay. They swooped and found Gotti hiding in the back of the lorry hiding behind some of the boxes.

While Gotti was out on bail, he was arrested again for stealing a cargo of cigarettes worth $500,000 from outside a restaurant in New Jersey. He was now in deep trouble, and Fatico hired the defence attorney Michael Coiro to represent the Gotti brothers and Ruggiero. Hiring Coiro paid off and Gotti was let off leniently, serving less than three years at Lewisburg prison.

When Gotti was released in January 1972, his wife forced him to get a legitimate job and he was put on the payroll of his father-in-law's construction company. Victoria got her wish, but deep down she knew her husband would never change and gave up asking questions about his underhand activities. Shortly after his release, their fifth child, Peter, was born.

WORKING HIS WAY UP

From their first introduction, Gotti and Aniello

Dellacroce hit it off, and the two men had many things in common. They were violent, foul-mouthed but clever, and also shared the bad habit of gambling. This friendship bought Gotti in close contact with the capo Garlo Gambino. As much as Dellacroce liked Gotti, the boss Paul Castellano hated him, or perhaps more accurately, feared him.

By the age of thirty-one Gotti became acting capo when Fatico was indicted for loan-sharking. Under the leadership of Gotti, the Bergin crew began to get restless, urging him to get involved in some of the richer pickings. They gradually drifted towards the dangerous game of drug trafficking, despite warnings from the Gambino family to steer clear.

Having ignored the rules of the family, the Gotti gang were caught selling drugs and they eventually disbanded. Dellacroce, who had been suffering from cancer, died on December 2, 1985. Unhappy with the way that Castellano was running the family, Gotti along with other family members, arranged for the assassination of the Gambino family boss. He was shot six times, along with his bodyguard, Thomas Bilotti, outside a restaurant in Manhattan on December 16, 1985.

With both Castellano and Dellacroce out of the way, Gotti had to play a waiting game. He didn't have to wait very long though, because within eight days Gotti was in charge of the biggest Mafia family in the nation. Gotti became the centre of attention and he loved it. He became nicknamed 'Dapper Don', wearing expensive hand-tailored suits and dining in the finest restaurants. He became famous for his lavish street parties and earned himself a reputation for keeping street crime at bay.

However, constantly being in the limelight had its disadvantages as it attracted the attention of the FBI. It was in the late 1980s that Gotti got his other nickname 'Teflon Don', due to the fact that he managed to avoid convictions on racketeering and assault charges in two seemingly watertight cases. In the first case, a man who had complained of being attacked by Gotti, changed his mind rapidly when someone 'tampered' with the brakes on his car. In the second case, Gotti was acquitted after he allegedly bribed the foreman of the jury. It didn't seem to matter what they did, the FBI seemed unable to make a charge stick against the Mafia boss.

THE FINAL TRIAL

Following their failure to have Gotti put behind bars, the FBI tightened their surveillance. They bugged his home, his club, his phones and all his known business premises. To get round this problem, Gotti decided to hold his clandestine business meetings while walking down the street, playing loud tapes of white noise. However, Gotti was caught. The FBI managed to get a recording of conversations in his 'headquarters', an apartment above the Ravenite Social Club. In the first tape he talked about one of his lawyers, who he suspected was leaking information. He ordered the man to shut up or suffer the consequences, i.e. a short trip down an elevator shaft. In another recording Gotti was heard to make defamatory remarks about his underboss Salvatore 'Sammy the Bull' Gravano. The tapes were recorded in late November 1989 by a bug the FBI had placed in the apartment.

Gotti was arrested on December 11, 1990 when FBI agents and New York City detectives raided the Ravenite Social Club. They arrested Gotti, Gravano, Frank Locascio and Thomas Gambino. The following morning the *New York Times* featured an article which sympathised over the arrest of John Gotti. Gotti didn't shun the media, in fact he loved them, he loved being a gangster. It would be fair to say that Gotti and the news media were born for each other. He became only the second Mafioso to make the cover of *Time* (Al Capone being the first), and responded by hanging a blown-up version of the cover on his office wall.

When Gravano heard the tapes with Gotti bad-mouthing him, he flipped, and it seemed as though with the evidence from the bugs, photographs and the testimony of Gravano, Gotti's fate was sealed. On April 2, 1992, Gotti was convicted on charges that included five murders, loansharking, racketeering, obstruction of justice, illegal gambling and tax evasion. He was sentenced to 100 years in prison and was sent to the maximum-security penitentiary in Marion, Illinois. For over nine years he spent twenty-three hours a day locked in solitary confinement in a cell that measured only eight feet by seven feet. He was allowed out one hour a day for solitary execise in a concrete-walled enclosure.

From behind bars, Gotti planned who would take over his role as capo, and the job fell to his son, John Gotti Jr, who acted as boss with the help of older members of the Gambino family.

Gotti's reign was finally over and even though he had managed to fight conviction for many years, he eventually lost his battle over throat cancer. He died on June 10, 2002, at the US Medical Center for Federal Prisoners in Springfield, Missouri. His funeral in New York was attended by over 130 members of the Gambino crime family and many of his personal friends and family.

Like many other gangsters before him, Gotti was a criminal mastermind, even though he was less sophisticated than the brutal Capone we know from the movies. Gotti's main aim within the Mafia was his constant strive to reach the top.

THE KRAYS

The Kray brothers grew up to become the UK's most famous and infamous gangsters. In comparison to the Mafia of Sicily or the Cosa Nostra in the USA, the Krays could be described as a bunch of ruffians rather than an evil organised crime cartel, but they still received notoriety for their acts of violence. These old-style cockney villains came close to building their own criminal empire with comparative ease, indicating just how backward the British authorities were in truly understanding the meaning of organised crime.

RAISED IN THE EAST END

The East End of London has been described as 'outcast London'. In the late 1950s and 1960s, it certainly could have been described as a world separated from the rest of London. It was an area that was dominated by trade and commerce, the profits of which were undoubtedly siphoned off into the pockets of criminal groups that operated there. The hugely over-populated area was rife with murder, extortion, theft, money lending and prostitution and this was where our brothers started out their lives.

Reggie Kray was born at 8.00 a.m. on October 24, 1933, and ten minutes later his identical twin Ronnie came into the world. Violet and Charlie Kray already had a seven-year-old son, Charlie, who over the years was rather dominated by his two younger brothers. The family lived in the Shoreditch area in the East End of London until 1939, when they moved to Bethnal Green. Their father lived a rather nomadic existence, often away on his travels buying and selling precious metals. Although this provided the family with a fairly regular, if not meagre, income, it also meant that the three boys had little contact with their father. Violet, by all accounts, was a good mother and she did her best to raise her three boys in difficult times.

At the start of World War II, Charlie senior was conscripted into the army and the family was evacuated to a small village in the Suffolk country-side. After the dirty, cramped streets of London, the Kray boys loved the freedom and spent hours playing in the fields. Had their mother not missed her friends and family so much back in the East End, the Krays would have had a very different life. Much to their dismay, they moved back to war-torn London within the year and the boys went back to having dodge the many street gangs that roamed the streets. Their father, who loved his freedom, did not fit into the routine of army life and he soon became a deserter from the British Army. The police and military were on the lookout for Charlie Kray and many a night the family would be woken up by a knock on the door. Charlie spent more and more time away from the family until eventually he became a virtual stranger.

In an effort to stay out of trouble, the three boys took up boxing. Charlie junior, proved to be a reasonable fighter, but it was the twins that soon started making the headlines as promising amateur boxers. Being called up to join the Army abruptly ended their boxing career, but it did little to stem the violence that was to be the hallmark of their lives.

GANGSTERS IN THE MAKING

When they were released from the Army, the Kray brothers turned quickly to a life of crime. They ran small-time protection rackets for local villains, but soon agreed they wanted to work for themselves. The turning point in their career came when they managed to save enough money to buy the lease on a seedy snooker club in Bethnal Green. Before they took over the club, it had a terrible reputation for fighting and it was constantly being smashed up by local thugs. When the Krays approached the owner asking if they could take over the lease, he jumped at the chance, telling the boys that the lease was theirs if they really felt they could sort the place out. They renamed the club The Regal, and within weeks they had turned it around and made it into a safe, profitable business venture. Many believed that they had been the perpetrators of the violence in the first place and it was their own reputation that put pay to any further trouble.

Shortly after they took over The Regal, a gang of thugs known as the Maltese mob tried to extract protection money from the Krays. This was a big mistake and for once the gang didn't get their own way. One member had a bayonet thrust through his hand, while the others were lucky to escape with their lives.

The Kray brothers loved to drink and frequented many late-night clubs and bars. In the Vienna Rooms off the Edgware Road, they met two of their heroes, Jack Spot and Billy Hill, who between them dominated the majority of London. Ronnie and Reggie could listen for hours to their stories and gleaned as much information as they could about organised crime. They worked for Spot for a while, providing protection for the bookmakers at the racecourses. While working for Spot they also came into contact with Mad Frankie Fraser, who at the time was working as a bucket boy for one of the bookmakers. A bucket boy was responsible for wiping the chalk off the bookies' boards. Mad

Frankie went on to become a notorious criminal and gang member who spent more than half of his life in prison for numerous violent offences.

TIME TO MOVE ON

Although the twins had learned a lot from their brief time with Spot and Hill, they knew in their hearts it was time to move on. They were already involved in virtually every type of scam, running protection rackets, hijacking and even made big business out of forging National Service exemption certificates. In 1957, Ronnie was arrested for grievous bodily harm (GBH) on a man called Terry Martin, outside a pub in Stepney. He was also charged with possessing a firearm and received a three-year prison sentence. Reggie was also charged with GBH, but the case did not hold up and he was found not guilty.

While Ronnie was off the scene, Reggie wasted no time in expanding The Firm, as the brothers liked to call it, opening another club called The Double R in Bow. Charlie was normally the brains and the money behind the operations while Reggie and Ronnie provided the brawn. The club soon flourished and it wasn't long before Reggie acquired many other clubs that were inexplicably burnt to the ground. Gradually, the Kray empire became bigger and bigger, until it is estimated that they owned more than thirty clubs and bars.

RON'S 'SICKNESS'

While Ronnie was in prison, Reggie and Charlie found that their operations ran a lot smoother, due to the fact that Reggie and Ronnie were frequently arguing about who was the boss. Ron, who seemed to be the more dominant twin, usually won the argument, which was often detrimental to their business. The trouble was, behind Ron's harsh exterior was a much softer heart. He would often have his hand in the tills and give money to what he felt was a deserving cause. Although this was highly commendable, it was not very good for their profits. For this reason, and because Ronnie could so easily break into a violent rage regardless of the consequences, the Kray's businesses thrived in his absence.

Ronnie spent his first year in Wandsworth prison but was later transferred to Camp Hill on the outskirts of Newport, on the Isle of Wight. While serving his time, Ron's favourite aunt Rose died, which seemed to tip him over the edge, and he had to be transferred to the psychiatric wing of Winchester prison. It was here he was diagnosed as being a paranoid schizophrenic and declared insane.

When Reggie was told the news and saw that his brother's health was deteriorating, he decided to do something about it. He blamed his ill health on the large doses of drugs that Ronnie was being administered, and decided he needed to get his brother out of prison. Luckily for Reg, they transferred his brother to the Long Grove mental hospital, which made it a lot easier for him to spring Ron. Reg's plan was to try and get a second opinion regarding his brother's sanity, and then when the diagnosis proved to be incorrect the authorities would have to rethink about having him returned to hospital. Being identical twins, the plan was simple, Reggie simply visited the hospital and changed places with his brother. By the time the doctors realised what had happened, Ronnie was long gone, and Reggie had to be released as well.

Ronnie remained on the run for five months, but it wasn't long before Reggie and Charlie realised what a big mistake they had made. It soon became apparent that Ronnie really was very ill. There were times that he was so bad that he didn't even recognise his own family and became paranoid that everyone was out to get him. It became evident that Ronnie needed to be readmitted to hospital and the Kray family had to do the unthinkable – turn their own brother over to the police.

The police raided the house and Ronnie was arrested without one word of protest. He was re-assessed and returned to prison, where he stayed until his release in May 1959.

When Ronnie was released, it was clear that he was still very sick and was subject to violent mood swings. He became a violent embarrassment and a liability to The Firm, and he was still paranoid that everyone was plotting against him. The family knew he desperately needed help and they took him to hospital for treatment. Unfortunately, this treatment involved taking drugs for the remainder of his life, which had a devastating affect on his appearance. Although the drugs helped to keep him calm, he gained a lot of weight, his speech became slurred and, in short, he was nothing like the man he used to be.

Reggie became his backbone and kept their businesses afloat, but he was arrested in 1959 for demanding money with menaces. He was given an eighteen month jail sentence and was sent to Wandsworth prison. While under lock and key, he associated with two hoods by the name of Jack 'the Hat' McVitie and 'The Mad Axeman' Frank Mitchell, two men who played a major part in the twins eventual downfall.

THE GOOD TIMES

At the beginning of the 1960s, the three brothers were back together and, with Ronnie back to his old self for a while, it appeared to be the start of some good times. Business was thriving and they were starting to make inroads into the West End club and gambling scene.

Their first foothold into the West End came when they opened an upmarket gambling club in Knightsbridge, called Esmerelda's Barn. To give the club an appearance of respectability they paid a peer to join them on the board. Lord Effingham, the sixth Earl of Effingham, used to stand at the door and welcome customers as they came into the club. The Krays were obsessed with celebrities and they lavishly entertained actors, pop stars, sports personalities, in fact anyone with any claim to fame.

The Krays also invested a lot of money into a coastal development in a place called Enugu in Nigeria. The project was set up by the Kray's business manager, Leslie Payne, and Ernest Shinwell, who was the son of the labour MP, Manny Shinwell. The first meeting to discuss the plans was between Ron, a man called Leslie Holt and a peer of the realm, Lord Boothby. However, the project collapsed and the money seemed to vanish into thin air. What did come out of the project was an alleged relationship between Ronnie and Lord Boothby. The couple originally met at one of the many gay parties they both regularly attended. Ronnie had realised that he was a homosexual at an early age when he had a crush on a boy that lived in the same street. He didn't attempt to hide his preference for men, but it wasn't really until the 1960s that it became public knowledge. In July 1964, the *Sunday Mirror* got scent of the relationship between Ronnie and Lord Boothby and decided to run a story saying that Scotland Yard were investigating an illicit romance. When Boothby was approached, he adamantly denied the relationship and explained away a photograph of them together by the fact that Ronnie simply loved to be photographed with celebrities. The *Sunday Mirror* immediately backed down, sacked its editor and paid Boothby £40,000 so that the matter didn't go to court. Leslie Holt, the third man at the meeting, died under very strange circumstances.

In 1965, the Kray twins were arrested again for demanding money with menaces from a man called Hew McGowan. He was the owner of a club called The Hideaway. Although they were remanded in custody in Brixton prison, by now their influence was so far-reaching that questions were asked in the House of Lords as to how long they were going to keep the Krays locked up without officially being charged. The question was raised by Ronnie's friend, Lord Boothby, which caused quite a sensation. However, it had the desired effect and when the case went to court they were cleared of all charges. Less than a month later they were the proud owners of The Hideaway, which then became known as El Morocco.

In April 1965, Reggie married twenty-one-year-old Francis Shea, who was the sister of his good friend, Frank. She was the love of his life and Reggie was devastated when the marriage ended in disaster eight months later, masterminded by his in-laws.

By the beginning of 1966, Ronnie and Reggie were moving into the world of organised crime in a big way. They forged links with the Mafia and even went to the USA to meet with some of their top men. They made some very useful connections during their visit and offered protection to any US celebrities visiting or performing in England.

CLASHES

Of course, the Krays were by no means the only gang operating in London and this led to them poaching on each other's territories, which nearly always ended up in violence. The Richardson brothers ran the south of London and had a reputation as being among London's most sadistic gangsters. They were also known as the 'Torture Gang' because their speciality was pinning victims to the floor with six inch nails and removing their victim's toes with bolt cutters. The Krays and the Richardsons crossed paths frequently.

One member of the Richardson gang who came into contact with the Krays was 'Mad' Frankie Fraser. He was an extremely violent and remorseless man who tried to take over a chain of gambling machines owned by his rivals, the Krays. They took out their revenge on the Richardsons by trying to bully the gang into sharing their profits from some of their other rackets with the Krays. This made another Richardson member angry, a man by the name of George Cornell. Cornell had worked with the Krays before jumping ship and joining the Richardsons, so the brothers were fully aware of his fearsome reputation.

In March 1966, a gun battle erupted outside a club called Mr Smiths in Catford, which resulted in a man called Richard Hart being shot dead. It is thought that the Richardson gang had gone there with the intention of trying to eradicate the Krays. However, there was only one member of the Kray family there, Richard Hart, who happened to be a cousin of the twins.

Family came first in the Kray organisation, and they immediately wanted revenge. On the night of March 9, 1966, Ronnie, Reggie and other members of The Firm were drinking in The Lion pub when they were told that Cornell was drinking in the Blind Beggar pub just down the road. At approximately 8.30 p.m. Ronnie and one of his associates walked into the Blind Beggar, only to be met by Cornell throwing abuse at them by calling Ronnie a 'fat poof'. Ronnie didn't waste any time in pulling out his pistol, shooting Cornell three times in the head. Although there was no proof that Cornell actually fired the shot that killed Richard Hart, all the other members of the Richardson gang were either in hospital or in prison at the time, so Cornell was the only one to bear the brunt of the Kray's revenge. Shortly after the killing of Cornell, Ronnie sank into another period of his psychotic depressions, and the good times seem to be coming to an end.

'THE MAD AXEMAN'

Towards the end of 1966, the Kray brothers decided to try and spring 'The Mad Axeman' Frank Mitchell from Dartmoor prison. He was serving a sentence for breaking into an elderly couple's house and holding them hostage with an axe, hence the nickname 'The Mad Axeman'. When he broke into the house he was on the run having only just escaped from prison, so when he was recaptured the authorities were not keen on giving him a new release date.

The plan the Krays hatched was to break Mitchell out of prison and keep him in hiding long enough for the media to run a story with the promise of his case being investigated. Mitchell would then give himself up and return to prison.

They were successful in springing him from Dartmoor, but there was no following investigation and the authorities started an intensive manhunt. Although Ronnie had been the main instigator in getting Mitchell out of prison he never made the effort to visit him while he was on the run. Mitchell saw this as a sign of disrespect and, added to this, he was getting restless being couped up in a cramped apartment. Mitchell started making threats, saying that if the twins didn't come and see him, then he would have to visit them. The Kray brothers knew they had to find a solution and fast. Frank Mitchell was found shot dead on December 23, 1966.

A BAD MOVE

Things were starting to look brighter for Reggie at the beginning of 1967. By June, it looked as if he would get the chance of getting back together with his wife Frances. What he didn't realise was that Frances had been unstable before they were married and following the break-up she had suffered a mental breakdown. Her parents had been the ones who instigated the separation, because they were not happy about her association with a local gangster with such a bad reputation. When she was eventually released from hospital, Reggie arranged for them to have a second honeymoon. However, the constant fighting between Reggie and her parents had taken its toll and the day they were to leave for Ibiza, Frances took an overdose and died. Reggie was broken hearted and went into a deep state of depression for months. To try and bury his sorrow, he took to drinking all the time and it was during this traumatic period that the Kray's world came crashing down around them.

Jack 'The Hat' McVitie had been an associate of the twins for a long time and, although he never actually belonged to The Firm, the twins often used him for odd jobs. McVitie got his name from the fact that he never removed his hat that was covering a bald patch. He was a dangerous man who had no fear of the twins, and was often heard badmouthing them. Added to this he was an alcoholic who took drugs and liked to beat up women.

Ronnie had given McVitie an advance payment to kill Leslie Payne, the twins ex-business manager, because he believed he was about to go to the police. However, he never fulfilled the contract and ran off with the money. As if this action wasn't stupid enough, McVitie was also threatening some of the bar owners who were under the Kray's protection and bragging about what he had done to Cornell. Despite numerous warnings from Reggie about his behaviour, McVitie continued to threaten until it was obvious he was riding for a fall.

On October 29, 1967, McVitie was invited to a party with some of his underworld associates and their families. What McVitie didn't know was that the twins had arrived early and had spent the last hour clearing the party of any guests. As soon as McVitie walked through the door, Reggie put a gun to his head and pulled the trigger.

McVitie couldn't believe his luck when the trigger jammed, but this caused Reggie to lose his temper even more and a scuffle broke out. Reggie threw down the gun and went for McVitie with a knife, stabbing him multiple times in the face, chest and stomach. This action proved to the last piece of violence to be carried out by the Krays and also culminated in the collapse of The Firm.

Although the authorities turned their backs in the past, this time the Kray brothers had overstepped the mark and had to be brought to justice.

THE END OF THE LINE

The Kray brothers were finally arrested by Scotland Yard on May 8, 1968. They appeared at the Old Bailey in 1969, along with other members of their gang. The trial started in January and lasted about six weeks, and the ten men who stood in the dock were all convicted of various charges, with the exception of one man Tony Barry, who was acquitted. Ronnie and Reggie Kray, who were thirty-five years old at the time, were both sentenced to thirty years for murder. Their forty-one-year-old brother, Charlie, was sentenced to ten years as an accessory to murder.

Prison did little to suppress the legend of the Kray twins, with both men writing best-selling books about their lives. In 1990, a full-length feature film was made that gave details of their exploits, including the murder of McVitie, which earned the Krays a princely sum of £255,000. Many people campaigned for their release, feeling that the sentences were too harsh as they had never killed any members of the general public. In 1993, several hundred people held a rally in Hyde Park, before marching to Downing Street to hand in a 10,000-signature petition.

Ronnie Kray died on March 17, 1995, after he collapsed in his ward at Broadmoor. Reggie was allowed out for one day to attend his funeral.

In 1997, Charlie was found guilty of masterminding a £39 million cocaine plot and was jailed for a further twelve years. He died in the prison hospital in April 2000.

In August 2000, the Home Secretary decided Reggie could be released on compassionate grounds due to his deteriorating health. Six weeks later on October 1, with his wife Roberta at his side, Reggie died in his sleep after a battle against cancer.

To this day, although their names are synonymous with violence, they are also remembered for having rid the streets of London of some of the most feared criminals. Women and children from the East End of London swore that they felt safe just as long as the Krays were on the streets.

THE BLOOD
BROTHERS

The Tijuana Cartel, also known as the Arellano Felix Organisation (AFO), was a Mexican drug cartel from Tijuana, in Baja California. The AFO was a family business led by Benjamin and Ramón Eduardo Arellano Félix. Ramón was considered to be the most violent of the seven brothers, a sociopath who seemed to thrive on murder. In fact the whole organisation had a reputation for extreme violence and Ramón ended up on the FBI's list of its ten most wanted men. In September 1998, Ramón ordered a hit which resulted in the mass murder of nineteen people in Ensenada, Baja California.

THE BROTHERS

Benjamin Arellano Félix, assumed leader of the Arellano Félix organization.

Ramón Eduardo Arellano Félix, considered to be the most violent brother, was responsible for the organisation's security, plucking members from the midst of violent street gangs. He was also responsible for dealing with rival drug dealers, law enforcement officials who the cartel could not bribe and any members of the AFO who didn't obey the rules.

Francisco Javier Arellano Félix, was the third-ranking of the cartel brothers, after Benjamin and Ramón, and controlled the organisation's finances.

Francisco Rafael Arellano Félix, was the eldest brother who was responsible for the buying and selling of the narcotics.

Eduardo Arellano and **Carlos Arellano Félix**, were both responsible for coordinating the smuggling of cocaine shipments to the USA.

Luis Fernando Arellano Félix, ran the family-owned businesses, which were allegedly used for money laundering the profits from the cartel's drug dealings.

THE CARTEL

The organisation that Ramón and his brothers ran was named after the violent border town, Tijuana, in which it was based. The US drug enforcement agencies were under no misapprehension about the power of the cartel, as it was considered to be one of the most powerful, violent and agressive drug trafficking organisations in the world. Their corruption and violence had such an impact that it even inspired a film, *Traffic*, which, if anything, was toned down to make it bearable to watch.

The Arellano Félix brothers were set up in the drug business by their cousin, Miguel Angel Félix Gallardo, who ran his own drug empire out of Culiacán, a city in north-western Mexico. Gallardo built his business up by trading locally grown marijuana and heroin across the border into the USA, but he was jailed for the murder of a DEA agent, Enrique Camarena, in 1989, which left his cartel in a state of disorder. The Félix brothers took advantage of the situation, inherited their uncle's business and saw this at their first big break.

The Félix brothers traded in a completely different direction, by trafficking cocaine, marijuana and amphetamines via a 160-km (100-mile) corridor between Tijuana and Mexicali, which lies directly on the border of California. The drugs literally poured across the border by car, by boat along the Pacific coast and even by tunnel.

In February 2002, following a tip-off, police searched a farm on the US side of the border. Underneath the stairs they discovered a safe, but when they broke into it, it was empty. They were about to move away and start their search elsewhere, when they noticed that the safe had a false bottom. When they removed the floor they found a deep shaft which descended to a 365-m (1,200-ft) tunnel, complete with electric lights and rails, which the police estimated had carried billions of dollars of drugs under the US–Mexican border.

Many of the Arellano Félix cartel were ruthless gunmen, who had literally been recruited off the streets in San Diego's Barrio Logan, an area noted for its violent gangs. The leader of the Barrio Logan assassins was an experienced gangster called David Barron Corona, who had earned the Félix brother's loyalty by saving two of the brothers from an ambush.

Despite the cartel's notoriety, they managed to remain untouched for thirteen years, due partially to bribes. They bought themselves protection by paying large amounts of cash to politicians and police, at an estimated $1 million a week. Anyone they couldn't buy, they simply killed. They murdered without giving it a second thought, and it is estimated their victims could amount to more than 1,000 people. Their targets were witnesses, innocent bystanders, federal police commanders, judges and even a Roman Catholic cardinal by the name Juan Jesus Posadas Ocampo. The cardinal was killed by mistake at Guadalajara airport in 1993, when members of the Félix gang mistook his car for that of a rival drug baron. The blunder meant that the gang had to adopt false names and lie low for a while, but it had little effect on their business transactions, apparently unafraid of capture.

In the end, the Félix organisation was a major embarrassment to the government in Mexico, as it was considered to be more powerful than the authorities themselves. They have been allowed to operate freely without being ever brought to justice.

TRAIL OF BLOOD

Wherever there was danger, Ramón seemed to be close at hand, and he was always the one who volunteered to carry out an assassination. Often he could be heard saying to his men, 'Let's go kill someone'. He killed out of simple ennui.

One of the worst examples of the AFO's blood-lust was at a fishing village called Ensenada, which just so happened to be the home of a small-time drug smuggler by the name of Fermín Castro Flores. Even though Fermín Castro had never faltered on a protection payment to the AFO, they eventually decided that he might become too competitive. On September 17, 1998, AFO gunmen arrived in the middle of the night and lined up every man, woman and child they could find in the village against a concrete wall. They were then brutally murdered by men dressed in black carrying AK-47s. Among the victims were: Fermín Castro Flores, 38, his wife and two-year-old son, his brother-in-law, Francisco Flores Altamirano, 30, Flores' 52-year-old mother, his sister, his wife and five children aged between four and thirteen years of age, and seven neighbours, including a pregnant woman. Fermín Castro survived the attack but remained unconscious for over a month and finally died. The only two survivors on that day were a fifteen-year-old girl and a twelve-year-old boy.

The Mexican police were convinced that it was a drug-related massacre and described it has the 'worst murder associated with organised crime ever to have occurred in this country'. The two surviving children were extremely traumatised and described the massacre as lasting an 'eternity', when it reality it probably took about fifteen minutes.

The AFO had broken the rule of the cartels that 'children are never touched'. This led for an intensive search for the gunmen, which ended with the arrest of fourteen suspects. Juan Carlos Moctezuma, José María Bernal, Francisco Javier Villalobos and José Torres were all tested for gun powder residue, and all four men were found to be positive.

In April 2000, a prosecutor named José Patino Moreno, along with two aides, a special prosecutor, Oscar Pompa Plaza and a Mexican army captain, Rafael Torres Bernal, disappeared into thin air from a Tijuana street. When their bodies were eventually discovered near Moreno's wrecked car, their bodies were hardly recognisable. Their heads had been crushed using some sort of industrial press and every single bone in their bodies were shattered. The local police ironically insisted that the men had died in a regrettable road accident, but it came to no surprise when the AFO started to lose their power, that two police commanders were charged with the murders.

'NARCO-JUNIORS'

Ramón would drive around in a flashy red Porsche, dressed in an outlandish mink jacket and heavy gold jewellery, cruising the streets of Tijuana. His arrogant attitude became a magnet for the bored sons of the city's rich and Ramón took advantage of this by recruiting several of them as his 'narco-juniors'. They became trusted hitmen who, when they were not killing for business, killed for fun.

Cristina and Alejandro Hodoyan were just such parents living in the middle class area of Tijuana. Their lives changed drastically when their eldest son, Alex, went missing in the mid-1990s. They soon discovered that he had been arrested and was suspected of having connections with the infamous Arellano Félix cartel.

Following months of confinement and brutal torture at the hands of the Mexican military, Alex eventually confessed to being involved with the cartel. Shortly afterwards, Alex's brother Alfredo was arrested in San Diego on gun charges. The Mexican government requested Alfredo's extradition to Mexico as he was suspected to have taken part in the murder of a federal prosecutor.

In a peculiar series of events, Alex was flown by Mexican authorities to the USA and handed over to the Drug Enforcement Agency (DEA). They tried to convince Alex to become a witness in their case against the Félix cartel and offered him a witness protection programme. Although Alex was in theory free, he was retained in a San Diego hotel room, but believing he would have to testify against his brother, he managed to escape back to Tijuana. Several days later, Alex was kidnapped while driving with his mother and has never been seen since and is presumed dead.

Alfredo was extradited to Mexico and held in a high security prison outside of the city awaiting trial. It was later discovered that the man responsible for kidnapping Alex, General Gutiérrez Rebollo, was working for a rival cartel, which shocked the US authorities.

Alex and Alfredo were part of the group of juniors who became entangled with gang members involved in the cocaine business. Although the Hodoyans had hoped to keep their children away from drugs, living in Tijuana it was hard when the majority of teenagers were exposed to temptation whenever they walked into a nightclub.

RAMÓN'S DEMISE

Ramón's exit from the world of drugs was as dramatic as his lifestyle. On September 17, 1998, he was driving a Volkswagen full of 'narco-juniors' down to the coastal town of Mazatlan. Their mission was to kill a rival gang leader, using the Mardi Gras carnival as their cover. However, Ramón made a mistake by driving down a one-way street the wrong way right into the arms of a patrol car. There was a shoot-out, which left three bodies lying on the streets amid the festivities of the carnaval.

One of the bodies had an identity card in the pocket of his clothing, which bore the name Jorge Perez Lopez – the equivalent of 'John Smith' in Mexican. However, by the time the police realised that the card was forged, the body had mysteriously disappeared. Some members of the AFO had seen to it that they relieved the terrified local undertaker of the body, threatening him into silence.

It wasn't until the police studied the photographs taken at the crime scene that they realised that could possibly have killed one of the FBI's most wanted men – Ramón Arellano Félix.

With Ramón gone, Benjamin, the cartel's mastermind, seemed to lose the will to carry on as head of the organisation and prepared to flee the country. He was apprehended by soldiers just as he was about to leave with his bags packed and his wallet stuffed full of $100 notes. The DEA and the authorities were celebrating and declared that it was 'a great day for law enforcement'.

However, despite their partial success in fighting the drug cartel, other people within the government were more cautious. They were well aware that the remaining Félix brothers would now try and gain control of the cartel and that their rivals would try and muscle in on some of their drug routes. The situation was very tenuous and it was feared that violence would escalate.

The youngest of the brothers, Francisco Javier, was captured on August 14, 2006, along with two assassins, just off the coast of Baja California. Authorities suspect that the notorious cartel is now being run by two more brothers, Javier and Eduardo Arellano Félix. They also believe that they were the two brothers who were responsible for the massive, sophisticated underground tunnels discovered in January 2006. The State Department currently has a $5 million reward out for both men for information leading to their arrest.

THE MEDELLIN CARTEL

Since the 1970s, Colombia in South America has been witness to some of the most violent and perhaps sophisticated drug trafficking organisations in the world. The Medellin cartel started off as a small-time cocaine smuggling business, but it quickly turned into a massive multi-national cocaine empire. It was masterminded by a man named Pablo Emilio Escobar Gaviria (better known as Pablo Escobar) and is believed to have been formed in 1978 when a man named Carlos Lehder purchased a large portion of Normans Cay, which was an island off the coast of the Bahamas. It was on this island that the six main kingpins of the cartel are said to have come together – Pablo Escobar, the Ochoa brothers, Jorge, Fabio and Juan, José Gonzalo Rodriguez Gacha (also known as 'The Mexican') and Carlos Lehder himself. Lehder convinced the men that they could fly cocaine in small aeroplanes directly into the USA, which would do away with the need for countless smaller suitcase trips. From then on the six men started using the island as a launching point for the exportation of their drugs.

The growing appetite for cocaine in the USA led to the Medellin cartel making huge profits, which resulted in them reinvesting much of their money into more sophisticated laboratories and better aeroplanes. However, their success had a much darker side. Pablo Escobar was an incredibly violent man who was considered to be one of the most brutally ruthless, ambitious and powerful drug dealers ever encountered.

PABLO ESCOBAR

Pablo was raised with his brother, Roberto, on the streets of Medellin, which is where his life of crime began. He was a tough street thug who put fear into the hearts of the local population, a population who saw him get richer and richer day by day. He worked his way into the cocaine trade by killing off the opposition, a well-known dealer by the name of Fabio Restrepo. Escobar then informed Restrepo's men that their leader was dead, and left them in no doubt as to who they were working for from now on.

In May 1976, Escobar and some of his men were arrested after returning from a drug run to Ecuador. Escobar attempted to bribe the judge but was unsuccessful. However, after two of the arresting officers were found dead, the case was dropped. From then on Escobar and his men used violence and strong-arm tactics with anyone who got in their way.

During the 1980s, the Medellin cartel revolted against the government's threats to extradite traffickers to the USA. The cartel, urged by Escobar, waged a war against the Colombian government and are thought to have been responsible for the murder of hundreds of government officials, police, prosecutors, judges, journalists and even innocent bystanders that happened to be in the wrong place at the wrong time.

It has also been claimed that Escobar was behind the the storming of the Colombian Supreme Court in 1985, which resulted in the murder of half the judges. At the time the Supreme Court was working on Colombia's extradition treaty with the USA, something which Escobar was desperate to stop.

At the height of his career, Escobar owned properties all over the world. In Medellin alone, he owned nineteen villas, all of which had helicopter pads. He also owned banks, apartments and huge tracts of land, a fleet of ships and aeroplanes and an army of white-collar criminals who laundered his money. In 1989, Escobar was rated by *Forbes* magazines as being the seventh-richest man in the world. It was estimated that the Medellin cartel was taking in anything up to $30 billion a year.

Despite his tough image, in his own town of Medellin, Escobar was seen as a hero. He helped the community, sponsored the building of sports stadiums and frequently distributed money to the less privileged. The population often helped Escobar by allowing him to hideout in their houses and did everything in their power to protect him from the authorities.

THE CALI CARTEL

The main rivals to the Medellin cartel were an organisation situated in the Colombian city of Cali. The Cali cartel was run by the Rodriguez Orejuela brothers and Santacruz Londoño. They ran a far more sophisticated set-up, learning from the mistakes made by some of the Medellin members. As opposed to the Medellin cartel, the Cali re-invested its money in legitimate businesses and also tried to establish good relationships with the government. In fact, the Cali were so highly regarded by the government that they received the nickname the 'gentlemen' while their main rivals were called the 'hoodlums'.

As competition became more violent, the Cali started to attack the Medellin cartel, and in particular Escobar. They formed an association called the PEPES, or People Against Pablo Escobar, which was designed to target his homes, businesses and crew members. They also secretly supplied the Colombian police and the DEA with information about Escobar's activities and some of his hideouts.

The Cali cartel instigated the eventual downfall of Pablo Escobar, and by 1991 he was on his own and running for his life. Escobar turned himself in to the Colombian government to avoid being assassinated by his rivals. As a reward for turning himself in, Escobar was allowed to build his own private prison, which became known as *La Catedral*. He bartered with his government and they agreed he would be jailed for a period of five years and would be guaranteed no extradition to the USA so long as his drug trafficking activities ceased. However, Escobar, as was the nature of the man, abused the agreement and was often seen outside the confines of his supposed prison. After the local media showed pictures of the luxurious *La Catedral*, claiming that several business associates had been murdered when they visited Escobar there, the public forced the government into taking action. They moved him to another jail, but on July 22, 1992, Escobar escaped, fearing that he was about to be extradited to the USA, where he knew he would face certain life imprisonment.

The Colombian police force formed a special unit called the Search Bloc and started an intensive manhunt to find Escobar. As the number of his enemies grew, a vigilante group called PEPES and financed by the Cali cartel, carried out a bloody campaign against Escobar's family and friends. In the end, about 300 people were killed and large amounts of the Medellin cartel's property were destroyed.

The hunt for Escobar ended on December 2, 1993, just one day after his forty-fourth birthday, as he tried desperately to elude the Search Bloc for the last time. An elite force of police and military commandos trapped the drug lord on a rooftop in Medellin. Escobar was killed in a hail of bullets and the troops celebrated by firing their weapons into the air and shouting, 'We won!'

The leaders of the Cali cartel were eventually tracked down and arrested in the mid-1990s.

COLOMBIA TODAY

After the Medellin and Cali cartels began to self-destruct, the cocaine business began to break up into splinter groups. One group smuggled drugs from Colombia to Mexico, while another controlled the laboratories. There are known links between Marxist guerilla groups and the cocaine trade, who use them to protect their fields and the more remote laboratories in exchange for a large fee. This is not good news for Colombia, because this means that both sides are reaping huge profits from the drug industry, which in turn are used to buy arms for further fighting. The DEA have estimated that there may be as many as 300 narcotic-linked organisations in Colombia today as cocaine is shipped to virtually every nation in the world. Although cocaine has been refined and distributed around the world for centuries, it is South America that has become the primary exporter of the drug. Colombia alone, with its many clandestine laboratories, accounts for an estimated seventy-five per cent of the world's cocaine supply, which is masterminded by just a few major kingpins in the world of narcotics.

PART FOUR

SPIES AND DOUBLE AGENTS

MATA HARI

Mata Hari was a beautiful, exotic dancer who became an espionage agent. The glamorous World War I spy was eventually shot by the French in 1917, despite the fact that there was never any evidence that she actually passed on anything of military importance.

She was born Margaretha Gertruida Zelle on August 7, 1876 in Leeuwarden, Holland. Her father, Adam Zelle, was a successful milliner who was married to Antje van der Meulen. Margaretha was the only girl in a family of four boys and, in a society noted for its fair complexions, blonde hair and blue eyes, she stood out from the crowd. She had an olive complexion, thick black hair and black eyes, and her father doted on her, often indulging his vivacious daughter.

The young Margaretha was beautiful, intelligent and, in many ways, showed a flair for dancing and dramatics from an early age. She loved to wear brightly coloured clothes and often told exaggerated tales about her exotic origins. Her friends listened to her stories of castles and princes, totally enthralled, although deep down they knew it was all a fantasy inside her head. She was a popular pupil who was quick to learn and seemed to have a natural aptitude for languages.

When Margaretha was only thirteen years old, disaster struck the Zelle family. Her father's business went bankrupt when he made some misguided investments on the stock market. They were forced to sell off their beautiful furniture and the family moved to a much smaller house in a shabby part of town. Her father decided to go to Amsterdam to see if he could earn some money, and he left his children in the care of his wife. Unfortunately, Antje found it all too much to handle and became mentally ill and died when Margaretha was only fifteen. The teenager took the death of her mother very hard, but her spirits lifted when her father returned home to attend the funeral.

Margaretha believed that she would now live with her beloved father, but she was wrong, as he left a few days later leaving her with her godfather, Heer Visser. Visser was not keen to take on the orphan and suggested that she started training to become a kindergarten teacher. Aware that she was not really wanted in the Visser household, Margaretha accepted a place at a teaching school in Leyde, run by Heer Wybrandus Haanstra. Even at this age, Margaretha at 178 cm (5 ft 10in) tall towered above most of the other female students.

Margaretha had one major problem at the school, and that was the proprietor Haanstra. He had developed an infatuation for the stunning young Margaretha, and forced his attentions on her. For a while it appears as though she welcomed his affections, but their affair became a subject of public scandal. The blame was placed on Margaretha, who was said to have made advances to the elderly man, and she was forced to leave the school in disgrace.

Confused, and unsure where to go, Margaretha ended up at the house of her uncle, Heer Taconis, in The Hague. Although he did not welcome her with open arms, Margaretha proved to be very helpful around the house and she was allowed to stay.

TIME FOR MARRIAGE

Margaretha had two main disadvantages when she started looking for a suitor. The first was her height, because the majority of men didn't like to have a wife taller than themselves, and the second was the size of her bosoms, which were uncommonly small in a time when the hour-glass figure was all the rage. Despite the fact that her exotic looks and style attracted many men, none seemed brave enough to approach her.

Eventually she found the solution in an advertisement placed in a local newspaper.

*Officer on home leave from Dutch East Indies
would like to meet a girl of pleasant character
– object matrimony.*

The gentleman in question was a thirty-eight-year-old man in the Dutch military by the name of Rudolph MacLeod. The advertisement had been placed in the newspaper by a friend without Rudolph's knowledge, so when he learned that a young lady would like to meet him he was surprised, but agreed. Rudolph had prematurely aged due to the fact that he was not only a heavy drinker, but also suffered from diabetes and rheumatism, and it was these health problems that had brought him home to Holland.

When the couple first met, Rudolph was smitten by the beautiful young woman and, despite their vast age difference Margaretha was also very taken by the military gentleman. She had always had a penchant for men in uniform and possibly seeing Rudolph adorning so many medals, swayed her affections somewhat. After a brief time, Rudolph proposed marriage and Margaretha accepted eagerly. The couple hit a snag, however, because in Holland the law stated that a female could marry at sixteen with a parent's consent but had to wait until they were thirty to marry without it. Margaretha had lied to Rudolph and told him that both her parents were dead, as she didn't want him to meet her now impoverished father. Aware that she would now have to tell the truth, she confessed to Rudolph that she had lied and then went to get permission from Adam Zelle.

Within three months of their engagement the couple were married. Their first child, Norman John, was born a year later on January 30, 1897. Although Rudolph was a loving, attentive husband for a while, after the birth of the first child he went back to his old ways of drinking and debauchery. Despite his own infidelity, he showed extreme jealousy if any man looked at his wife, and he took to beating Margaretha. She tried to ignore her husbands behaviour and continued to act the loving mother and wife.

A NEW START

Margaretha became excited when Rudolph told her he had been transferred to Java. She imagined a new exotic lifestyle in a land that she had heard so much about. When they arrived in Abawara, a city in the middle of the island, Margaretha was not disappointed and found the place enchanting. She loved to wear the native sarong, but it wasn't long before the old problems reared their ugly head. Rudolph became more and more bad tempered, spending much of his time in a drunken stupor. He took to raping his wife and also took a young native woman as his concubine. Margaretha discovered she was pregnant with her second child during the heavy monsoon season. Unable to get down the flooded roads, she was forced to stay at home and soon she became extremely bored. With the help of her servants she quickly mastered the Malay tongue, despite her husband strictly forbidding it.

Their daughter, Jeanne Louise, was born on May 2, 1898. Margaretha hoped that a daughter would change her husband's moods, but she couldn't have been proved more wrong – in fact he despised the fact that it was a girl.

A year later, Rudolph was called to Sumatra, but he told Margaretha that he was unable to take his family with him. He promised to send her money and placed her in the care of the comptroller. Once again, Margaretha found herself in a place where she wasn't really wanted, and she hated being totally dependent on the family when her husband forgot to send any monetary support. She was delighted when he eventually called her to say that she could join him in Medan.

As a commander, Rudolph lived in a spacious, well-furnished house, and it was Margaretha's job as his wife to hold lavish parties. She took the responsibility readily and dressed in beautiful dresses sent to her from Amsterdam, conversing easily with their visitors, very often in their native tongue. For once Rudolph realised that his stunning wife was a major asset and for a while their marriage was revived. He felt proud of her and was grateful that she had made him such a social success.

On the night of June 27, 1899, Margaretha had just settled into bed after a night of entertaining, when she heard screams coming from the nursery. She rushed upstairs and as she entered the room she was overcome by the stench of vomit. As she looked into their beds she noticed that the vomit was a strange black colour and that both children were convulsed with pain. She screamed to Rudolph to get a doctor as she hugged her children in desperation.

By the time the doctor arrived Norman was already dead, but Jeanne Louise was rushed to hospital and her life was saved. After an autopsy it was discovered that both children had been poisoned and, although it was never proved, there were whispers that it may have been one of the servants who had been abused once too often by Mr MacLeod.

Both Margaretha and Rudolph were completely devastated by the loss of their son, but instead of pulling together in their grief, they gradually drifted apart. They returned to Java, where Rudolph's drinking became a major problem, often blaming his wife for the loss of their child.

Margaretha fell ill with typhoid, which made Rudolph even more angry, complaining that her illness was costing him a lot of money. The marriage deteriorated day by day, and shortly after her recovery Rudolph announced they were to return to Europe. They had only just settled into their new home, when Rudolph left Margaretha, taking their daughter with him.

Margaretha filed for legal separation with an Amsterdam tribunal, which was an exceptionally brave move as it was scandalous for a woman to seek a divorce. To her surprise, the tribunal granted her a divorce and also custody of their daughter. However, Margaretha had no work and was unable to support her daughter because Rudolph had flatly refused to pay her any maintenance. Reluctantly, she was forced to hand her over to Rudolph's custody once again, and Margaretha sought refuge in Paris.

MATA HARI EMERGES

Margaretha was dazzled by the bright lights of Paris and she started dreaming about what sort of job she could do. She hoped to join a theatre or perhaps become a model, but nothing was forthcoming and she was forced to return home penniless. Margaretha had hit rock bottom – no husband, no child, no home, no money – she felt life had nothing left to offer her. In a last desperate effort she scraped enough money together to return to Paris, determined this time she was going to be a success.

Wanting to put her old life behind her, she

changed her name to Mata Hari, which in Malay translated as 'eye of dawn'. It was using her new identity that she got a job as an exotic dancer in the Musé Guimet on March 13, 1905. She wore an elaborate costume and accessories and try to enhance what nature had failed to provide by stuffing the cups of her costume with cotton wool. When she had completed her dance, completely drained of any energy, Mata Hari was met with rapturous applause. She was literally an overnight success and soon her new art form took her to many European countries. At last she was famous and she loved it.

Mata Hari's heyday lasted from 1905 until 1912. As she approached forty, Mata Hari's dancing started to lose its vitality and her career gradually turned to that of a courtesan. She had relationships with many high-ranking military officers, politicians and others in influential positions, captivating them with her eroticism. Her liaisons took her across international borders, but as World War I took hold, this proved to be her downfall.

DOUBLE AGENT

One of Mata Hari's rich associates was a man called Traugott von Jagow. He was allegedly in charge of German espionage and gave orders to his mistress to spy on France. It is believed that Mata Hari attended a so-called 'spy school' in Antwerp, Belgium, which was run by a woman named Elsbeth Schragmüller. At the school Mata Hari was given the code name 'H21', and she spent her time learning codes, ciphers, and the study of chemicals and their uses and she also memorized maps, charts and photographs.

The animosity between France and Germany was gradually starting to build and Mata Hari asked permission to leave Germany just before World War I broke out. Although she managed to get into Switzerland, she was immediately sent back to Germany because of problems with her papers. She eventually ended up in Amsterdam, but made many journeys between Paris and Amsterdam.

Paris, being the capital of a country now at war, was deeply concerned about its security and the authorities were aware there might be spies in their midst. Mata Hari became a prime suspect, due to the fact that she had recently had a German lover, and they started to put a tail on her movements.

It was around this time that Mata Hari met the love of her life, a twenty-one-year-old Russian officer by the name of Vadim. Despite the age difference a passionate romance blossomed until Vadim was ordered back to the Front. Vadim was injured and was in danger of losing the sight of one eye. When Mata Hari heard that her lover was hurt, she returned to being a courtesan in an effort to raise money to get him medical help. While trying to get permission to visit Vadim in an official war zone, Mata Hari met a man named Georges Ladoux, who was instrumental in her downfall.

Ladoux was a captain in the French army who was in charge of organising counter-espionage. Mata Hari was having difficulty getting permission to visit Vadim because the authorities suspected that she was a spy and some friends recommended that she contact Ladoux. She told him her story and said that as a Dutch citizen she should be considered neutral, but she pointed out that her sympathies were with France. Ladoux said he would be prepared to help her if she would considering spying against the Germans for France.

Mata Hari said she needed time to think about it, aware that being a spy could be exceptionally dangerous. However, she knew she needed to earn a lot of money if she wanted to help Vadim, and she decided to take a chance.

Ladoux made arrangements for Mata Hari to go to Brussels, where she met up with a businessman by the name of Wurfbein. He supplied food to the German army and was therefore a useful contact. The plan was that Wurfbein would introduce her to General Moritz Ferdinand von Bissing, whom she intended to seduce and hopefully gain some useful information via pillow talk. Because of the war it was necessary for Mata Hari to take a circuitous route to Belgium – via Spain, Britain, Holland and eventually Belgium.

However, as soon as she landed in Britain things started to go wrong. The British were very suspicious of Mata Hari as they thought she was working for the Germans. As soon as the boat landed the police were waiting for her and took her back to Scotland Yard for questioning. Apparently she had been mistaken for a spy by the name of Clara Benedix who was similar in appearance. Mata Hari told Scotland Yard that they had made a terrible mistake, and they contacted Ladoux for his advice. Ladoux told them to send her back to Spain.

Mata Hari was angry and still unable to get to see her lover. She met and had a romance with a German officer named Major Arnold Kalle, and during their time together she attempted to extract secret information from her lover. She hoped to use it to please her French spymasters so that she could at least receive some payment for her services. The information that Kalle passed on to her was that he was 'trying to arrange for a submarine to drop off some German and Turkish officers in the French zone of Morocco.'

Believing that she had obtained a very important secret, Mata Hari wrote a coded letter to Ladoux. However, it had all been a plot because the French already knew about the submarine and Kalle wanted to know whether she was spying for the French by giving her some stale information. Mata Hari, who was unaware that her secrets weren't really secrets at all, decided to return to Paris to reap the rewards of her spying. When she eventually got in to see Ladoux, he told her that he was not prepared to pay her any money as the information she passed on was not up to date. Mata Hari was despondent and sat around waiting for another assignment.

The alarm over Mata Hari being a German spy went off when a message came through to Ladoux which read:

> *H21 informs us: Princess George of Greece, Marie Bonaparte, is using her 'intimate relations' with Briand [Aristide Briande, the then prime minister of France] to get French support for her husband's access to the Greek throne. She says Briand's enemies would welcome further defeats in the war to overthrow him. Britain has political and military control of France. French are afraid to speak up. General offensive planned for next spring.*

Although the message itself was pretty meaningless, it was the fact that Mata Hari had been allotted a code name recognizable by the Germans, that alerted the French authorities. It appeared that the Germans wanted to alert the French to Mata Hari by revealing her code, so that they would do their dirty work for them.

CONDEMNED TO DEATH

Mata Hari was arrested for espionage by the French authorities on February 13, 1917. France was hungry for a scapegoat, as it was at a low point in the war. She was interrogated many times by Captain Pierre Bouchardon while she was held at Saint-Lazarre Prison. She continued to deny being a double agent saying, 'I am innocent. Someone is playing with me – French counter-espionage, since I am in its service, and I have acted only on its instructions.'

The only visitor allowed in to see Mata Hari was her attorney, seventy-four-year-old Edouard Clunet. They had once been lovers and he continued to have feelings for her. However, despite still having an alert legal mind, he proved to have lost his skills at the handling the court and proved to be more of a disadvantage during the trial.

Mata Hari's arrest was kept secret until her case came to trial on July 24, 1917, at the Palace of Justice. The courtroom was full to the brim with people who wanted to see the once beautiful, exotic dancer who became a spy. Presiding over the trial was Lieutenant-Colonel Albert-Ernest Somprou, while the chief prosecutor was André Mornet. Mornet carefully outlined the case against Mata Hari and said she had been under suspicion and surveillance since her arrival in Paris in May 1916. Despite a distinct lack of evidence, the court found

Mata Hari guilty of being a double agent, an offence which was punishable by death.

When Mata Hari heard the sentence, she seemed to be in a state of shock, staring transfixed at the floor. Her attorney, Clunet, wept with his head in his hands. Although Mata Hari hoped for a reprieve during her last months in prison, it was not to be, and she was executed by a firing squad on October 15, 1917, at the age of forty-one.

No one ever claimed the body of Mata Hari and it was taken away to be used for medical studies. Her head was embalmed and kept in the Museum of Anatomy in Paris, until it mysteriously disappeared in the 1950s.

In the years since her death, Mata Hari has become a legend, despite the fact that her career as a spy was very short-lived and unproductive. She is remembered in history as the 'greatest woman spy', which is sadly grossly exaggerated. The truth of the matter is she really made her fame as an exotic dancer and a pleaser of men. Sadly her daughter died in her sleep at the age of twenty-one, the night before she was supposed to travel to the Dutch East Indies to become a teacher.

ALDRICH AMES

Aldrich Hazen Ames was paid over two million dollars by the KGB for revealing the names of every US spy in the Soviet Union. Because of this he put dozens of CIA officers at risk, and he is still considered to be the most damaging mole in the history of the CIA. He began selling secrets in 1985 and within a decade he had revealed more than 100 covert operations and caused the death of several CIA agents.

IN HIS BLOOD

When Ames was interviewed he joked that 'spying was in his blood', although he was unaware in his early years that his father, Carleton Ames, worked secretly for the CIA. At the beginning of 1957, his father suggested that Ames, or Rick as he was known by his friends and family, should apply for a summer job at the agency. This was offered exclusively to children of agency employees. Ames spent time at the secret training camp of the CIA, where he learned to make counterfeit money.

Ames was a bright pupil at Langley High School, where his mother, Rachel, was a teacher. He loved to play-act and would spend his leisure time in imaginary covert missions, even devising his own secret languange.

After graduation, Ames went to the University of Chicago, but he failed to get any grades due to the fact that he spent so much time in drama club. His father, who was displeased with his sons attitude, suggested that he went to work for the CIA. Consequently, in 1962 Ames spent his days being trained as a case officer for the covert branch of the CIA and his evenings attending college to further his education. His love of dramatics came into play at the CIA, when he was told it was imperative to lie, cheat and deceive to become a good agent. He was also told that he would need to adopt different identities in undercover work, something that Ames was already exceptionally good at.

After his training Ames was assigned to the Soviet branch of the CIA and went to Ankara in Turkey to pose as a military officer. His job was to recruit Turks as spies for the CIA, but his mission was a dismal failure and he only managed to find one suitable candidate. When Ames returned to Washington, he was told by his superior that he would never make a successful case officer as he obviously did not have the skill to manipulate. Ames was devastated and even considered leaving the CIA, but the agency had other plans for him and he was sent to its foreign language school. Here it was a different story, and he quickly mastered the Russian language, which opened up new opportunities for him. His first big break came in 1974 when he was asked to oversee a Soviet diplomat, Alexander Dmitrievich Ogorodnik, in Langley, Virginia. Ogorodnik, code name Trigon, had been blackmailed into becoming a spy by some Colombian intelligence agents, but he refused to work with them and had asked to be turned over to the CIA. One of the first things that Orogodnik asked for from Ames, was a cyanide pill, which he said he would take in the event that he was caught. Orogodnik soon became a valuable informant for the CIA when he was assigned to the Soviet foreign ministry in Moscow, but he was exposed by a Czechoslovak translator and was forced to commit suicide in 1977.

The CIA were highly impressed with the way Ames had handled the Orogodnik case. He was sent to New York City, which was considered to be part of a major spy network because it was home to the United Nations. Here, Ames was assigned to a nuclear arms expert by the name of Sergey Fedorenko, whose code name was Pyrrhic. Before Fedorenko was called back to Russia, Ames claimed that he had managed to obtain vital missile information off him and that the two men had become very close friends.

In 1978, Ames was given a third assignment – to get close to Ambassador Nikolaevich Shevchenko, who had been secretly spying for the USA for over two years. Ames helped to protect Shevchenko from the KGB and had to comfort him when his wife mysteriously committed suicide.

With several successful missions under his belt, Ames was now at the top of his game. However, his personal life was now a mess and he grew further and further apart from his wife, Nancy. He started going on drinking binges and it was not surprising that when it came to the time for promotion within the CIA, Ames was passed over. He became bitter and many of his associates at the CIA said they were concerned about his growing bitterness and aggression.

Shortly after his divorce from Nancy, Ames's financial situation took a nosedive. He started to fantasise about ways to earn large amounts of money and before long his bank account swelled with money being deposited on a regular basis, in a way that he could not admit to any of his colleagues.

CO-CONSPIRATOR

Ames married Maria del Rosario Casa Depuy one hot afternoon in August 1985. She was the cultural attaché for the Colombian Embassy in Mexico and was introduced to Ames by one of his associates at the CIA. Their relationship, which was clandestine at first, was frowned upon by the CIA. Agents are not supposed to have affairs with or marry foreign national, yet Ames was seemingly successful on both counts.

However, the marriage between Ames and Depuy was nothing compared to the secret they held, which would eventually become too large to hide. When Ames was trying to think of ways of earning cash, he remembered that the KGB had once offered one of his CIA subordinates $50,000 to spy for them.

Over the period of the next nine years, Ames, with his considerable knowledge of Soviet operations and experience in clandestine missions, he succeeded in obtaining a vast amount of money from the KGB without being detected by either the CIA or FBI. Using his counter-intelligence job within the CIA to obtain access to active cases, Ames contacted selected Soviet officials, using an assumed name and fake job description. He identified himself as a Soviet Union expert with the Intelligence Community Staff and, using this cover, he met with one particular Soviet official for almost a year. Ames allegedly sold the KGB the names of Soviet agents who had been recruited by the CIA, as well as many valuable secrets about US spies working against the Soviet Union. During these years Ames and his wife made numerous large cash deposits into two Virginia banks in the USA and abroad. All the money was allegedly paid by the Soviet Union in exchange for national security secrets. Using this information the KGB started rounding up the CIA's secret spies, beginning with two men: Motorin and Martynov. They were both brutally interrogated in Moscow and eventually executed.

In July 1986, Ames was transferred to Rome in Italy, where he continued his meetings with the KGB. When his assignment in Rome was complete, Ames returned to Washington DC, where he continued to pass classified documents to the KGB using predetermined hiding places. Ames would leave his documents in the 'dead drop', which would be replaced by an envelope containing money. Eventually his clandestine operations netted him over $1.8 billion.

MONEY AROUSES SUSPICION

By 1993, the CIA and the FBI were suspicious about the Ames's new-found wealth. The FBI opened an investigation in May 1993, and they carried out intensive surveillance of both Ames and his wife for the next ten months. When the FBI searched the Ames's residence, they found documents and other information which linked them to the KGB. They went through his rubbish and found a computer printer ribbon which showed that Ames had written several long letters to the

Russians. The key piece of information, and a major blunder on the part of Ames, was the fact that he had recently updated his word processing programme on his computer. What he had failed to realise was that the programme automatically made copies of any documents that he typed, giving the FBI details of his counter-espionage activities.

On October 13, 1993, agents watching Ames saw him put a chalk mark on a mailbox, indicating that he intended to meet with KGB members in Bogota, Colombia. Ames was tailed and was seen speaking to his Russian contact in Bogota. When Ames applied for a trip to Moscow as part of his official CIA duties, the FBI decided to take action. Scared that Ames might try and bolt, on February 21, 1994, he was lured from his house on the pretext that he was urgently needed at the office. As he got into his Jaguar to leave, his car was surrounded by FBI officers. Inside the house, his wife was also arrested, surrounded by evidence of her obvious gluttony. Row upon row of priceless dresses, shoes, jewellery and lingerie, some of which hadn't even been removed from their boxes.

Ames, now 52, and his wife, 41, were arrested in Arlington, Virginia, and both were charged with conspiracy to commit espionage. Ames offered to confess if the government would release his wife, but the Justice Department refused to bargain with him. Little did Ames know, that in another room

Rosario was turning against her husband, stating that she had simply got caught up in his lies, deceit and manipulation.

Ames was eventually sentenced to life imprisonment while Rosario received five years. As soon as her parole came up in 1999, she was deported to Colombia, where she still lives today.

The case of Aldrich Ames is considered to be the worst betrayal of intelligence in the history of the USA. No one has really ever assessed the true extent of the damage, but it is obvious that Ames knew all the true names of virtually every Soviet agent being recruited by the CIA. There is no doubt that Ames was a 'super' criminal mastermind who sent shock-waves through the US intelligence community, causing the deaths of at least ten US agents.

A man who never made any attempt at hiding his love of excesses, Ames eventually expressed bitter regret at what he had done, saying:

No punishment by this court can balance or ease the profound shame and guilt I bear.

KLAUS FUCHS

Klaus Emil Julius Fuchs was a scientist who was responsible for many of the theoretical calculations relating to early models of the hydrogen bomb. Through a series of blunders he was allowed to provide British and US nuclear secrets to the Soviet Union which turned out to be of major significance.

Klaus Fuchs was born on December 29, 1911, in Rüsselsheim, Germany. His father was a Lutheran minister who was deeply committed to socialist ideology. He taught his son to stand up for what he believed, even if his beliefs were at odds with accepted codes of ethic.

Fuchs came to the UK in 1933 as a communist refugee. As a student at both Leipzig and Kiel Universities, Fuchs became active in politics and joined the Social Democratic Party of Germany. In 1932, he became a member of the Communist Party, but after Adolf Hitler became Chancellor of Germany in 1933, his political affiliations made him a target for the Nazis. Fuchs was forced into hiding and managed to flee to France. From there, using family connections, he managed to escape to Bristol, England. As a German refugee, Fuchs was entitled to aid, including a scholarship to Bristol University. By 1937, he had graduated from Bristol with a doctorate in Physics and continued his education with advanced Physics at Edinburgh University. His paper on quantum mechanics entitled *Proceedings of the Royal Society* gained him a teaching position at Edinburgh, until the outbreak of war in 1939.

By 1940, the war in Europe had escalated and the UK began to fear for its national security. Any Germans living in the UK were taken into custody and put into internment camps. Fuchs was first taken to the Isle of Man but was later transferred to Quebec in Canada, where he stayed from June to December 1940. However, Professor Max Born, who Fuchs had studied under at Edinburgh, intervened and managed to obtain special treatment for the talented, young physicist.

By early 1941, Fuchs had temporarily returned to Edinburgh. Within months, Fuchs was approached by Rudolf Peierls of the University of Birmingham to work on the British 'Tube Alloys' programme – the British atomic bomb research project. Despite wartime restrictions, Fuchs was granted British citizenship in 1942 and was asked to sign the Official Secrets Act. It was around this time that Fuchs contacted a former friend in the German Communist Party, who put him in touch with a man at the Soviet Embassy in the UK, whose code name was 'Rest'.

PASSING OVER SECRETS

In 1943, Fuchs was transferred, along with Rudolf Peierls, to the Columbia University in New York City. It was here that Fuchs began work on the Manhattan Project, which was the US atomic bomb programme. In August 1944, Fuchs' work took him to the Los Alamos, New Mexico, research facility, where he was seen as a first-rate scientist and researcher. His colleages later remarked that he was a serious man who focused with great intensity on his work. No one suspected that Fuchs had in fact been passing detailed information regarding the bomb project to a Soviet connection called Harry Gold, code name 'Raymond'. Fuchs made contact with Gold almost as soon as he arrived in the USA, and at one of their meetings in Santa Fe he gave his contact a precise drawing with measurements of the 'Fat Man' bomb. This was the bomb that the USA eventually dropped on Nagasaki at the end of World War II.

When the war ended, Fuchs knew everything there was to know about making hydrogen bombs. In April 1946, he attended a three-day, top secret conference at Los Alamos, which outlined the details of work on the new 'super bomb'.

When Fuchs was asked to return to the UK to continue his work, he made sure he read every document in the Los Alamos archives on thermo-nuclear weapon designs. Once back in the UK, Fuchs started work at the Harwell Atomic Research facility. However, it wasn't long before he had re-established contact with his Soviet friends.

In 1947, Fuchs met his new contact, Alexander Feklisov, in a pub in north London. Feklisov primed him for details of the new super bomb, and Fuchs described in detail certain structural characteristics of the new weapon. They met for a second time in March 1948, and this time Fuchs handed over specific information that some Russian physicists now say proved to be of great importance to the Soviet hydrogen bomb.

Fuchs' world of espionage started to crumble at the end of 1949. In 1948, the Venona cables were starting to be deciphered. The Venona Project was a top-secret US effort to gather and decrypt messages sent in the 1940s by agents of what is now called the KGB and the GRU, the Soviet military intelligence agency. These cables revealed the identities of numerous Americans who were spying for the Soviet Union, including Klaus Fuchs.

One of these cables was a report on the progress of the atomic bomb research, which had been written by Fuchs. At first it was not obvious whether Fuchs had in fact written the report for the Soviets,

c.1933: US bank robbers and lovers Clyde Barrow (1909–34) and Bonnie Parker (1911–34), *popularly known as Bonnie and Clyde.*

c.1934: US bank robber John Dillinger (1903–34), who went from small-time crook to the USA's 'Most Wanted' after an ill-fated bank robbery left a police officer dead.

Head shot of Italian-born gangster Lucky Luciano (1897–1962). Luciano was considered the father of modern organised crime and the mastermind of the massive post-war expansion of the international heroine trade.

English actor Charles Gray (1928–2000) as SPECTRE founder Ernst Stavro Blofeld in the James Bond film Diamonds Are Forever, *which was directed by Guy Hamilton in 1971.*

c.1975: Four members of the 'Cambridge Five' graduates of Trinity College, Cambridge, who passed information from British Intelligence to the Soviet Union in the 1940s and 1950s. Clockwise from top left, Anthony Blunt (1907–83), Donald Duart Maclean (1913–83), Kim Philby (1912–88) and Guy Burgess (1911–63).

Phoolan Devi, the reformed bandit queen who spent eleven years in jail for the massacre of 22 men, is pictured in front of a statue of India's founding father, Mahatma Gandhi, in June 1996.

The notorious Carlos, known as 'The Jackal', who virtually invented late-twentieth-century-style terrorism.
Carlos reportedly helped coordinate an assassination attempt on the Shah of Persia in June 1979. He was finally caught in 1995.

Nick Leeson, the British futures market dealer who brought about the downfall of Barings Bank while working for their Singapore offices.

or whether they had obtained it by other means. Whatever the truth, it was definite proof that the Russians had penetrated the secret of the Manhattan Project.

On December 21, 1949, a British intelligence officer told Fuchs that he was suspected of having given away classified information on nuclear weapons to the Soviet Union. Although Fuchs repeatedly denied the accusations, he eventually broke down under interrogation and agreed to make a statement. He confessed to his part in the theft of atomic secrets and his trial took place at the Old Bailey in London on March 1, 1950. The court was packed, with over eighty reporters, two US Embassy representatives, the mayor of London and the Duchess of Kent. The chief prosecutor was attorney General Hartley Shawcross, who had made a name for himself at the famous Nuremberg Trials.

The trial only lasted for two hours after Fuchs pleaded guilty, and he was sentenced to fourteen years in prison, which was the maximum possible punishment under British law for the passing of military secrets to a friendly nation. When Fuchs was passing his secrets, the USSR was not an enemy.

Fuchs only served nine years of his sentence, after which he was allowed to leave the UK to relocate in East Germany. He resumed his scientific career and lectured on his beloved Physics. In 1959, he married a friend of his from his years as a student,

Margarete Keilson. Fuchs was elected to the Academy of Sciences and the Communist Party central committee, and he was later appointed as deputy director for the Institute for Nuclear Research in Rossendorf. He eventually retired in 1979 and died on January 28, 1988.

Whether the information Fuchs passed on regarding neclear weapons was useful is still a matter of debate. Many believe that by the time Fuchs left the project in 1946, too little information was known about the workings of the hydrogen bomb to be deemed of any use. British security were highly criticised after the trial of Fuchs for failing to make appropriate checks on a man who never denied having communist connections.

Ten months after Fuchs was jailed, another Harwell scientist, Professor Bruno Pontecorvo, went missing, and it was later discovered that he had fled to Russia.

THE CAMBRIDGE SPIES

In the 1930s, a number of bright young students at Cambridge University, who were destined for careers in the Foreign Office or the intelligence agencies, became famous for passing information to the Soviet Union over a period of about thirty years. In the KGB they were known as the 'magnificent five', but in the UK they were better known as the Cambridge spies. The four men were Kim Philby, Guy Burgess, Donald Mclean and Anthony Blunt. There was believed to be a fifth man, John Cairncross, but there is insufficient proof to confirm that he was actually involved. The information they passed on was accurate and reliable, and they became major assets to the KGB. None of the men were motivated by any form of financial gain, but by the fact that they believed capitalism to be corrupt.

The Cambridge spies were informally led by Harold 'Kim' Philby, who allegedly served the KGB for over fifty years. He is believed to have caused the most damage to both British and US intelligence, providing classified information that caused the deaths of numerous agents. Burgess and Maclean were most productive for around twelve years, until they defected to Russia in 1951. Anthony Blunt was the most aristocratic of the infamous Cambridge spy ring. He was a discreet homosexual, a distant relative of the Queen and keeper of the royal family's pictures and drawings.

THE BEGINNING

The story of the Cambridge spies really started during the time of the Great Depression. The world was plunged into an economic crisis after the Wall Street Crash of 1929. At colleges and universities, Socialist groups were beginning to make their presence known, and this included a group of young men at Cambridge University. Young people who had become fed up with capitalist ideals had gone to fight for Franco and the Nationalist cause in the Spanish Civil War. Others, who wanted to see what Communism was like, went to the Soviet Union. The men mentioned above decided to take matters into their own hands to try and help the Socialist cause.

ANTHONY BLUNT

Anthony Blunt, the son of a London vicar, was the first of the four to enter Cambridge. He joined in

1926 to study the History of Art, and shortly afterwards he became a member of the Cambridge Apostles. This was an elite secret society, which was essentially a debating club that based its beliefs on those of Marxism.

Blunt went to Russia in 1933, and it was probably while he was there that he was recruited by the NKVD, a branch of secret communist police. Although it is not certain, it is thought that Blunt recruited the other members of the Cambridge spies, especially targeting homosexuals. At a time when homosexuality was illegal, Blunt kept his affair with fellow student, Guy de Moncey Burgess, under wraps.

When war broke out, Blunt was working as Deputy Director for the Courtauld Institute of Art. Although he volunteered to work in Military Intelligence, because of his links with communism, his application was rejected. Ironically, he was later given a job in MI5 on the recommendations of a friend. For the next five years he secretly sabotaged counter-espionage operations. He provided Moscow with the names of double agents within the KGB and also intercepted diplomatic documents and communications. Blunt worked closely with his lover, Guy, and they often met up to prepare their reports for the Kremlin.

When the war finished, with the permission of Moscow, Blunt left MI5, but not the services of the

KGB. Blunt effected the perfect cover by taking the job as Surveyor of the King's Pictures. He felt that no one would suspect him of running messages and collecting information while he was a member of the King's staff.

Not only did he prove to be indispensable to Russia, but also to his friends Philby, Burgess and McLean, who fled to Moscow in 1951. Aware that the authorities would want to search Burgess's flat, Blunt, who was in possession of a key, made sure he was there to let them in. While they were searching the flat, Blunt noticed three letters that would implicate his friends in espionage, so he quickly concealed them in his pocket. As a valuable asset, and because they knew he would be interrogated, the Russians advised Blunt to defect immediately. Blunt, who was so pleased with his new royal position, was not so keen to leave the UK, and he told the Russians that he would be able to withstand any type of interrogation. He proved this fact when, for the next twelve years Blunt was interrogated eleven times, and on not one occasion did he crack.

In 1963, Blunt's luck ran out. A former university friend was offered a job as art consultant to President Kennedy. However, before taking the job he decided to clear his conscience and named Blunt as the Soviet agent who had recruited him. When Blunt was accused by an MI5 agent, he was told that if he confessed he would be immune from prosecution. Blunt confessed, and the slate was wiped clean. During his confession, Blunt told MI5 the names of other people he had recruited, but also gave them some misleading advice to protect his friends, Burgess, McLean and Philby.

No one really knows why Blunt was offered immunity, but many believe it was because of his royal connections. In 1946, he was asked to go on a mission to Germany to retrieve some papers. Although the full details of this mission have never been revealed it resulted in him not only being presented with the Commander of the Royal Victorian Order but a knighthood as well.

It wasn't until 1979, when a book was published about the Cambridge Spies, that Blunt was publicly exposed and stripped of all of his titles. He died in disgrace in 1983.

GUY BURGESS

Guy Francis de Moncy Burgess, was the rather eccentric son of a naval commander. He was at Cambridge University from 1930 studying History. He met Anthony Blunt when he joined the Cambridge Apostles, but was often an embarrassment to the society due to his heavy drinking and open homosexuality.

Burgess became a personal assistant to Jack

McNamara, a Conservative MP, and quickly fitted into the rich and influential lifestyle. As well as working for McNamara, Burgess also worked for the BBC, which gave him the opportunity to meet influential people and obtain important information, which he subsequently passed on to Moscow. Using his contacts he managed to ingratiate himself with members of the British intelligence, and in 1939, he was offered a full-time job with MI6.

At the beginning of the war the Secret Service were desperate for new recruits, and Burgess was given the job of finding suitable candidates. He chose to look for these men in the elite drinking clubs of London, but by the 1950s his heavy drinking lost him his job. He was posted to Washington, where Kim Philby took him under his wing and tried to get him to amend his ways. This was something that he later regretted, when he asked Burgess to do him a favour.

British intelligence had got wind that another member of the Cambridge spies, Donald McLean, was spying for Russia. Both Philby and the Russians were worried about him cracking under interrogation and it was decided to send him to Moscow without delay. Burgess was sent to make sure that McLean stayed one step ahead of MI6. When Burgess learned how close the MI6 were, he packed up his car and headed to McLean's house, and drove them to Southampton. Nothing was heard from either of them for a few months, when they eventually turned up in Moscow. McLean was supposed to travel on his own, but Burgess decided he would be his travelling companion, much to the disgust of Philby and the KGB.

Guy Burgess, who never really gave up his drinking lifestyle, died in misery in Russia in 1963. He never settled in his new homeland and was said to have always felt out of place.

DONALD McLEAN

Donald McLean was rather shy, the son of a puritanical Liberal MP. He arrived at Cambridge in 1931 and studied French. In 1935, he passed the entrance exam to join the Foreign Office and was posted to Paris. He soon made a name for himself in the Diplomatic Corps, and in 1944 was made Head of Chancery at the embassy in Washington. The KGB could not believe their luck, as secret documents about the heads of the UK, Canada and the USA landed on their desks.

Russia was even more delighted when McLean was made secretary of the combined Policy Committee, which was dealing with the classified Manhattan Project. He passed secret after secret, making himself one of the best agents the KGB had ever used.

By the early 1950s, just like Burgess, the strains of

a double life were starting to take their toll. He was drinking heavily and started making indiscreet comments in inappropriate places. However, instead of losing his job, he was transferred to a high position in Cairo where his anti-American opinions became too much of an embarrassment. He was arrested and deported back to the UK where he was told he had to 'sort himself out'. After a few months he was given the job as head of the American Desk at the Foreign Office, which left the floodgates open for him to pass information on to Moscow about America's involvement in the Korean War.

Following the decoding of the Venona Transcripts, McLean was named as one of the spies involved in passing nuclear secrets. Moscow was frightened that he would crack under interrogation and ordered him to flee the country. He arrived in Moscow with his friend Burgess, where he was given a job in the Soviet Foreign Office. He died in 1983, an unhappy man, because his wife had left him and gone to live with Kim Philby.

KIM PHILBY

Harold Adrian Russell Philby was the son of St John Philby, a British diplomat, an explorer, author and adviser to King Ibn Sa'ud of Saudi Arabia. He got his nickname 'Kim' from a book of the same name by Rudyard Kipling, which was a story about a young Irish-Indian boy who was a spy for the British in India. Philby studied History and Economics at Cambridge from 1929.

Philby became a committed communist and went to Vienna to help refugees who were fleeing Nazi Germany. He even went as far as marrying his landlady's daughter, Litzi Friedman, a Jewish communist, to help her flee Austria as a British subject.

On the orders of Moscow, in 1936, Philby toned down his communist beliefs, appearing at Anglo-German meetings and editing a pro-Hitler magazine. In 1937, as a freelance journalist, Philby went to Spain to report on the war from Franco's point of view. A car he was travelling in with three other journalists was hit by a shell, and Philby was the only one to survive. Franco was grateful for his support and in 1938 awarded him the Red Cross of Military Merit.

In 1940, Guy Burgess introduced Philby to the chief of staff, Marjorie Maxse, at MI6, and suggested that she should recruit him. Philby impressed Maxse and after being given security clearance by Guy Liddell of MI5, he was given a key job in Iberia. His aim was to try and counter Nazi spies that had penetrated Spain and Portugal.

Later the same year a senior Soviet intelligence officer, Walter Krivitsky, who had defected to the West, was brought back to London to be questioned by MI5. Krivitsky spilled the beans and gave details of sixty-one agents who were working in the UK. Although he was unable to disclose any names the description of one particular man – a journalist who had worked for a British newspaper during the Civil War – fitted Philby exactly. Another man he described was a Scotsman who had been educated at Eton and Cambridge, an idealist who worked for the Russians for no remuneration – just like Donald McLean. MI5 were not convinced with the Russian's testimony and they decided not to follow up any of his leads.

On February 10, 1941, Walter Krivitsky was found dead in the Bellevue Hotel in Washington. The first reports were that he had committed suicide, but most people within intelligence believed that his hiding place had been disclosed by a Soviet mole working for the MI5 and that he had been murdered by Soviet agents.

During World War II, Philby was placed in charge of a propaganda training programme for the Special Operations Executive. By 1943 he was responsible for Spanish, French, Italian and African affairs and was so successful that he caught the attention of Major General Stewart Menzies. Menzies was the Director-General of MI6, and he was so impressed with Philby that he placed him in charge of Section IX, which was responsible for Soviet Affairs.

When the war was over, Philby was assigned to monitoring Soviet espionage. This was the perfect role for him because it meant he was able to protect his good friends, Burgess, McLean and Blunt. Their security was under threat in September 1945, when a Russian diplomat by the name of Constantin Volkhov approached the British vice-consul in Istanbul in Turkey. He said that he had information regarding three Soviet agents who were working within the Foreign Office. Philby was able to tell the KGB, who quickly arrested Volkhov and had him returned to the Soviet Union. Later the same month a cipher clerk in the Russian Legation who had defected to the West was also interviewed by MI5. However, even though he said he had evidence of a Soviet spy ring based in the UK, MI5 seemed to show little interest in the matter and no action was taken.

In 1949, Philby was appointed as a liaison officer for MI6 in Washington. While in this post, he discovered that the SIS planned to overthrow Enver Hoxha, the communist dictator of Albania. Philby passed this information on to the KGB, who arrested all the Albanians involved in the plot and had them executed. Philby's betrayal had cost 300 Albanians their lives.

In 1950, Philby was put forward for the job as Director General of MI6. However, there was concern about the way Philby had been so willing to switch from being a communist sympathiser to a supporter of pro-fascist organisations and they decided to produce a report on him. When delving into his past, MI6 realised for the first time that the descriptions given to them by Krivitsky and Gouzenko were so close to that of Philby, that there was every possibility that he was a double agent.

When Burgess and McLean defected to Russia in 1951, the finger pointed at Philby as the man who had tipped them off that they were being investigated by MI5. Under pressure from the prime minister, Clement Attlee, and several heads of MI5, Philby was interrogated by MI6. However, he was exonerated, but was recalled to London by the CIA. Due to pressure, Philby resigned his position at MI6 but continued to work for them on a part-time basis and was also paid £4,000 to compensate him for the loss of his job.

The headlines in the *New York Sunday Times* on October 23, 1955, reported that Kim Philby was a Soviet spy. There was uproar in the House of Commons when politicians demanded to know if the prime minister had decided to cover up the dubious activites of Philby. Although the prime minister, then Anthony Eden, refused to give a reply, the foreign secretary, Harold Macmillan issued a statement a couple of days later:

> *While in government service he [Philby]*
> *carried out his duties ably and conscientiously,*
> *and I have no reason to conclude that Mr*

*Philby has at any time betrayed the interests
of his country, or to identify him with the so-
called 'Third Man', if indeed there was one.*

Although Macmillan knew that Philby was a spy,
there was little he could do about it as there was no
concrete evidence, other than order MI6 never to
use him again. Philby, who now realised that he was
safe, called a press conference, adamantly denying
that he was a spy.

*I have never been a communist and the last
time I spoke to a communist knowing he was
one, was in 1934.*

Unbelievably, MI6 ignored the advice of
Macmillan and continued to use the services of
Philby, but on a more casual basis. Philby moved to
the Middle East where he worked as a foreign
correspondent for *The Observer* and *The Economist*,
using this post as cover. While in the Middle East
the CIA decided to keep him under observation.

In 1961, a KGB agent by the name of Anatoli
Golitsin, defected to the CIA and gave a very
detailed debriefing about a man named Philby who
had tipped off McLean and also as the man who
lead a KGB operation in the Arab states. Golitsin
was immediately flown to the USA and placed in a
safe house called Ashford Farm near Washington.

When MI5 interviewed Golitsin, he provided firm evidence that suggested that Philby had been a member of a ring of four, maybe five, agents who were based in the UK.

The MI6 sent one of his agents, Nicholas Elliott, to Beirut to interview Philby. The Attorney General gave him instructions that Philby could be offered immunity from prosecution if he made a full confession. The KGB were one step ahead, and aware that Philby was about to be interrogated and planned an escape route for him. However, Philby was unable to run, because he knew it would endanger the informer who had warned Russia that he was in trouble. Instead, Philby made a carefully worded confession, full of misleading statements, which was designed to protect KGB moles in the UK. Philby signed his statement and the MI6 agent then flew back to the USA to show it to the CIA.

Aware that he was on the verge of being arrested, Philby planned his own escape. On the night of January 23, 1963, when he was on his way to a dinner party with a female friend, he sent a message to London to say that he would be a little later. In fact he never arrived, and he turned up in Moscow six months later.

Philby settled into his life in Moscow far better than Burgess and McLean. He was given a senior position in the KGB and was awarded the Order of the Red Banner and full Russian citizenship. He wrote a book in 1968 called *My Silent War*, in which he openly admitted that he had been a Soviet spy for over thirty years. Kim Philby died in 1988 in Russia and was buried with full military honours.

Of course, if communism had not fallen in 1989, the full story of these four remarkable pro-Soviet spies would never have been told. The most bitter fight between the Soviet Union and the West during the fifty years of the Cold War was on the espionage front. The aim of each side was to try and steal secrets and peer inside the inner depths of the enemy. In this new political climate, it allowed the Cambridge Spies to become notorious for being the most devastatingly successful spies in the history of modern intelligence. The four men had very little in common, except for their mutual belief in communism, and it is remarkable that they actually remained loyal to each other over such a long period of time. They were idealists, who were driven, above all, by their abhorration of fascism. Philby, the most successful of the four, had always dreamed of being a spy, thriving on the adventure and excitement. The greatest sacrifice all four men made was having to run away to Moscow, which was rather ironic as they spent the majority of their life doing everything for the Soviet Union. However, when they were actually forced to live there, they found it an incredibly grim place.

'FALCON' AND 'SNOWMAN'

Between April 1975 and January 1977, two young men, one a drug dealer and the other an intelligent dropout, sold sensitive US government secrets to the Soviet Union. The two men were Christopher Boyce, nicknamed 'The Falcon' because of his love of falconry, and his childhood friend, Andrew Daulton Lee, a heroin and cocaine dealer by trade, hence his nickname 'The Snowman'.

INSIGHT INTO THEIR BACKGROUNDS

Christopher Boyce was born on February 16, 1953, in Santa Monica, California. Christopher's father, Charles, a former FBI agent, had moved west after he resigned from the intelligence services to work as a security executive for an aircraft manufacturer. Boyce was the eldest of nine children and was brought up under the strict Catholic beliefs of his mother, Noreen. The children grew up surrounded by law enforcement agents and police officers who loved to exchange stories about their work, and from an early age Boyce became enthralled with the thoughts of adventure and excitement. To him, undercover work sounded thrilling, feeding his already daredevil spirit and love of taking uncalculated risks. Very often Boyce's love of adventure had disastrous consequences.

Boyce's best friend at the St John Fisher elementary school was Andrew Daulton Lee (more commonly known as Daulton), the adopted son of a wealthy physician. Daulton also had a pious Catholic upbringing, and the two boys attended the same church, both becoming altar boys. Although the boys spent much of their time together, their academic levels were very different. Boyce achieved 'A' grades with ease, while his friend struggled to obtain 'C's. Daulton found it hard at school, preferring to work with his hands rather than his mind.

As a teenager, Boyce joined a falconry club and, unlike his friends who drifted off to pursue other sports, Boyce became an expert. Daulton also shared his passion for the hunting birds and this caused the two teenagers to form an even closer bond.

By sixteen, Boyce had grown into a handsome young man with an exceptionally amiable personality, which made him very popular with his fellow pupils. However, at school his grades started to slip as he found that some of the subjects were starting to get boring. He also suffered a crisis of faith and began to doubt many of the Catholic beliefs. He was becoming more and more disillusioned with the country he was living in as night after night he watched horrific pictures of the Vietnam War. He also began to doubt US politics during the Watergate scandal, and he questioned the abilities of the people who were supposed to be in charge of his country.

Daulton, on the other hand, had very different problems. Neither his appearance or his personality attracted any close friends, and he became obsessed with his height, which was only 157 cm (5 ft 2 in). He developed a complex and became extremely obsessed by his appearance, believing that he was not attractive to the opposite sex. Although his grades were poor, Daulton showed a great talent in woodworking and impressed his teachers with intricate and detailed work. He decided he would like to become a carpenter, but his idea was ridiculed as he lived in a neighbourhood where people were respected for their brains not their brawn.

Daulton soon found a way of making himself popular and numbing his feelings of worthlessness – he turned to marijuana and cocaine. Like many of his schoolmates he loved the false sense of security these substances provided, but Daulton went one step further in exchanging the drugs for sex.

When Daulton left high school, his occupation was primarily a drug dealer. It was a life he enjoyed, which reaped large rewards and meant he had a lot more spare time than a regular job. His speciality became cocaine, which earned him the nickname 'The Snowman'.

Boyce struggled when he left school, dropping out of one college after another, unsure of what he wanted to do. Eventually, in desperation, his father called a friend who worked for TRW Defence and Space Systems Group. It was a private company that had a contract to design US spy satellites. By the age of twenty-one, Boyce was hired as a $140 per week general clerk.

A HIGH-SECURITY RISK

Boyce was issued with a security badge and was forced to sign a Secrecy Act document, saying that he would not pass on any classified information to any unauthorised person or agency. He was employed in the Classified Material Control, which, as the name suggests, gave him access to a lot of classified information.

During his first months at TRW, Boyce did not have the authority to enter the Black Vault, a special room that required high security clearance from the FBI, the CIA and the National Security Agency. Boyce was flattered when he was offered this clearance within his first few months of joining the company. The atmosphere within the Black Vault was light-hearted and jovial and the workers talked freely. One of his co-workers was a Vietnam War veteran, and he talked in detail about his experiences, little realising that he was fuelling Boyce's growing dislike of US superpowers. Added to this, Boyce had access to highly secret telex documents that passed between the US government and TRW, the contents of which made him hate the country in which he lived, even more.

Boyce's protests against US policy were not open and public, like many protesters. He chose to express his dislike for the USA in a far more secretive and illegal manner. He started to betray his country and he enlisted his close friend, Daulton, to help him.

Boyce knew that his friend loved money, and so he approached him and told him he could make far more profit by dealing with the USA's chief enemy, the Soviet Union. He told Daulton that he would smuggle information out of the Black Vault and that his friend could act as the courier, taking it to a Russian embassy in a different country. At first Daulton laughed, not believing his friend. However, when he realised that Boyce was serious, he jumped at the chance, aware that this was an opportunity to make big bucks.

DODGY DEALINGS

In April 1975, Daulton travelled to Mexico City and

headed for the Russian embassy. When he reached the reception he told the man standing behind the desk that he had some important information regarding spy satellites that he thought might be of interest. Daulton was introduced to a Soviet official by the name of Vasily Okana.

At first Okana was suspicious of the American with the unkempt hairdo and moustache, but he thought he would listen to what he had to say. He was invited to sit down and was offered a glass of Vodka and some caviar. Daulton told Okana that before he would release any classified information, he would need to know how much he was going to get paid, bearing in mind that his associate had access to top-secret material on a daily basis. Okana remained doubtful, so Daulton passed him an envelope. Inside this envelope was a brief note saying:

Enclosed is a computer card from a National Security Agency crypto system. If you want do do business, please advise the courier.

As the note said, inside the envelope were some computer programming cards and a 30 cm (12 in) piece of paper tape used in the KG-13 and KW-7 crypto machines at TRW.

Okana left the room, taking the envelope with him. He returned a short while later carrying an envelope, which contained $250 and handed it over to Daulton.

Okana said that under no circumstances was Daulton to return to the embassy and that from now on they should use code names. Okana said he should call him 'John' while Daulton was given the name 'Luis'. Okana also told him that in future they would meet at a designated location and would use coded messages and passwords to recognise one another.

As Boyce continued to take photographs and steal vital information, Daulton made more and more visits to Mexico. Each time he went, Okana kept pushing him for details of his informant and where he worked. Although the Soviets paid for every piece of information that the two men supplied, sometimes there were complaints that the photographs were too fuzzy and asked for more details. However, when Daulton phoned his friend to ask for these details, very often Boyce could not give him the information he needed and this led to squabbles between the two men. Tension mounted and Boyce was nervous because of his friend's addiction to heroin. He felt that this might make him careless and let information slip. He also doubted that Daulton was being honest about the money he received, and worried that he was not getting his fair share.

In almost two years of passing information to the Soviet Union, Boyce only earned himself around $20,000. His motive was never really the money. It was the excitement of the danger and the fact that he was pulling one over on US intelligence.

Eventually, Boyce told Daulton that he had had enough and that he wanted to get out of the spying game before they were caught. Daulton, on the other hand, said there was still a lot of money to be made and urged his friend to reconsider.

Meanwhile, the Russians were still eager to meet the man who was giving them so much information. Daulton was not keen on them meeting Boyce, because he felt his friend might double-cross him. After all if they had the main man, then they would have no need of a courier. Eventually, the pressure was too great and a meeting was set up, with Boyce accompanying Daulton to Mexico City.

The meeting did not go well. The Russians demanded code room transmission frequencies, but when Boyce told them he did not have access to that kind of information, it reflected badly on Daulton who had said it was only a matter of time.

DISASTROUS DEALINGS

At the time Boyce decided to tender his resignation from TRW in 1973, the company had just received a contract to design the 'Pyramider'. It was a top secret project for a huge communication satellite that resembled an open umbrella. Before he left Boyce managed to take several photographs of the prototype, which he intended to pass on to his friends in the Soviet Union. Boyce had decided to leave work and go back to college full time, but in the meantime he would continue with his espionage work. Daulton, armed with his photos of the Pyramider, had returned to Mexico. He had become rather blasé about his missions and when he arrived at the embassy, finding it shut, he simply threw a message inside the gates. Little did he realise that he was being watched and within seconds he was surrounded by police officers.

The police wanted to know what he had thrown and Daulton answered casually that it was just a packet of cigarettes. The Mexican police did not believe his story, because a member of an anti-government terrorist group had recently been arrested for doing a similar thing. As Daulton argued with the police, they were overheard by Eileen Heaphy, who was an officer working at the US embassy. Daulton hoped that because he was a US citizen, he would get her support. When he was asked to go with the police for questioning, the Mexicans said it would be all right for members of the US embassy to be present. Daulton was therefore accompanied by both a vice-consul and a CIA agent.

Back at the station, Daulton was asked to empty his pockets and put everything he was holding on the desk in front of him. The first thing that intrigued the investigating officer was a fake post-card, which Daulton had been given to show his designated meeting place. The officer then opened the plain, brown envelope that Daulton had been carrying, and found some photographic film inside marked 'Top Secret'. Daulton tried to explain that it was just a photograph that was to be used in an advertising campaign, but his story did not wash with the official. The officer said he would have the film developed and that the US officials should come back after one hour.

When the investigating officer told Daulton that he was being charged with *aesisinato*, he asked them to explain exactly what it meant. When they said the word 'murder', Daulton's face turned white and he felt as if he had been hit by a bolt of lightning. He panicked and started planning what he was going to say.

Over the next few days he was interrogated for hours on end, but still he denied any knowledge of a murder and that he was simply a tourist. At one point in the proceedings, Daulton changed his story and said that he and an associate, Christopher Boyce, worked for the CIA. Once again the police said he was guilty of killing a policeman. The reason they believed he was the murderer was because the fake postcard showed a picture of the junction where the policeman had been killed. Daulton continued to plead innocence and eventually the Mexican police lost their patience. They ordered him to take off all his clothes and an officer threatened to cut off his genitals. They also held his head over a filthy toilet bowl and dunked his head in it three times. In between questioning Daulton was made to lie blindfolded with his hands tied behind his back. He was given nothing to drink except tap water which upset his stomach, and he was left lying in his own faeces.

Eventually, the Mexican police allowed the FBI to talk to their prisoner. He told them the same story that he had fed to the Mexicans, saying that he worked for the CIA but that he had fed false information to confuse the Russians. The FBI contacted the CIA, the Pentagon and the White House, and they were ordered to bring Daulton back to the USA to stand trial.

Christopher Boyce was arrested in January 1977. It only took him a couple of days of interrogation before he confessed to spying and selling secrets to the Soviet Union. The two men were tried separately and eventually they were both convincted of espionage and sent to Lompoc Federal Prison in California. Boyce was sentenced to forty years, but he escaped in January 1980 by hiding in a drainage hole for over three hours. While on the run he carried out several bank robberies in Idaho and Washington. He was arrested in Idaho in August 1981 after the authorities received a tip-off about his whereabouts. He was eventually released from prison on May 15, 2003, but he will remain on parole until his original release date of 2046.

Andrew Daulton was given a life sentence. He received a heavier sentence than Boyce because of his prior criminal record. He was released on parole in 1998 and, apparently, at some point after his release, Daulton was hired by the actor Sean Penn to be his personal assistant.

PART FIVE

MURDERERS, OUTLAWS AND THIEVES

JACK SHEPPARD

Jack Sheppard, one of England's most notorious historical criminals, was a non-violent legend in his own time. During his two-year crime career he mixed with the criminal elite of the day and was known as a thorn in the side of the infamous Jonathan Wild. He was hailed by the people and hated and pursued by the law.

Jack Sheppard, née John, was born into a poor London family on March 4, 1702. The area in which he was born was famous for the presence of high-waymen, but Sheppard managed to start his life out on the right track. Sheppard's father died when he was very young, and when he was six years old his mother decided that she could no longer care for her sons and sent them to a boarding school to learn carpentry. He started to work for and apprentice with various carpenters before he started working for the man with whom he would stay with the longest, William Kneebone.

By the time Sheppard was in his late teens he showed great promise in his chosen career. The young criminal mastermind in the making was known to frequent a pub near his place of work. Despite his slight stutter he was considered to be quite witty. It was only when Sheppard looked to expand his social horizons by going to a different tavern than his usual haunt, that he began to realise that there was more in the world than carpentry. Sheppard started to frequent another pub near his work called The Black Lion. He met some of the day's most notorious criminals including his future arch-enemy, Jonathan Wild and future partner in crime Joseph 'Blueskin' Blake. It was while drinking at the same establishment that Sheppard became attracted to Elizabeth Lyon, a prostitute who went by the nickname of Edgeworth Bess.

Because of Sheppard's growing interest in drink and his love interest, his work life suffered. Elizabeth was not only Sheppard's love interest she also served to advise him. It was partly due to her misguided advice that Sheppard started his career, albeit a short one, in crime. His first crime is believed to be the theft of a pair of silver spoons from a local tavern while making a delivery for his boss. Sheppard's crimes went unnoticed and his youthful overconfidence construed this as a sign of his criminal prowess. He began to steal on a regular basis, pilfering from homes and businesses in which he was doing carpentry work. It was not long before Sheppard began to work with the gang of master criminal, Jonathan Wild. It was also around this time that Sheppard decided to hand in his resignation, with just two years left of his apprenticeship.

Meanwhile the relationship between Sheppard and Lyon was blossoming and they decided to move away and live together and found a home in Fulham, London. A short time later they moved to Piccadilly and within a very brief period Lyon was arrested and jailed for a petty crime. When Sheppard was told he could not visit her he defied the guards' instructions, broke Elizabeth from her cell and they made their escape. This was to be the beginning of several journeys to and from jail for Sheppard, only next time it would be him who was behind bars.

On February 5, 1724, Sheppard, along with his girlfriend and his brother Tom, plundered 'Clare's Market', a meat shop in greater London. Sheppard's brother already had a criminal record and had the scars to prove it. Tom was arrested for this crime and leaked the details of who was involved in attempt to ease his sentence. Because of this information, the police started looking for Jack and Elizabeth. Sheppard was arrested after another criminal, who was also associated with Jonathan Wild, called James Sykes, informed the police as to his whereabouts. His interest was limited to the cash reward. Jack was sent to St. Giles Roadhouse and imprisoned on the top floor.

Sheppard had not been in prison for more than three hours, before he escaped with a makeshift rope fashioned from bed clothes. His ingenuity did not end there. Sheppard joined the crowd who had gathered at the commotion of his escape and pointed to the roof exclaiming that he could see himself escaping. With this distraction in place and the crowd fooled, Sheppard fled the scene.

It was not long before Jack was re-arrested. He was caught red-handed picking pockets on the city streets. He was sent back to the same prison that he had recently escaped from. Because of primitive law enforcement methods he was simply placed back in a cell, something he had proved he could easily circumvent. On the second day of his latest incarceration Elizabeth came to visit him. The guards recognised her and put her in the cell with Jack. They went to court and were sent to New Prison in Clerkenwell by Judge Walters. It was a short-lived prison stay, however, because the two seasoned outlaws scaled the near twenty-foot prison perimeter wall to their freedom.

Jack Sheppard's reputation circulated throughout the criminal underworld and soon caught the attention of Jonathan Wild. Wild was a clever man, holding the position of number one gangster in England, while appearing to be England's number one policeman. This of course gave him enormous power and influence and he used it when he ordered the arrest of Sheppard. Wild had a group of his men spy on Sheppard in an effort to learn more about his movements. The appointed group informed on Sheppard to Wild just as he was getting ready to pull off yet any another robbery. Sheppard started working with Joseph 'Blueskin' Blake and the two robbed Sheppard's previous employer, William Kneebone.

Wild was becoming irritated with this criminal, because he could not get him under his direct control. He doubled his efforts to get him arrested. Wild used Lyon to get to Sheppard by getting her drunk and asking her questions, until she gave vital information about Sheppard's whereabouts. After a short time, on July 23, 1724, Sheppard was arrested at his partner's mother's liquor shop. Wild had got what he wanted, although the seemingly invincible Sheppard was not going to stay locked up for long!

Sheppard once again found himself at Newgate Prison awaiting trial. When he eventually faced the jury he was charged with three crimes but the first two were dismissed for lack of evidence. Sheppard was, however, convicted of the burglary at the Kneebones. William Kneebone, Jonathan Wild and one of Wild's henchmen, testified at Sheppard's trial and the sentence was passed on August 12, 1724. Sheppard was sentenced to death but before the death warrant could be issued, less than six days after the conviction, Sheppard escaped and fled to nearby Blackfriars Stairs. The news of his latest escape delighted the public who saw him as a folk hero. Sheppard quickly went into deeper hiding but Jonathan Wild was in pursuit. By the beginning of September 1724 Wild had assembled a posse and they started to hunt for Sheppard. On September 9, Wild's gang was hot on Sheppard's heels and he was arrested and dragged back to his cell at Newgate Prison. For the next few weeks Sheppard tried to escape a few more times but his attempts were prevented by the watchful eye of the prison guards. They found cutting and grinding implements in his cell and decided that, after repeated threats that he would escape easily, to lock Sheppard in metal arm and leg irons. When Sheppard bragged even more about how easily he could escape and how it was useless to try and hold him, the guards only tightened his bindings. It was during this time that Sheppard's co-hort Blake was arrested. On October 15, 1724, Sheppard used the distraction created during the trial by none other than his ex-partner Blake to escape the confines of the prison.

Sheppard worked himself free from the bindings and, still wearing leg irons, made his way through the prison towards freedom. He got past one barred door after another and climbed multiple floors with makeshift ropes made of blankets, as he had done many times before. Once he was outside of the prison Sheppard took to hiding in a barn. When he was discovered by the farmer Sheppard told him a completely concocted story about why he was wearing the irons. A few days later, Sheppard bribed a blacksmith to cut him free of the bindings. Sheppard did not have long before he was recaptured but he made the best he could of the time. He disguised himself as a beggar and broke into a pawn shop and stole many valuable items including a new suit. He wore the suit and for a few days lived the highlife in London, enjoying everything the city had to offer.

Sheppard was finally arrested again November 1, 1724. He was apprehended while he was drunk and dragged once again, back to prison. Once there the guards placed him in the highest security cell they had in the middle of the prison, where he could be watched at all times. He became something of a celebrity and admission was charged for people to come and view him. Sheppard's exploits had reached such acclaim, that wealthy people wrote to the Royal Family to have charges against him reduced to exile. A famous artist of the time was even commissioned to come and paint Jack Sheppard. On November 16, 1724, Jack Sheppard was executed by way of hanging. Those noose was placed round his neck, but after the usual fifteen minutes he was still alive. The execution crew cut him down and the crowd that had gathered around to watch, fell upon Sheppard.

That evening Sheppard's badly mutilated remains were taken and buried.

Jack Sheppard became a legend in his own time but it wasn't until after his death that public interest in his exploits exploded. Many plays, books, operas and short stories were written, produced and performed with rave reviews. People delighted in his crime adventures well over a hundred years after his death. After some controversy and claims that the plays and books telling of Sheppard's life caused people to misbehave and, in some cases, commit murder, in 1840, any publication with the name 'Jack Sheppard' was banned. This ban was to last for a period of forty years. Jack is still referenced today almost three-hundred years after he committed his crimes and baffled the police.

MACHINE GUN
KELLY

George Kelly Barnes, the man remembered by most as 'Machine Gun' Kelly was one of the few non-murderous gangster figures in the American Prohibition era. His misguided exploits took him through one robbery after another and it wasn't until he came into contact with the big boys of crime at the time that he truly developed a talent for robbery. Kelly was constantly trying to aspire to the image that the media and his associates painted of him.

George Kelly Barnes was born on July 18, 1896, in Memphis, Tennessee. Unlike most of his soon to be gangster brethren George was born into a wealthy, respected family. He enjoyed a model childhood and started life out on a track that could not have been further from organised crime. His school life was somewhat troubled and he spent a lot of time in detention. Although he tried hard he would only earn mediocre grades. During his final year of high school George met Geneva Ramsay and fell head over heels in love with her. He decided to leave High School early to marry her and started looking for work to support his now growing family. George, who was tired of working for little pay decided that he would use less conventional means to make ends meet. It was around this time when George was nineteen, that he began socialising with bootlegging gangsters.

It was not long before George's activities got him into trouble and he was arrested for illegal trafficking. He decided that preserving the good name of his family was important to him, so he took his own family and headed west. It was around that time that George adopted an alias, also in an effort to protect his family's good name. He took the name George R. Kelly and by 1927 was known by law enforcement and in the criminal underworld as a seasoned gangster. He ran into trouble with the law a few more times and was jailed for a short time. Kelly did not, however, learn his lesson as he committed just one offence too many, until he was caught for his most serious crime yet.

In 1928, George was arrested after he was apprehended smuggling alcohol onto an Indian Reservation. His latest offence was a more serious crime and carried a much more severe punishment that would make his previous incarcerations seem like a slap on the wrist. Kelly was jailed for a three-year sentence at the Kansas State High Security

Prison, the world renowned, Leavenworth. Some of America's worst criminals were his prison mates there. They took the troubled, minor offender and turned him into a hardened professional. While Kelly was incarcerated Geneva left him and took their new child with her. Kelly had the benefit of leaving prison with more friends in the criminal underworld than when he had entered.

Upon his release from another stint in prison, while living in Oklahoma, George met Kathryn Thorne. Thorne was a hardened criminal in her own right. She was the attractive mistress of Kelly's newest crime contact, Steve Anderson. Kelly fell for Thorne, possibly attracted to her family's long association with burglaries and prostitution. Rumour at the time held that Kathryn had killed her previous husband who had also been a bootlegging gangster, but the official investigation maintains he took his own life. Kelly married Kathryn after several months of courting each other's affections in Minneapolis in September 1930.

So far the criminal life of George Kelly had been relatively unremarkable and unimpressive. The latest edition to his family in the form of Kathryn was to change his entire image, both to the criminal underworld and to media. It would be under her guidance that his crimes would escalate him to the most wanted list and quickly rise to 'Public Enemy Number One'. Kathryn was anything but an ordinary housewife to Kelly as she pumped up his image to other members of organised crime and to the media. Kathryn bought George a Thompson machine gun and encouraged him to hone his skills with the menacing weapon, a favourite of gangsters. It is said that she distributed shell casings from his practise sessions as mementos to other gangsters and anyone else who would listen. She coined George Kelly's third and final name, 'Machine Gun' Kelly. It was because of this relentless and shameless promotion of her husband that, when the police issued wanted posters in August 1933, the poster listed Kelly as 'an excellent machine gunner'.

In July 1933 Machine Gun Kelly and his wife masterminded the kidnapping of a wealthy oil tycoon, Charles Urchil. Kelly and two accomplices broke into Urchil's Oklahoma home and found him playing Bridge with a companion. Kelly shouted his threats to kill both men and took them hostage, as he was not sure which one of them was Charles Urchil. Kelly and his team loaded the two men into their waiting car and searched them for identification. The man with Urchil was Walter Jarrett. They robbed him of the $51 that was in his wallet and abandoned him on the roadside. Kelly wanted Urchil and took him to a ranch in Texas where they held him for a ransom of $200,000.

A family friend of the Urchil's agreed to pay the ransom and make the drop at the place that George and his accomplices had demanded. That place was near the La Salle Hotel in Kansas City. The terrible ordeal ended on July 30, 1933, just eight days after it had began. Kelly held true to his word and released Urchil in Oklahoma where he is reported to have casually walked into a restaurant and telephoned for a taxi. Urchil was the wrong man for Kelly to capture as he had the connections and the intelligence to lead the police right back to him. Urchil had no intention of allowing Kelly to just get away with what he did, so he left his fingerprints on everything he could and remained vigilant of his surroundings during his capture. This careful planning on Urchil's part proved invaluable during the FBI investigation.

Kelly's gang split up and went their separate ways. George Kelly and his wife had to keep on the move and stay ahead of the law enforcement that was now motivated for more reasons than one to capture them. It was only a short time later that part of the gang was apprehended at the ranch where Urchil had been held. The police used the serial numbers on the ransom money to track Kelly's purchases. Kelly earned his reputation and his rank on the most wanted men list as the gang continued to elude police by changing their appearance and dying their hair. They hid for several weeks but decided to head back to Kelly's hometown of Memphis to stay with a long-time friend, John Tichenor.

On the morning of September 26, 1933, FBI and police, in a combined effort, surrounded the Tichenor property. When they forced their way in, they found Kelly and his wife in a state which rendered them unable to resist the lawmen. Kelly had passed out in a drunken state from the previous evenings drinking, and Kathryn was still asleep. Kelly is said to have shouted, 'Don't shooot, G-men!' referring to the Federal agents on the scene. It has since been accepted that it was Kelly that coined the phrase G-men that is still in use to this day. The couple were arrested and taken to trial in Oklahoma where they each received life sentences for kidnapping Urchil. George R. Kelly was sent back to the first prison he had ever been held at, Leavenworth in Kansas. His wife, Kathryn, was sent to a high security facility in Cincinnati, Ohio. Not long after Kelly was jailed he bragged to the media that he would escape from Leavenworth, break his wife out of prison and they would spend Christmas together. The authorities did not take the threats lightly and decided that they should send him to the new, high security prison off the San Francisco coast, Alcatraz.

During Kelly's stay at the dreaded prison island Alcatraz he was under the strict rules of the new facility. There was to be no talking between inmates and they were on the tightest schedule and discipline of any prison in the United States, ever.

Because of the position of Alcatraz, an imprisoned island in the middle of freezing water in direct view of San Francisco the prospect of escape was practically non-existent. Instead of trying to flee, Kelly became a model inmate and was said to keep mostly to himself except for one rather humorous detail. Kelly repeatedly bragged to other inmates such as the 1930's bank robber, Alvin Karpis, about crimes that he had never been involved with. Karpis said, 'he never tired of telling of his escapades'. Kelly remained at Alcatraz for many years until he was transferred back to Leavenworth.

George 'Machine Gun' Kelly died at Leavenworth prison on his fifty-ninth birthday. It was not the prison or the inmates that killed him but rather the natural cause that claims so many lives, a heart attack. His wife was released from prison in 1958 and went on to live a normal life in Oklahoma. Machine Gun Kelly's name is remembered with the hardened gangsters like Karpis and Capone but the one major factor that separated him from the likes of them is he never killed anybody. Kelly was a misguided man who died serving his time, his name continues to echo through pop culture almost seventy-five years since he held the rank of Public Enemy Number One.

BONNIE AND CLYDE

Bonnie Parker and Clyde Barrow were the all-American romantic legends of the depression era and beyond. They are probably best remembered as the bank robbers and outlaws 'Bonnie and Clyde'. These two notorious outlaws led law enforcement on a two-year manhunt that spanned across seven states. On the numerous occasions that the police closed in on them, they would shoot their way to safety. In their acts of theft, combined with violence, they killed nine police officers and several civilians.

Bonnie Elizabeth Parker was born on October 1, 1910, in Rowena, Texas. Despite the troubled future that awaited her, Bonnie started out life on the right track. Her father died when she was very young and as a result her mother took their family to live in Cement City. Bonnie was below average height and tiny at around 41 kg (18½ lb), and an attractive child with her red hair and light freckles. She liked to follow fashion and favoured the colour red. She worked hard in school and achieved high grades. She was a prolific young writer and showed promise when she won the country literary contest. In her mid-teens, Bonnie married Roy Thornton and despite common belief, remained married to him for the rest of her life. Their marriage was troubled and they became estranged after just three years. Thornton went to prison shortly after on a charge of theft. Bonnie started working as a waitress to make the money she needed to survive. One day, while caring for a friend who had been injured in a fall, she met her future lover and cohort, Clyde Barrow, who was also visiting their mutual friend.

Clyde Chestnut 'Champion' Barrow was born on March 24, 1909, in Teleco, Texas, just south of Dallas in Ellis County. He was born into a very poor farming family. When Clyde was a child his family operated a petrol station and they lived in a small one-bedroom home. Clyde grew up to be a good looking, lovable rogue at 170 cm (5ft 7in), with slicked back hair and dark eyes and was described as irresistible by many. Clyde and his brother Ivan 'Buck' Barrow were at odds with the law from very early in life, working as a team and commiting minor offenses. One noted crime was the theft and attempted sale of a series of turkeys. Because of their growing reputation, when a crime was committed in their home town, it was usually suspected that the Barrow Boys had something to do with it. However, Clyde seemed to have a deep, unrelenting, unquenchable anger. These strong emotions were possibly due to his family and their financial situation, or possibly the state of his country which was deep in an economic depression of its own. His anger fuelled his excellent trigger finger and many said if you made Clyde Barrow draw, you were a dead man.

While Clyde was serving time at Eastham Prison for one of his crimes, he became acquainted with two men, Ray Hamilton and Ralph Fults, who would later join him as members of the infamous Barrow Gang. After Clyde was released he returned to break Hamilton and Fults from jail. It was also around this time that Clyde shot a police officer who was apprehending him for being drunk in public.

The first robbery that his now lover, Bonnie, was involved in was that of a hardware shop in Kauffman, Texas. During their high-speed getaway from the shop Clyde slammed on the breaks and ordered Bonnie to get out of the car. He gave her a wad of the stolen cash and drove away. Although she had been ejected from the car and had the embarrassment of walking back to the town they had just plundered, she knew that Clyde's reasons were honourable and it just made her desire to be with him more intense. Shortly after this incident, which netted little profit, Clyde and his friend and cohort Hamilton decided to plan another robbery. It was also during this time that Ralph Fults, who had been involved in the raid on the hardware shop, was arrested. Spooked, but still determined, Clyde and Hamilton decided to enter the home of the Buchers, owners of a Hillsboro, Texas, grocery shop and hold them at gunpoint while they opened the safe for them. While the safe was being opened, Hamilton, who was holding the gun to the store owner's head, was surprised and he accidentally fired the trigger. Mr Bucher, the store owner, was suddenly dead before them and Clyde and Hamilton were fugitives. They made their escape, but Clyde asked Bonnie to join them on what would be a continuous run from the law. She eagerly accepted and it was at this moment that the partnership of Bonnie and Clyde as outlaws was really born.

In the following weeks and months, Bonnie, Clyde and Hamilton would commit more crimes, many of which ended in murder. The gang brought another newcomer aboard, W. D. Jones, a thief of only seventeen years old. The media portrayed the dangerous gang as Robin Hood-like characters and Americans everywhere delighted in the exploits of the soap opera gang. Bonnie and Clyde became aware of this new-found status and began to carry a camera and photograph each other in various 'gangster' poses. This just fuelled an already growing public interest in their adventures. It was around this time that Clyde's brother and his wife Blanche joined the gang. The Barrow Gang was now five-strong and continued to lead the police on a deadly chase, leaving nothing but havoc in the shops, petrol stations and banks they entered.

During one of the many getaways in a stolen car driven at excess speed, the car flew off a bridge that was still under construction, and Bonnie became pinned beneath the wrecked machine. Despite the best efforts of Clyde and Jones to free her, she remained stuck. The car became engulfed in flames and before they were able to work Bonnie loose from the wreckage, she sustained severe burns to all parts of her body, including her legs and face. After this tragic incident, Bonnie's left leg was seriously deformed, and subsequently Clyde always carried Bonnie in the copious photographs taken during their violent exploits.

The gang did not go long before crashing another vehicle, this time while the police were pursuing them, Clyde ploughed the car into a tree stump. The car subsequently lurched into a ditch at the side of the road, and the police riddled the car with bullets. Bonnie, Clyde and the gang escaped with minor injuries. To many it seemed that the gang had more than one life each.

In July of 1933, the gang was in Dexfield Park and found themselves surrounded by police. A gun battle ensued and the police were partially victorious. Ivan 'Buck' Barrow was hit in the back, captured and a few days later died in hospital after the onset of pneumonia. His wife, Blanche, who had only sustained minor injuries in previous engagements, was hit by flying glass. Blanche was arrested and sent to Missouri State Penitentiary. She was charged with assault with intent to kill and sentenced to ten years.

In November 1933, Bonnie and Clyde were visiting their families when they were caught once again in the crossfire of the Texas Department of Public Safety. Bonnie and Clyde were hit in the legs. Bonnie's condition and her deformed leg only worsened from this most recent assault.

In January of 1934, Clyde masterminded yet another prison break. This time it was his goal to spring ex-Barrow Gang member, Ray Hamilton, Henry Methvin and other prisoners from the Eastham Prison. It was during this prison break that the Barrow gang shot yet another series of police officers and prison guards.

In April of that year, Clyde and Methvin killed two Texas Highway Patrol officers and shortly after that the gang was responsible for another officer's death. This latest batch of killing sullied the public's interest in the adventures of the Barrow Gang and gave the police a serious incentive to end the Barrow Gang reign of terror. Law enforcement officials decided that they needed to bring out the big guns to stop what seemed like, until that time, a set of unstoppable criminals.

On May 20, 1934, a posse consisting of Deputies Bob Alcorn, Ted Hinton, ex-Texas Ranger B. M. 'Manny' Gault, Bienville Parish, Sheriff Henderson Jordan, Deputy Prentiss Oakley and led by retired Texas Ranger, Frank Hamer, observed the gang's movements and lay in wait at a well used drop point for Bonnie and Clyde. They only had a few hours to wait for the two outlaws to arrive and when the infamous two showed up and stopped their car, the team opened fire on their vehicle with automatic weapons. Bonnie and Clyde were struck multiple times in all parts of their bodies. Some of the bullets travelled through the car door, through Bonnie's body, entered Clyde and exited the vehicle on the other side. Because Bonnie and Clyde had survived so many skirmishes in the past, the police approached the bullet-riddled car with caution, but Bonnie and Clyde were slumped over dead. Bonnie was holding her weapon but neither she nor her lover had the chance to use them. The car was towed to Arcadia, Louisiana, with their bodies still inside the cabin. When the bodies of the two were autopsied, they each had in excess of sixty bullet wounds. Just after the posse gunned down Bonnie and Clyde, they searched their stolen vehicle and found multiple firearms, thousands of rounds of ammunition and licence plates from many different states.

Bonnie's mother refused to allow her daughter to be buried next to her long-time lover, and she lies at

Crown Hill Memorial Park in Dallas, Texas, on the opposite side of town from Clyde's final resting place.

Bonnie and Clyde's adventures inspired the 1967 film starring Fay Dunnaway as Bonnie and Warren Beatty as Clyde. The film was met by rave reviews and won critical acclaim. Today, Bonnie and Clyde's death car is on display in a little town called Primm, at the Whiskey Peaks hotel near the State line where Nevada meets California. The car is enclosed in a glass display, along with replica artefacts from the famous adventures of these ever-lasting romantics. Bonnie and Clyde continue to be featured in popular culture on a regular basis and their romantic image is sure to never die. The legend lives on to this day, now almost a century after their manic, but memorable, crime spree. People visit the site of their final battle in Louisiana and every year a festival is held by enthusiasts in Gibsland in honour of their memory.

'PRETTY BOY' FLOYD

Charles Arthur Floyd, one of the twentieth century's most recognised and notorious criminals, was no typical bank robber. Donning the nickname 'Pretty Boy' Floyd, he was responsible for the deaths of ten men. Like many investigations in history, many of Floyd's actions, including his final encounter with law enforcement, are shrouded in controversy. Charles Arthur Floyd was a man with a problem with society and absolutely no idea how to express his distaste. Unlike most people who might conduct peaceful demonstrations, Floyd brought his emotions to fruition in acts of disgusting violence.

Charles Arthur Floyd was born on February 3, 1906, in Georgia, into a large, poor farming family. His parents were constantly trying to avoid bankruptcy and in desperation turned to bootlegging to feed their family. In 1921, Floyd married Ruby Hargrove, and like many young couples they decided to find a new place to live and start their family. After numerous failed attempts to find work, Floyd decided that he would have to get money through less conventional means. It was around this time he decided to invest some of the little money he had and buy a gun.

When Charles was eighteen years old he committed his first major offence by holding up the local post office and stealing $350 in pennies. The police immediately suspected him and he was arrested, but they had to release him because his father had given him a solid alibi. It was only a short time later that Floyd committed his second major offence, this time travelling to St Louis and robbing a supermarket. Floyd took $16,000 that was held in the store safe and fled home with his pockets overflowing with packaged bills. It was not long before the money started to burn a hole in his pocket and he purchased some very expensive items. He spent the money on anything and everything he wanted, from new clothes to expensive meals in restaurants. The police finally became suspicious when Floyd was seen driving a brand new car. They arrested Floyd on this evidence and, when they searched his home, they found the money still in wrappers. His guilt was clear and the evidence was incontrovertible. He was convicted and sentenced to five years in prison for the crime. After serving only three years in Jefferson City Penitentiary, Floyd was parolled. He hated prison so much, that on his release he vowed that he would never return – and he didn't. While Floyd was in prison his wife gave birth to their son and then she divorced him.

It was after Floyd was released from prison that he committed his first murder. The murder, though in cold blood, was not unprovoked. Floyd was given the news that his father had been killed in a shoot-out with his neighbour. The enraged Floyd took his father's hunting rifle and went next door to claim his revenge. Their neighbour, J. Mills, did not live another day. Floyd's anger festered and he soon became a hit man in Liverpool, Ohio. He worked jobs for bootleggers, possibly feeling by protecting them he was somehow honouring his father. His crimes became known in the criminal underworld and to law enforcement alike. Floyd moved to Kansas City, where many gangsters and other harsh criminals were known to frequent. He learned how to effectively use a machine gun, a weapon favoured by the gangsters of the time. It was also during this time that Floyd got his famous nickname 'Pretty Boy', a name given to him by a brothel madam by the name of Beulah Baird Ash. Although he hated the pseudonym, it stuck with him through the remainder of his career.

Floyd committed his first bank robbery at the Farmers and Merchants Bank in Sylvania, Ohio. Floyd's crimes continued over the next decade in the surrounding states, and he was officially blamed for the death of ten men and the robbing of as many as thirty banks. He was known for making notches in his pocket watch for every man that he killed. Floyd was never one to hide himself from his victims and never wore a mask. He was also exceptionally polite to those in the places he robbed. Floyd was always well presented and kept his hair in order by slicking it back.

Charles Arthur Floyd first killed a police officer on April 16, 1931. The shoot-out with the police started after Floyd was shopping with William Miller who was also known as 'Bill the Killer', Beulah and her sister Rose. It was only after they left the shop that the police arrived. The bloody shoot-out on the city street left police officer Ralph Castner and William Miller dead, the twenty-one-year-old Beulah was injured by crossfire and Rose was captured by the police. The ever clever and resourceful Floyd escaped in a car.

Floyd is associated with many violent crimes but few as destructive as the one remembered as the 'Union Station Massacre'. On July 17, 1933, Floyd and his cohort Adam Richetti allegedly took part in the killing of five men. Among the slaughtered that day was an FBI agent by the name of Raymond Caffrey. The men were killed as they tried to stop Floyd from freeing underworld ganger Frank 'Gentleman' Nash. Floyd maintained to his dying breath that he had nothing to do with the deaths of those men or the plot to release Frank Nash and was not present for the entire affair. Because of the crimes that they committed together, especially the major Union Station incident, the entire crime fighting body of the USA was on hot pursuit of Pretty Boy Floyd and his associate Richetti. Because of the death of the notorious criminal, John Dillinger, on July 22, 1933, Floyd was promoted to the acclaim of 'Public Enemy Number One' on the FBI most wanted list. The establishment put a reward on his head of $23,000 for his capture – dead or alive.

The end was near for Floyd, even he was not invincible, although so far the police had been unable to keep him locked up. On October 19, 1934, after robbing a series of banks in the surrounding area, Floyd and Richetti were recognised and the police showed up to apprehend the two men. After a shoot-out the police scored a victory in the form of the capture of Adam Richetti. Floyd escaped capture by stealing a car and fleeing.

On October 22, 1934, just three days since the capture of his long-time buddy, Pretty Boy Floyd's luck finally ran out. Floyd was just getting in the car that would take him to the bus station when the police came up the road. He fled the vehicle and ran for the cover of the nearby forest. The police officers involved, led by Chief McDermott, ordered Floyd to halt and surrender. When Floyd drew his .45 calibre handgun another police officer on the scene, Chester Smith, opened fire with his rifle. The shot struck Floyd in his wrist and he dropped his gun. Determined not to be captured Floyd fled yet again as the police continued to shout orders to stop. The police team opened fire on Floyd with full force and took him down. He died minutes later from his injuries but not before he uttered the words, 'I am Charles Arthur Floyd'. Tucked in his belt was a second handgun, one that Floyd never got to use. In fact, Floyd was killed in a shoot-out where he never fired a single shot. Richetti was executed in 1938 after a series of appeals, including one that tried to claim he was insane.

Following the death of the USA's Public Enemy Number One, there was much controversy. It was said that the circumstances surrounding his death were not as they had been told previously by the police. He was thought that Floyd had in fact been shot at point-blank range in execution style by the police, after they had shot him multiple times already. This has never been proven and does not exist in the official account from the FBI of the day's events.

Floyd's mother did not allow what the public wanted most of all, a open casket. His coffin was shipped back to Oklahoma, where it was viewed by many thousands of mourners and curious on-lookers, before being placed in the ground. Floyd's funeral was attended by 20,000 people. Floyd's body rests in Atkins, Oklahoma, where he had told his mother he wanted to be buried a year prior to his death.

The life and exploits of the eternal lawbreaker Pretty Boy Floyd were immortalized in a song by Woodie Guthrie in 1939, just five years following Floyd's death. Floyd's gravestone was stolen in 1985 and had to be replaced. The marker that stands on the site of the final battle was stolen in 1995, but has since been recovered and re-erected. Several movies have been made that chronicle the life and times of Floyd. His name has become part of pop culture and he remains a household name three-quarters of a century after his death. As Woodie Gurthrie put it so well in his song, 'some will rob you with a six gun and some with a fountain pen'. There could be no better way to describe Floyd's distaste for authority. He felt like it was all just some form of robbery, but of course it all depends on how you look at it. Floyd wasted his life in such an inferno of hatred for the society he could never participate in and perhaps always knew it would end in his own downfall.

NED KELLY

Ned Kelly is one of those criminals who polarizes opinion. Some remember him as a folk hero and masterful criminal, along the lines of the mythical Robin Hood. Others regard him as a common ill-educated convict who got his just desserts. He was, what the Australians call, a bushranger, which basically means a felon who conceals his where-abouts in the wilderness, or 'bush', as it is called down under. He was the equivalent of a highway-men in the UK or an outlaw in the USA.

Edward (Ned) Kelly was the first son born into a family of eight children in the winter of 1854–55. His parents were of Irish stock, impoverished and socially disadvantaged. His father died when he was eleven years old, having been convicted of cattle rustling and harshly treated in jail. This left an embittered Ned and his brothers with the respon-sibility of supporting their mother and sisters. With-out the prospect of securing decent jobs, the brothers turned to petty crime as a way of making ends meet. Consequently, they became acquainted with the protectors of the law from an early age and so the die was cast.

Ned's first serious brush with the law came at the age of fourteen, when he assaulted and robbed a Chinese pig farmer named Ah Fook, for which he served ten days in custody. Following this experience he fell in with an established bushranger named Harry Power – real name Henry Johnson – who was Ned's senior by thirty-six years. Power's influence led to his being arrested and sentenced to three months hard labour for violent intimidation. He had assaulted a costermonger named Jeremiah McCormack, and then delivered an indecent note to the man's wife, Kelly McCormack, which was accompanied in its envelope by a calf's testicles. From that point onwards Ned's reputations was established and the only way was down, or up, depending on one's point of view.

Following his release from prison, another bushranger, Isiah (Wild) Wright, lent Ned a stolen horse, which he used to ride to the town of Greta. The horse was recognised and Ned was apprehended, but not before an attempt to resist arrest which saw Ned overpower and humiliate the arresting officer, Constable Hall. This time Ned was sent down for three years, having enjoyed only a few weeks of freedom. Ned had become a repeat offender, a recidivist.

When Ned was next released he had transformed

into the true villain of the peace. Before long he became involved in a large-scale cattle-rustling operation with his new father-in-law and his brothers. Constable Fitzpatrick, who attempted to put a stop to their criminal activities, ended up with injuries, including a broken wrist. Ned and his brother Dan went into hiding, knowing that they faced certain imprisonment for both the cattle rustling and the assault of a police officer. Now Ned had the title 'wanted fugitive' to add to his growing criminal resume. This was the start of the infamous Kelly Gang, which terrorised the area of north-east Victoria for two years from 1878.

THE GANG

Ned and Dan Kelly were joined by Joe Byrne and Steve Hart. The four of them secreted themselves in a wooded area north of Mansfield in Victoria, known as the Wombat Range. In late October 1878, four undercover police officers set about trying to capture them, or at least return with their bodies, for the members of the gang each had prices on their heads. The officers disguised themselves as gold prospectors and set off on their mission. Their names were Kennedy, Lonigan, McIntyre and Scanlan.

By chance the policemen set up camp only a mile away from the Kelly Gang, who were alerted to the presence of the officers when they used their guns to bring down some birds for food. When the Kelly Gang arrived to recce the strangers' camp, they immediately realised that the law was upon them despite their masquerade. Only two officers were in camp at the time so the gang decided to overpower them and so improve their chances of escaping from the area.

However, one officer was killed and the other was made hostage. Then a shoot-out resulted in the other two officers dying when they returned to the camp. One of the hapless victims had been executed as a measure of mercy to put him out of his misery, having already received a fatal injury, but this was seen as an act of unimaginable brutality by the Australian authorities. Ned also took and discarded the dying man's note to his wife. The Kelly Gang had become public enemy number one.

Perhaps concluding that they now had nothing to lose, but their lives, the Kelly Gang now evolved into a troop of bank robbers. Their first heist saw them take £2,000 from the National Bank at a place called Euroa on December 10. They took a number of staff and general public hostage in the process, but they escaped without harming anyone – well, not physically anyway. The next bank job took place on February 8–10, 1879, in the town of Jerilderie. They took a number of hostages and then robbed the bank of another £2,000.

Sometime before the Jerilderie robbery, Ned

Kelly suddenly decided to declare himself – in writing – a political dissident in defence of his criminal activities. His Jerilderie Letter, sets out his agenda; his political manifesto. In the 8,000 word letter, he attempted to absolve himself of any blame by voicing his disgust at the prejudicial and unjust treatment of Irish Catholics in Australia, the USA and Ireland itself. He also attempted to explain that all of his former wrongdoings were the result of police antagonism and conspiracy. The letter was left behind when the gang departed with the request that it should be published as a pamphlet for general distribution. It never was.

Ned also burned all of the Jerilderie townsfolk's mortgage deeds, apparently to set them free of their debts. This gesture did not go unnoticed by the everyday population of Australia, who subsequently began to view him as something of a man of the ordinary people instead of just a lowly criminal – 'taking from the rich and giving to the poor'. Others chose to read between the lines of his letter, concluding that his true ambition was to plan an armed uprising, a coup, against the British Empire and declare north-east Victoria an independent state, presumably with him as rebel leader.

Following the events at Jerilderie, the police made a concerted effort to close in on the Kelly Gang. They got their first lucky break over a year later when the gang turned to revenge and retribution. An old friend of theirs had turned police informer, so they decided to punish him by death. Joe Byrne murdered Aaron Sherrit at his home on June 26, 1880. The killing was witnessed by four policemen who, in fear for their own lives, hid the whole night long before reporting the murder.

The Kelly Gang had presumed that the death had been reported the previous evening, so they set up an ambush for early the next day. They took around seventy hostages in a place called Glenrowan and set about sabotaging the railway's tracks so that the police train would derail. However, the unexpected delay gave a hostage an opportunity to warn the police by waving a candle, as night time had by then fallen.

The gang evaded capture by holing themselves up in the Glenrowan Inn for the night with a number of hostages. At dawn they made their final stand wearing their famous armour, which was fashioned from iron plough parts. Each had a helmet and various body plates, which weighed a total of around 44 kg (7 stone). With so much additional weight and the armour so crudely designed, it only served to encumber their movements rather than provide protection.

Ned Kelly was the only one to leave the confines of the Glenrowan Inn. He boldly walked through the front door into a hail of bullets and kept on walking straight towards the barrage, firing his guns all the while. Slugs ricocheted off his helmet, saving him from immediate death, but he was brought down by a number of shots aimed at his lower legs, which were unprotected. The other three gang members, Dan Kelly, Joe Byrne and Steve Hart, all died inside the building. Joe Byrne was shot in the upper leg and died from loss of blood. The other two men took poison rather than be killed by the police. Unfortunately, a number of the hostages were fatally wounded by crossfire.

Ned, the only gang member to survive, was duly indicted for his crimes and treated for his injuries. Some four months later he was well enough to stand trial. By that time, his story had generated a certain level of empathy. Some 32,000 people had signed a petition against his receiving the death penalty, which was prompted by the notion that he was a political activist and voice of the Australian underclass.

Unfortunately for Kelly, the presiding judge, Sir Redmond Barry, was himself a Catholic Irishman who had become a British colonial judge when he emigrated to Australia. He did not share the sentiments of the petitioners as he was a leading player in the government of Victoria, which had been created in 1855 – coincidentally the very year of Kelly's birth. To him, Kelly was nothing but an ill-educated thug from the wrong side of the tracks, whom he had seen progress from one crime to the next in an inevitable march towards execution.

When Sir Redmond sentenced Kelly to death by hanging he commented: 'May God have mercy on your soul'. Kelly, who saw Redmond as a traitor to the Irish and so his natural enemy, retorted: 'I will go further than that and say; I will see you there when I go'. As it turned out, Redmond had been suffering from a carbuncle, or multiple boil, on his neck. Only twelve days following Kelly's execution Redmond died from pneumonia brought on by a bacterial infection.

There is some contention about Ned Kelly's last words on November 11, 1880, before he went for the drop, because he mumbled under his breath, having been prompted to say something at the last minute. It was reported that he said: 'Ah well, I suppose it has come to this. Such is life.' or perhaps just the last sentence: 'Such is life.' Whatever it was exactly, it was dismissive and indicative of a man who couldn't see that his fate had actually been in his own hands rather than those of others.

To that extent, it seems that Judge Barry was correct in his assessment of Kelly. To blame society for the outcome of his life was, to him, typical of those with deviant minds. To the judge, if you really did want to make your mark on society you got yourself educated and promoted yourself to a position of influence, which is exactly what he had done himself. That is why views on Ned Kelly are so disparate to this day.

Those able to achieve success themselves by orthodox routes tend to have the conservative view that he embarked on a criminal career because he was fundamentally a lowlife. Those who believe that social disadvantage has prevented them from progressing tend to have the sympathetic view that he was making the best of a bad situation. He certainly seems to have been more intelligent than your typical criminal mind, but whether he was a 'criminal mastermind' is a matter for debate.

He did end up walking to the gallows, having left a trail of death in his wake and ultimately got himself caught. But then again, he did also show that he had a burgeoning social conscience and surprised people by his ingenuity and courage. There is something inside most people that likes to see individuals rebelling against authority, simply because it gives them a chance to live vicariously in a world otherwise rather ordered and predictable. Perhaps that is why Ned Kelly holds a certain appeal as a cultural icon, because he held two fingers up to law and order but, at the same time, demonstrated that we wouldn't really be better off without them.

CHARLES MANSON

Charles Manson, one of the modern world's most dangerous criminal masterminds, was born on November 12, 1934, in Cincinnati General Hospital, Ohio. Manson was the illegitimate child to a sixteen-year-old prostitute and alcoholic mother, Kathleen Maddox. Maddox was overwhelmed by the new responsibility of motherhood and often left her baby in the care of her family. After committing strong-arm robbery, Kathleen Maddox was sentenced to five years in prison, and Charles was left in the loving care of his devoutly religious aunt and uncle in West Virginia.

Charles Manson's lifetime of disregard for the law started from a very young age. Throughout his childhood, Charles dreamed of a life with his mother and, on the one occasion he managed to find her, she rejected him. Because of his mother's apparent disinterest in him, Manson became disillusioned with society. Before the age of twenty he had been in and out of detention centres and boys homes. Unable to settle into the cold, unfamiliar surroundings, he often escaped. After a while Manson adjusted to being institutionalised and relished the attention that he got. By 1954, Manson had become a model inmate and was paroled.

In January 1955, while living in Virginia, Manson married seventeen-year-old Rosalie Jean Willis. The couple decided to move to California and start a new life. In order to effect the relocation, Manson stole a car and they headed west. On arriving in California, he was arrested and charged with grand theft auto. Soon after Manson's arrest, Rosalie gave birth to their son, Charles Manson Jr and, shortly afterwards decided to leave Charles for another man. Manson served two years for the grand theft auto conviction and was paroled again. It was not long before the prison-hardened Manson offended again, only next time it would be a federal offence and carry a more severe punishment.

It was while serving a ten-year sentence at McNeil Island Penitentiary in Washington State for attempting to cash a forged treasury cheque that Manson became very interested in music, specifically the guitar. It was also during this term in prison that Manson developed his warped philosophy. Surrounded by convicts, there was no one to tell Manson that his ideas were bordered on the insane. Manson's interest in guitar was satiated by the expert tutelage of Alvin Karpis, a hardened bank robber of the 1930s. Karpis took Manson under his wing and taught him how to play the guitar, as he felt some responsibility to show Manson some much needed affection. Karpis was aware of Manson's troubled and unfortunate past and was sure that he would never put the time into learning how to play the guitar. Manson surprised Karpis by becoming quite proficient with the instrument and even showing interest in becoming a musician and performing in Las Vegas, where Karpis had connections and still had influence. Karpis might have been able to help Manson with his new dream had Manson not been transferred to a California prison in 1967. Manson was released that year having only served seven years out of the ten-year sentence.

In March of 1967, at the age of thirty-two, Manson was released from prison despite announcing his wishes to remain incarcerated. The authorities should have obeyed his wishes, as his crimes escalated at this time to the crimes that he is most noted for orchestrating and committing. It was his belief that he could not adjust to life in the real world as, at that point in his life, he had been in prison for more than half of his years. The skills that he had developed in prison, including an aptitude for the power of positive thinking would serve him well in the new world in which he found himself. This new world of Flower Power and the young ruling the streets, suited Manson perfectly and he blended in with this new breed.

Not long after his release from prison, and while living in San Francisco, Manson began attracting the interest of a group of young people. His strange, twenty-five 'devotees' and as many as sixty other 'associates' which became known collectively as the 'Manson Family'. Manson and his new family took up residence in an abandoned film-set owned by a blind man called George Spahn. Manson presided over the breaking and rebuilding of the families personal identities. He used several methods, including drugs and sex to maintain control. Manson made use of LSD to control the family, although he was not using the drugs himself because he felt he needed to maintain control of his own faculties. Meanwhile, he used sex to control the female members of the family and used the 'sale' of sex from the women in the family that he considered most enticing to buy the loyalty and support of his male disciples. The group that Manson surrounded himself with consisted of mostly young women who were quite willing to give up their comfortable, middle-class lives to follow Manson on his strange quest, which only he ultimately knew the full meaning of.

One day, while the Manson family was in Los Angeles, Dennis Wilson, a member of the popular music band, The Beach Boys, picked up two female members of the Manson Family and took them to his home. It was only a short while later that

Manson and the rest of the family moved in with Wilson. Manson's plan was to use Wilson to get his music recorded. Manson is bitter to this day that his music was never widely distributed or appreciated. Soon fascination with the Beatles, coupled with his growing philosophy for rebellion against society, generated a new objective.

Manson's new plan, dubbed 'Helter Skelter' named after the Beatles song, predicted a race war between blacks and whites where the blacks would eventually win. Manson believed that even if the blacks won the war, they would be unable to sustain supremacy and would eventually have to rely on the whites who had survived 'Helter Skelter'. Later in 1968, the family spent time in a remote area of Death Valley, California, called Barker Ranch. Later that year the family moved back to the Los Angeles area. Shortly after the Manson Family moved back to Los Angeles, Manson told his followers that he believed that he had killed an Afro-American man who he thought was a member of 'The Black Panthers', a political and civil rights activist party. Anticipating an angry reprisal from the party forced Manson into laying low for much of mid-1969.

On August 9, 1969, Manson ordered a small team from his group to infiltrate the home of famous film producer Roman Polanski and his wife Sharon Tate, one of the most photographed women of the 1960s. Manson was ordering nothing short of a slaughter when he sent a team that consisted of Manson Family members Charles 'Tex' Watson, Patricia Krenwinkel, Susan Atkins and Linda Kasabian to invade and kill the occupants of the house. In a flurry of violence, the inhabitants of the home were brutally murdered by stabbing, gunshots and bludgeoning. Among the dead were Jay Sebring, founder of Sebring International and a noted hairstylist, Abigail Folger, the wealthy coffee heiress, Wojciech Frykowski, a polish writer, Steven Parent, an eighteen-year-old friend of the caretaker at the home, Sharon Tate and her unborn child. The gang left the scene of carnage with the word 'Pig' written in blood on the door.

As if he had embarked on a Holy War, Charles Manson decided to carry out even further attacks the following evening. Manson and family members Watson, Krenwinkel and Leslie Van Houten invaded the home of Leno and Rosemary Labianca at 3301 Waverly Drive in Los Angeles. Manson entered the property first and tied up the occupants. He then assured the Labiancas they would be robbed but left unhurt, and then proceeded to tell the team waiting outside to enter the property and kill them. The murders were as brutal as those at the home of the Tates' the night before. The word 'War' was carved in Mr Labianca's stomach and he had a carving knife jammed in his neck. Mrs Labianca had been brutally stabbed multiple times in the back. The walls were scrawled with the words 'death to pigs' and 'Rise' written in the victims' blood. On the door the word 'helter skelter' was also written in blood. At the time the police investigation did not link the murder of the Tates and Labiancas, and believed that the murder of the Labiancas was a 'copycat' crime. The word 'Rise' made the police think the crime was ritual-related. Although Manson was not present for these crimes, the command he held over his followers coerced them into committing these acts of disgusting, inhumane violence. Without Manson's hypnotic suggestions, these crimes may not have not occurred.

Later in 1969, when a few members of the Manson family were incarcerated yet again for car theft, one of the family members bragged to another inmate that they had been involved in the Tate and Labianca murders. This information was later given to the police, and the events that Manson thought he had so skilfully orchestrated started to unravel before him.

In December 1969, after a lengthy investigation, Charles Manson and members of the family were arrested at their hide out at Barker Ranch and charged with the Tate and Labianca murders. Manson wanted to serve as his own attorney but the court denied him the right. Linda Kasabian, who had been the getaway car driver for the invaders on the nights of the murders, volunteered to testify against the family in exchange for immunity. The family was banned from the court room after repeated disruptions and mocking the proceedings. In July 1970, Manson and the other three women on trial for the murders carved X's in their foreheads to signify their exclusion from society. The 'X' carving remains on Manson's forehead to this day but now resembles a swastika. In an unexpected flurry of violence, Manson lunged at the judge as if to attack, but he did not reach him.

On November 16, 1970, the trial ended. On January 25, 1971, the four family members – Charles Manson, Leslie Van Houten, Pat Krenwinkel and Susan Atkins – were found guilty of conspiracy to commit murder and murder in the first degree. They were sentenced to die in the gas chamber. Watson was tried in a separate trial and found guilty of the same crimes and sentenced to death. In 1972, the Supreme Court temporarily ruled against the death penalty and their sentences were reduced to life imprisonment.

Charles Manson went back to prison, the one place in the world where he had always fitted in. It had been his home for a good deal of his life and most likely will serve as his home for the rest of his days. Manson is currently an inmate at Corcoran State Prison in California. It is well over one-quarter of a century after these brutal crimes and he remains unremorseful. His psychological state is a precarious one. On most of the occasions Manson has been interviewed, he has been verbally abusive and very unpleasant to the interviewer, going as far as to threaten to beat the interviewer to death with a book that was on the table in front of him. He said, 'I would do it as easily as you would walk to the drug store'. Manson blames society for the way that he has behaved and remains adamant that he never controlled the members of the Manson family and that he had nothing to do with their actions. Manson is due to be considered for parole again in 2007.

> *I never broke nobody's will. I never told anybody to do anything other than what they wanted to do ... I said you do what's best for you ... what you do is up to you ... it has nothing to do with me.*
>
> CHARLES MANSON

PART SIX

TERRORISTS

ABU NIDAL

During the 1980s, Abu Nidal headed one of the longest-running terrorist campaigns against the Western world in general, and Israeli interests in particular. A veteran Palestinian freedom fighter, over his career Abu Nidal's operations became more and more violent, until he and his organization were acting more or less as a mercenary force rather than as pro-Arab political campaigners. Throughout the mid-1980s, the Abu Nidal Organization (ANO) was regarded as the most dangerous terrorist group in the world, and it mounted major terrorist attacks in over twenty countries, killing a total of around 300 people and injuring many more.

However, despite his many crimes, from masterminding assassinations of leading political figures to hijacking aeroplanes, for many years Abu Nidal remained at large. For a long time, he was able to gain protection from the authorities by making cunning alliances with rogue Arab states, such as Iraq, Libya and Syria, who were also highly critical of the West, and moved his training camps to these countries to continue his campaign of destruction.

However, in the end he even alienated these governments, and one by one they expelled him from their soil, until he literally had nowhere to run. His demise came in 2002, when he was shot dead in mysterious circumstances at his home in a suburb of Baghdad. At the time of his death he was facing a charge of treason from the Iraqi government, and is thought to have been suffering from leukaemia.

'FATHER OF STRUGGLE'

Born Sabri al-Banna in 1931, the man who later grew up to be one of the most feared terrorists in the world, spent his early years in the town of Jaffa (now part of Tel Aviv). He came from a very rich Palestinian farming family who owned miles of orange groves and orchards, but his childhood was far from secure and peaceful. In 1948, when war broke out between the Arabs and the Israelis, the family were forced to flee as refugees to the West Bank. In addition to this political upheaval, Sabri had to endure upheaval in his family life.

His father Khalil had thirteen wives and twenty-four children. Sabri was the son of his second wife, but this woman had very low status in the family, since she had been a maid when she joined them, and had only been sixteen years old when Khalil married her. The family disapproved of the marriage, and thus Sabri was treated badly by his many brothers and sisters. The situation took a turn for the worse when Sabri was seven: his father died, and the family threw his mother out of the house. Sabri was sent to a strict Muslim school and was shunned by the rest of the family, thus finding himself alone in the world at a young age. Many commentators have suggested that these experiences gave him a paranoid, and later, psychopathic personality, so that he was unable to trust anyone throughout his life.

As a young man, he became a teacher and joined the Ba'ath party during the 1950s. In the late sixties, he joined the Palestinian Liberation Organization (PLO), aiming to fight to reclaim the land and position that his family had lost in the war. Adopting the *nom de guerre* Abu Nidal, meaning 'father of struggle', he aligned himself with the radical wing of the PLO, headed by Yasser Arafat. However, his co-existence with Arafat in the party did not last long. In 1974, he split with the organization, regarding them as too conservative in their programme of reform. The PLO were fighting to create a Palestinian state step by step, first setting up a national authority in the West Bank and the Gaza Strip. However, Nidal saw this as a timid response to the situation, and recommended all-out warfare with Israel instead.

SHOOT-OUT AT THE SYNAGOGUE

Along with other radicals from the PLO, Nidal

formed his own organization, the Fatah Revolutionary Council. This was the group that later became known as the Abu Nidal Organization (ANO). Nidal was uncompromising in his position: not only did he believe that peace negotiations between the Arabs and the Israelis should be immediately halted, he also believed that moderate Arab leaders should be attacked.

During the 1980s, the ANO's targets were wide ranging, taking place in Europe, Asia and the Middle East. The ANO are believed to have been behind many assassinations, mass shootings and hijackings during this period. In June 1982, the organization made an assassination attempt on Shlomo Argov in London, prompting the Israeli invasion of the Lebanon. Three years later, it attacked El Al airport counters in Rome and Vienna, killing eighteen people and injuring over 100 more. That same year, a Pan Am Flight to Karachi was hijacked, killing twenty-two people. The following year, in 1986, there was a shoot-out at the Neve Shalom Synagogue in Istanbul, killing twenty-two, believed to have been the work of the ANO.

In the 1990s, the attacks continued, with the assassination of Abu Iyyad, PLO leader Yasser Arafat's right-hand man and the assassination of Naeb Imran Maaytah, a top Jordanian diplomat. The ANO was also suspected of attacking a cruise ship, the *City of Poros*, which left nine people dead and almost 100 injured, and of planting a car bomb outside the Israeli embassy in Cyprus, killing three people.

SADISTIC PURGES

As well as conducting these horrific attacks, the Abu Nidal Organization also began to act as a mercenary force for radical Arab governments, including Syria, Libya and Iraq. In return for this, these countries offered the terrorists a safe haven, allowing them to train soldiers at camps on their soil. However, in each case, when international pressure became extreme, the organization was banned from the country, in order to avoid problems such as sanctions and political ostracism from the West.

Chillingly, news then began to spread of internal purges in the Abu Nidal Organization itself. It is thought that around 150 of the organization's own members met their deaths as a result of torture and execution, in a series of bizarre trials for conspiracy. By this time, Nidal had begun to show signs of extreme paranoia, refusing to let any ANO members leave the organization, and suspecting them of being double agents. New recruits were required to write out their life story by hand, agreeing to be executed if any of the facts were found not to be true. When mistakes were made, members were tortured until a confession was extracted out of them. Escaped recruits told of terrible tortures, such as being buried alive, having their genitals placed in boiling oil and being killed by having a feeding tube forced into their mouths and a gun fired into their guts. According to reliable sources, mass purges also took place: in November 1987, 170 members were machine-gunned to death in a single night, while not long afterwards, 150 more were shot and buried in a mass grave.

MASTER OF CUNNING

Not surprisingly, the effectiveness of the organization began to decline during the 1990s, but despite his declining mental health, Nidal was still a master of cunning, escaping capture for many years. During this time he conducted a massive banking scam, through the BCCI bank, trading under the name of a company called SAS Trade and Investment and using the name Shakar Farhan. The business was actually an arms dealing one, selling European and American-made guns, armoured cars, grenade launchers and other accoutrements of war to Middle Eastern clients. An astute businessman, Nidal always kept a large slice of the profits for himself.

THE FINAL SHOWDOWN

At the end of the 1990s, Nidal was expelled from Libya, where he had set up his operation, because Colonel Gaddafi wanted to improve his relations with the West in the wake of the Lockerbie disaster. Nidal is rumoured to have been involved with the bombing of this aircraft as well as other terrorist attacks during this period. He went to live in Iraq, and was allowed to stay there, despite the fact that the Jordanian government wanted to extradite him. On August 19, 2002, he was reported to have died of gunshot wounds in a house owned by the Iraqi secret service in the well-to-do neighbourhood of al-Jadriya in Baghdad. Iraq's chief security man alleged that Nidal had committed suicide, shooting himself through the mouth when security forces paid him a visit to accuse him of conspiracy to bring down the Iraqi leader Saddam Hussein. Other sources suggest that it was the Iraqi secret service, known as the Mukhabarat, that shot Nidal. According to these reports, Nidal was assassinated by a hit squad . of thirty officers in a surprise attack on his house, and died of multiple gunshot wounds. He was rushed to hospital, where he died after eight hours.

Given the number of assassinations, mass shootings, hijackings and other terror attacks that Abu Nidal had masterminded since the 1970s – not to mention his numerous financial scams and arms dealing activities – it is extraordinary that he managed to evade capture for over three decades, during which time he became one of the most wanted international criminals of all time.

BAADER-MEINHOF GANG

The Baader-Meinhof Gang, also known as the Red Army Faction or Fraction, was a terrorist group that was active in Germany for almost thirty years, beginning in the 1970s. Its aim was to mount a left-wing campaign against what it saw as the repressive German state by organising a series of terror attacks. These included bombings of military, police and media targets, the kidnapping and murder of leading German politicians and businessmen, and hijackings. In all, the gang killed thirty-four people in their attacks, and injured many more.

ARSON ATTACKS

The campaign had its roots in the student protest movement of the 1960s, which began peacefully but became violent when students demonstrated against the visit of the Shah of Persia to West Berlin. During the demonstrations, a student named Benno Ohnesorg was shot dead by police. His death became a rallying point for left-wing activists, who now decided to respond to what they saw as police brutality by burning down a number of department stores. The group included Andreaas Baader, Gudrin Ensslin, Horst Söhnlein and Thorwald Proll. They were arrested and, while on trial, their story was sympathetically covered by a journalist, Ulrike Meinhof.

Next, to add fuel to the fire, the leading student activist of the day, Rudi Dutschke, was badly injured in a demonstration, further alienating the activists from the mainstream of German political life. They now became known as the Red Army Fraction, a name inspired by the Japanese Red Army, a left-wing paramilitary group in Japan. However, the press and the public informally referred to them as the Baader-Meinhof Gang. Ulrike Meinhof never led the gang, but her close involvement with it and public support of the actions ensured that she became permanently associated with it.

The main leaders of the gang were soon arrested and imprisoned, but the trouble was far from over. The prisoners were put into solitary confinement, and saw themselves as political martyrs, winning a great deal of support for their cause from the student population. The situation worsened when the prisoners went on hunger strike and had to be force fed. One of them, Holger Meins, died on November 9, 1974, causing a public outcry.

SERIES OF BOMBINGS

Meanwhile, the terror attacks continued, perpetrated by a new generation of Red Army activists, who had taken over from the founders of the group. In 1972, the gang carried out a series of bombings. On May 11, they bombed a US barracks in Frankfurt, killing one person and injuring thirteen; the following day, they bombed a police station in Augsburg and a Criminal Investigations Agency in Munich, injuring five people. A few days later, the bombings started again, with the bombing of the car of a federal judge, whose wife was injured in the attack, and the bombing of the Axel Springer Verlag, a newspaper and magazine publisher, which caused seventeen injuries. Next, there was a more serious attack on the Military Intelligence Headquarters of the US army in Heidelberg, killing three people and injuring five. The following year, four people were killed when the West German embassy in Stockholm was taken over; two of these were members of the gang.

CONSPIRACY THEORIES

In 1975, the Stammheim trial, named after a district in the city of Stuttgart, took place. This became one of the longest and most controversial criminal trials in Germany. Most of the culprits were convicted and imprisoned, but in May 1976, Ulrike Meinhof was found hanged in her cell. On April 28, 1977, Raspe was found with a gunshot wound in his cell at Stammheim prison. He died soon after being taken to hospital. The same morning, Andreas Baader and Gudrun Ensslin were found dead in their cells. Another prisoner, Irmgard Möller, was also found wounded, stabbed in the chest, but survived. An official enquiry concluded that the prisoners committed suicide; however, Red Army supporters were convinced that the deaths were suspicious, and many conspiracy theories arose as to how the activists had met their deaths.

Meanwhile, despite the fact that the main leaders of the gang were now locked away or dead, the killings continued. Throughout the 1970s and 1980s, there were a series of kidnaps, murders, hijackings and bombings. In 1977, the situation reached crisis point, in what became known as 'German Autumn'. The head of a major German bank, Jürgen Ponto, was shot and killed in front of his house; one of the members of the gang who killed him was his own god-daughter, Susanne Albrecht. When they were arrested, tried and convicted of the crime, the backlash started, with a series of more ambitious attacks that terrorized the German public.

'GERMAN AUTUMN'

First, a Lufthansa aircraft was hijacked at Palma De Majorca. The hijacking came to an end in a commando-style operation that left three hijackers dead. Next, Hanns-Martin Schleyer, the Chairman of the German Employers' Organization was kidnapped and shot; three police officers and a driver were also killed during the kidnapping. Then Alexander Haig, the Supreme Allied Commander of NATO, narrowly avoided an assassination attempt. Clearly, the fact that the first generation of Red Army leaders were out of the picture had not ended the organization's rule of terror; indeed, their imprisonment and subsequent death appeared to have incited more attacks, escalating the violence to an alarming degree.

During the 1980s, there were more attacks, though by now they were more sporadic. On August 8, 1985, a Volkswagen minibus exploded in a car park at a military air base near Frankfurt. Two people were killed, and twenty injured. It later transpired that a soldier had been kidnapped and killed the night before the attack, and his ID card stolen to gain access to the base. The following year, a leading industrialist, Karl Heinz Beckurts and his driver were shot, and banker Alfred Herrhausen was the victim of a bomb attack. In 1993, another attack took place, when explosives were thrown at the construction site of a new prison, causing millions of dollars' worth of damage; thankfully, no one was killed in this attack.

Thus it was that the Baader-Meinhof gang managed to mastermind a series of terror attacks over a period of three decades. In the wake of the attacks, there have been many questions as to why it was that such a violent group of generally well-educated, middle-class young people could take to crime in this way, and attract such a lot of support from their peers at universities and educational establishments across the country.

THE END OF AN ERA

One theory is that young people in Germany in the 1970s felt extremely guilty about the events of World War II, in particular the Nazi regime, and were trying to absolve themselves in a negative way from that sense of guilt by attacking the establishment, in the shape of the police, the military, the government and the business and industrial leaders of the nation. It has also been pointed out that the The Baader-Meinhof Gang also represented a kind of 'rock' aesthetic, and that they appealed to young people because they dressed in a trendy way, with leather jackets and long hair. The presence of young women dressed as gangsters, in dark glasses and black clothes, was also a draw to young, impressionable students. Moreover, the gang consciously referenced such leaders as Che Guevara, not only in their style of dress, but in their actions. Many of the terror attacks they undertook were influenced by the theories of guerrilla warfare put forward by Guevara and others during the Cuban revolution.

However, instead of fighting for justice in a poor, oppressed society such as that of Cuba, the Baader-Meinhof Gang were trying to lead a revolution in Germany, which by the late 1960s had become one of Europe's richest nations. For this reason, among others, they failed to do more than mount a series of extremely damaging attacks on individuals – whether heads of banks, military figures or simply those who happened to be nearby at the time – earning themselves a reputation as cold-blooded killers rather than as revolutionaries or visionaries.

Today, most commentators regard the influence of the Baader-Meinhof Gang as negligible. In general, the political left, which arose out of the student protests of the 1960s, has given rise to positive initiatives such as the anti-nuclear and green movements, both of which have increased in popularity since that time. By contrast, the extremism of the Baader-Meinhof Gang, to the relief of most of the German people, appears to have reached a dead end. (Interestingly, one of its founding members, Horst Mahler, who was released from prison in the early 1980s, is now a leading neo-Nazi figure, having completely reversed his politics.) It is still remarkable, however, that the group managed to maintain a presence for so long in German society, terrorizing some of the most influential and powerful figures in the nation, and causing the government a series of extremely humiliating episodes.

OSAMA BIN LADEN

Today, Osama bin Laden is probably the most famous terrorist in the world, having been identified as the mastermind behind al-Qaeda, the organization that carried out the attacks of September 11, 2001. As well as this horrific attack, which killed almost 3,000 people in the biggest single terror offensive of all time, he and al-Qaeda are believed to have been behind a series of US embassy bombings, the Bali nightclub bombings, the USS *Cole* bombing and the Madrid bombings. Al-Qaeda is also thought to be responsible for terror attacks in the Jordanian capital Amman, and the Sinai peninsula of Egypt.

Although bin Laden has now publicly claimed responsibility for the September 11 attacks, to date the US security services do not have enough hard evidence to link him to the events and he has not been indicted for these. However, he has been indicted on the embassy bombings in Africa, and is currently on the FBI's Ten Most Wanted Fugitives list. Strenuous attempts have been made to capture him, but at present his whereabouts are unknown, although he is thought to be living in rural

Afghanistan. There have also been several reports of his death, though these are unsubstantiated.

MILLIONAIRE FATHER

The story of bin Laden is a strange one, and it still remains something of a mystery as to why this intelligent, well-educated man, who was born and raised in the lap of luxury, should have become one of the greatest mass murderers of our time. Osama bin Laden was born in Riyadh, Saudi Arabia, on March 10, 1957. His father, Muhammed Awad bin Laden, was an extremely wealthy man, building palaces for the billionaire Saudi royal family and, in the process, amassing a huge fortune. As was the custom for men of wealth and position, Muhammed had many wives, who bore him, in total, fifty-five offspring. Osama was the son of Muhammed's tenth wife, Hamida al-Attas, a Syrian-born woman. The marriage did not last long (Muhammed was married twenty-two times, though he only had four wives at a time, in accordance with Islamic law).

Soon after Osama's birth, his parents divorced, and his mother Hamida married Muhammed al-Attas, one of her former husband's employees. The couple went on to have four children, and Osama became part of a new step-family. Raised as a devout Sunni Muslim, at school and university, Osama came under the influence of Islamic fundamentalist teachers who had been banned for their extremist views from other Arab countries. Some of these teachers preached a philosophy of anti-Western 'jihad', and Osama, as was later to become clear, was deeply influenced by their views.

As a young man, bin Laden gained degrees in civil engineering, business and public administration and economics; he also became an expert in Islamic jurisprudence. He went on to marry several times, as was the custom, and is thought to have fathered between twelve and twenty children. As a result of his family's business interests, and his own, he was an extremely wealthy man, and because of his funda-mentalist views, began to support the mujahideen, a radical group of Muslim guerrillas fighting for control of Afghanistan after the invasion of the country by the Soviet Union in 1979. He co-ordinated his efforts with a former university teacher of his, Abdullah Azzam, who had moved to Peshawar, Pakistan, and was running a resistance campaign on the border with Afghanistan.

BANK-ROLLING THE MUJAHIDEEN

After bin Laden graduated from Jeddah University, he not only continued to bankroll Azzam's opera-tion, but also went to Peshawar himself to fight for the cause. Together, he and Azzam set up an organization called Maktab al-Khadamat (MAK) whose aim was to channel arms, money and mujahideen soldiers into Afghanistan. In this way, bin Laden established an international network of covert activities and contacts that was to become the basis for his later anti-American terrorist activities. According to some sources, he was helped at this time by the CIA, who were keen to topple the Soviet regime in Afghanistan and were willing to make alliances with any group that also wished for its demise. As we now know, this strategy was to prove disastrous for the United States in later years.

After splitting from MAK in 1988, bin Laden formed al-Qaeda, a specifically Arab nationalist organization with its own army of 12,000 armed men. When Iraq invaded Kuwait, bin Laden offered the Saudi government his army, but instead, the Saudis accepted help from the US government. This absolutely incensed bin Laden, who had a loathing for the values of Western democracy, and firmly believed that US troops should never be allowed on to Saudi Arabian soil. From this time on, he publicly denounced the Saudi royal family, and he was forced to become an exile from Saudi Arabia as a result.

THE 'FATWA'

Bin Laden's next port of call was Khartoum, Sudan, where he set up a new base for his operations. These included training camps, which recruited soldiers from all over the world and educated them both in Islamic law and military strategy. An astute business-man, bin Laden also set up a large road construction company and agricultural corporation in Sudan, assisted by friends in high places, such as the Sudanese political leader, Hassan al Turabi. How-ever, even though he had the protection of Turabi, bin Laden was eventually forced to leave Sudan, under pressure from the international community.

Forced into exile once again, bin Laden now decided to move to the heart of the fundamentalist world, to the new Afghan government of the Taliban, whose headquarters were at Kandahar. Here, he not only bankrolled new regime but was suspected of financing and organizing a series of horrific anti-Western terror attacks and atrocities around the world, including the Luxor massacre in Egypt in 1997.

In 1998, along with one of the leaders of the Egyptian Islamic Jihad, Ayman al-Zawahiri, bin Laden issued a 'fatwa', or religious edict, threatening to kill all Americans and their allies, whether civilian or military. He declared that it was the duty of every good Muslim to do this, so as to liberate the Muslim people. There followed, in 1998, a series of US embassy bombings across the world. Bin Laden was held responsible and US president Bill Clinton ordered that his assets should be frozen. He also signed an order authorizing bin

Laden's arrest and offered a five-million dollar reward for his capture. The same year, the United States launched a cruise missile attack on Afghanistan. Bin Laden escaped unharmed, but the missile killed nineteen others, causing controversy over the US action.

DISASTER STRIKES

The worst was still to come, however. On the morning of September 11, in Manhattan, the world watched in horror as two planes crashed into the North and South Towers of the World Trade Center, setting fire to the buildings and bringing them crashing down. On the same morning, another hijacked aeroplane crashed into the Pentagon headquarters at Arlington County, Virginia, destroying part of the building, and a fourth hijacked plane crashed into a field in Pennsylvania, killing the entire crew and passengers, as well as the hijackers themselves.

The fact that the terrorists had managed to destroy some of the greatest symbols of Western power and economic might, in the heart of New York and Washington, killing around 3,000 people, was extraordinary. When news emerged that the suicide bombers had simply boarded the planes armed only with box cutters, it became clear that the West was now under threat from a very extremist group that would stop at nothing. Bin Laden immediately came under suspicion, and although he initially denied involvement in the events, he later admitted his involvement.

AFTERMATH

After these events, which are now referred to as 9/11, a special commission was set up to enquire into what had happened. Eventually, after three years of investigation, the report identified nineteen hijackers, all of whom belonged to Al-Qaeda. The terrorists mostly came from Saudi Arabia, but also from the United Arab Emirates, Lebanon and Egypt, and had entered the United States earlier that year. They had been trained by the terrorist group Al-Qaeda, and the plan had the full approval and backing of Osama bin Laden.

Today, bin Laden is still in hiding, and is currently thought to be living somewhere on the border between Pakistan and Afghanistan. Rumours abound as to his whereabouts and state of health. He suffers from a kidney disease, which needs to be treated with highly technological medical equipment, and is rumoured to be unwell. In recent years, several sightings of him have been reported, but none of them have yet led to his capture. According to some reports, he may even have died, either of his illness, or from a disease such as typhoid. But whatever the true story, the fact remains that, the mastermind behind the atrocities of 9/11 and many other bombings around the world has still not been captured and brought to justice. In addition, the events of 9/11 have plunged the West into increasing disputes with the Arab nations, and the conflicts look set to continue well into the new millennium.

CARLOS THE JACKAL

Carlos the Jackal was the name given to Ilich Ramirez Sanchez, a Venezuelan national who masterminded some of the most outrageous terror attacks of the twentieth century. Like Abu Nidal, Sanchez began his career as something of an idealist, but soon lost all sense of his political cause and began to kill at random, out of bloodlust and greed. During his long career of terror attacks, he also emerged as a man who loved to show off his fame and wealth, and who thoroughly enjoyed his position as one of the world's most notorious criminals. For over two decades, he terrorised the general public of many countries in Europe with a series of brutal, senseless attacks, until he was driven underground and eventually handed over to the authorities for trial in France. Sanchez was convicted of three murders and given a life sentence for these crimes, but to date, he still has not been tried for all the attacks that he masterminded.

TERRORIST EDUCATION

Born in 1949 in Caracas, Venezuela, Ilich Ramirez Sanchez was named after the Russian revolutionary Vladimir Ilich Lenin. (In fact, the three sons of the family each took one of the the famous Russian leader's names: Vladimir was the eldest, Ilich was the middle son, and Lenin the youngest.) His father was a millionaire, a lawyer who had made a fortune, but at the same time espoused extremely left-wing views. Sanchez grew up in this contradictory environment, being educated by left-wing militants while living in the lap of luxury. Some commentators have argued that this strange dichotomy, coupled with the instabilities of his parents' relationship, may have caused Sanchez to become violent in later life, but that remains a matter of conjecture.

As a child, young Ilich attended a local school in Caracas. In his teenage years, encouraged by his father, he joined the youth movement of the national communist party. He learned to speak Arabic, Russian, English and French, as well as his native Spanish, which aided him in his later career as an international criminal, as he often posed as a language teacher in the different countries he visited. In 1966, he attended a training camp for guerrilla warfare in Cuba, learning some of the ideology and skills that were to shape his adult life as a terrorist.

'CARLOS THE JACKAL'

In 1966, Sanchez' parents divorced, and he moved with his mother and brothers to London, England, where he continued his education. As a young man, he enrolled at Patrice Lumumba University in Moscow, where he came into contact with the Communist Party there. From the start, he made it clear that his political interests lay in the problems of the Middle East, and thus he began to carve out a career for himself as an agitator on behalf of the Palestinian cause.

In the 1970s, Sanchez was sent to Amman, Jordan, to train as a guerrilla fighter for the PFLP (Popular Front for the Liberation of Palestine). It was during this period that he began to use the name 'Carlos'. (Later, 'The Jackal' was added, when a copy of the Frederick Forsyth spy thriller *The Day of the Jackal* was found by police at one of his many hideouts.) After this spell in the Middle East, he returned to London. There, possibly under orders from the PFLP, he performed his first terrorist act, shooting and seriously wounding British business-man Edward Seiff, as part of a protest against Jewish actions in Palestine. Seiff was a prominent Jewish figure, head of the department store Marks and Spencer, and the attack was apparently made to draw attention to the situation in the Middle East. Yet it was a strangely random episode: Sanchez called on Seiff's house, forced his way in past the staff, brandishing a gun, and cornered Seiff, before shooting him in the head and running off, thinking that he had killed his victim. However, by sheer chance the bullet that lodged in Seiff's head did not kill him, but only injured him severely. It later emerged that Sanchez' attack was prompted by the assassination of Mohamed Boudia, a theatre director thought to be a Palestinian activist, by the Israeli secret service Mossad.

SENSELESS VIOLENCE

Sanchez' career as a terrorist continued with a failed bomb attack on a Jewish bank in London, and more bomb attacks on three pro-Israeli newspapers in France. In addition, Sanchez claimed responsibility for a grenade thrown at a Parisian restaurant that killed two people and injured thirty more. He was also involved in two grenade attacks on the Jewish airline, El Al, at Orly Airport near Paris.

Up to this point, the casualties in Sanchez' attacks had been relatively limited. However, as his career as a terrorist progressed, his subsequent attacks became more brutal and reckless. In 1975, he led a team of terrorists to seize over sixty hostages at an OPEC meeting in Vienna, storming the meeting and demanding that a political statement he had written should be read on radio throughout the

Middle East. During this attack, three people were killed. The terrorists then left with their hostages, including ministers from eleven OPEC states. After negotiations with the Austrian government, the hostages were released and the terrorists were granted political asylum.

It now became clear that Sanchez was enjoying his notoriety. Like Abu Nidal, who also began his career as a committed Palestinian activist, Sanchez appeared to have entirely lost the political rationale for his actions, and his attacks were becoming more sense-lessly violent. The attacks continued and seemed more and more arbitrary in nature: in 1982, for example, one person was killed and sixty-three injured when a car bomb exploded in the centre of Paris.

PLAYBOY TERRORIST

Not surprisingly, the antics of 'Carlos the Jackal' engendered a great deal of antipathy towards the Palestinian cause among the general public and the media; consequently, the Palestinian groups that had protected him in the past now began to withdraw their support. Unfortunately, this did not stop Sanchez from pursuing his terrorist activities, and he continued to perpetrate bomb attacks across Europe throughout the next decade, killing dozens of people in the process and injuring hundreds.

Despite his unpopularity with the Palestinian

activists, and his obviously violent personality, Sanchez continued to find that he had friends in high places. Although he was a known terrorist, and was wanted by the authorities of many countries in Europe, he was given asylum at various times by radical Arab regimes in Iraq, Libya, Syria, Yemen and Lebanon. He was protected by the governments of these countries from the agencies who were legitimately pursuing him for his crimes: from the CIA, Interpol and French intelligence in particular. Even when it became clear that Sanchez was acting as a mercenary, the Arab regimes continued to protect him. Sanchez' career as a mercenary, selling himself and his men as guns for hire, is thought to have amassed him a fortune, and he was able to live in luxury while pursuing his taste for violence. He clearly enjoyed his wealth, and acquired a reputation as a flamboyant playboy and womaniser who enjoyed living the high life.

LIFE ON THE RUN

In 1982, Sanchez became involved in an attack on a nuclear reactor in France, but the attempt failed. However, two members of the group were arrested, including Sanchez' wife, Magdalena Kopp, who was closely connected to the Bader-Meinhof Gang in Germany. In order to intimidate the authorities into freeing the suspects, Sanchez contacted the police, threatening to launch a series of attacks unless the suspects were released. When the authorities refused to give them up, he went on to launch a series of bombings, including one attack on a French passenger train that killed five people and injured dozens more. However, in the long term, Sanchez' plan failed, and far from releasing the jailed suspects, the authorities brought them to trial, where they were eventually convicted of their crimes. Magdalena Kopp received a sentence of six years' imprisonment, after which she returned to live with her terrorist husband.

By now, Sanchez' brutal attacks were becoming legendary, and the radical Arab countries who had previously supported him were beginning to back away from giving him protection. Moreover, the Soviet bloc countries were also removing their support, realising that Sanchez had now become a thug rather than a political activist with any clear plan of action. He was eventually allowed to settle in Syria, but was only tolerated there on condition that his terrorist activities ceased. Political events in the Middle East then caused another twist in the tale, when rumours spread that Saddam Hussein wanted to hire Sanchez to make a terrorist strike on the United States. At this point, Syria exiled Sanchez from the country, and he was forced to move around the Middle East as an underground operative.

It was not long before Sanchez found his way to

the Sudan, which had a reputation for harbouring terrorist activists such as Osama bin Laden. In the Sudan, an Islamic sheikh offered him protection, but the relationship did not last long. Sanchez was a Westernized playboy who delighted in gratifying his lusts, and not surprisingly, this openly debauched behaviour caused disapproval from the fundamentalist sheikh, who arranged for him to be handed over to the French police. He was finally arrested in Khartoum, Sudan, in 1994. From there, he was taken to France, where, he was held for three years in solitary confinement. In 1997, he was tried, convicted and given a life sentence. Today, he continues to serve his sentence, all but forgotten as one of the most vicious criminal masterminds of the twentieth century.

OKLAHOMA BOMBER

Timothy McVeigh, otherwise known as the Oklahoma bomber, committed one of the most deadly terror attacks in the history of the United States. In 1995, he detonated a bomb at the Federal Building of Oklahoma, killing 168 people and injuring many more. He was convicted of the crime and executed by lethal injection, becoming the first person to undergo this punishment in the state of Oklahoma. The media often portrayed him as mentally unbalanced, but his conviction rested on the belief that he knowingly committed the crime, in a rational state of mind. It was also widely conjectured that he was acting as part of a political conspiracy to undermine the US government, but no hard evidence emerged to support this idea.

THE MAKING OF A KILLER

Born in Pendleton, near Buffalo, in 1968, McVeigh spent his childhood years in upstate New York. His parents were unhappily married, and his parents split up many times, beginning when Timothy was ten, until they finally separated and divorced for good. After the split, Timothy and his siblings went to live with his father, a devout Catholic, and often attended mass. As a teenager, he was shy and withdrawn, with few friends. He was also not confident with girls and did not date any at high school. However, up to this point he did not show any remarkable anti-social traits, but was on the face of it simply an insecure, inexperienced teenager with a troubled family background.

In 1986, McVeigh graduated from high school and attended business college, working part time flipping hamburgers. He did not complete his studies, however, and instead began work as a security guard in Buffalo. As part of his job, he received a gun permit, and began to become fascinated, if not obsessed, by guns and weaponry. According to co-workers, he also began to exhibit early signs of paranoia at this time. He became convinced that the end of civilisation was nigh, and therefore began to hoard food and weapons to save himself in this eventuality. In 1988, he bought a ten-acre plot of land with a friend and began to use it as a shooting range, before enlisting in the US army.

GULF WAR VETERAN

Initially, it seemed that army life would help McVeigh to gain an identity and to succeed in building a career for himself. He was a hardworking soldier with a great deal of skill as a gunner, derived from his many hours of practise on his shooting range as a civilian. He served in the Gulf War, and was decorated with a Bronze Star medal. However, despite his success in the Gulf, it was there that his disillusionment with the government began, as he witnessed at first hand some of the worst excesses of the war. Even so, he was promoted, and decided on his return to further his career by joining the Green Berets, the Special Operations Force of the US army.

In a pattern that was to repeat itself throughout his life, McVeigh then dropped out of his planned career, quite suddenly. He was required to take a physical fitness test, but failed he it because he got blisters on his feet during a long march and could not walk. This minor setback appeared to under-mine him completely, and instead of continuing to further his career in the army, he decided to leave. In 1991, he was discharged. This move was to prove his most fatal yet.

DRUG-INDUCED PARANOIA

As a soldier, McVeigh had become interested in extremist politics and had often spoken to his colleagues about a novel, *The Turner Diaries*, gener-ally considered to be racist and anti-Semitic. His experience in the Gulf War had left him disillusioned and cynical about the way the US government operated, and he now adopted a full-blown survivalist philosophy. He believed, along with many others in the United States, that the rights of the individual were paramount, especially the right to bear arms and defend oneself. He also believed that the establishment was entirely corrupt and evil, and it should be brought down in any way possible.

After McVeigh's discharge from the army, his erratic behaviour became more pronounced, and he began to move around from city to city, working as a security guard. He lived in a succession of trailer parks and motels, becoming more and more alienated from society and eccentric in his behaviour. His only friends during this period were his former army colleagues, whom he visited from time to time around the country. However, he never stayed anywhere for very long, and would become restless and leave after a few days. He is also known to have been experimenting with drugs, particularly methamphetamine, which is known to cause extreme paranoia in some users.

MAKING BOMBS

In 1993, the Waco incident rocked the United States. What happened at Waco was that a cult community known as the branch Davidians, a religious group that had originated in the Seventh-Day Adventist Church, were accused of crimes such as paedophilia. Federal agents then targeted the commune, and the authorities proceeded to mount a siege at their compound. While this was happening, there was outrage in the press and among many commentators, at the heavy-handed way in which the police and the authorities were dealing with the incident. In particular, what horrified the nation was that during the siege, many cult members met their deaths, including the Davidians' leader, David Koresh.

Along with many other Americans, McVeigh visited the scene of the siege, and he became infuriated by the way the authorities were handling the incident. It seemed to sum up the way in which, in their eyes, individual liberties were being eroded by the modern-day state. McVeigh's hatred of the government intensified, with results that were to prove disastrous.

It was at around this time that McVeigh began to make bombs, assisted by one of his former army friends, Terry Nichols. The pair then devised a plan to detonate a bomb at the Alfred P. Murrah Federal Building in Oklahoma City. In this way, they hoped to undermine the state. Whether or not they realised how much loss of life and injury it would cause to innocent citizens, including many children, is unclear, but it seems likely that they did.

THE OKLAHOMA TERROR ATTACK

McVeigh chose to make his attack in the morning, a time of day when he knew there would be a lot of people arriving at their offices to start the day. He method was breathtakingly simple: he drove a truck loaded with bombs to the building, set a timed fuse, ignited it, and then walked away. He then got into his getaway car, and sped off down the highway, leaving a trail of devastation behind him.

When the bomb detonated, minutes later, it killed and wounded hundreds of people who were in and around the building, including many children who were attending a day care centre there. Meanwhile, McVeigh was driving out of the city, thinking that he had got away with the attack. He was wrong, however. Police soon picked him up for speeding, and it was then found that he was driving without a licence and carrying a gun.

He was about to be released for these minor offences when news came in that a manhunt had been launched to find the perpetrator of the Oklahoma bombing. It then became clear that, by chance, the police had found their man.

EXECUTED BY LETHAL INJECTION

Not surprisingly, McVeigh's trial was a highly controversial one, with outraged members of the public and the press baying for his blood, and others urging a calmer approach. The fact that McVeigh had managed to kill and injure so many children made him especially unpopular. In 1997, after a high-profile trial, McVeigh was convicted of the atrocity and received the death sentence. Co-conspirator Terry Nichols was given a sentence of life imprisonment.

Despite McVeigh's protestations that he had acted alone and taking full responsibility for the crime, many believed that this was not the case, and that he was part of a group of political activists – including Nichols' brother James – who had planned the attack together. Many conspiracy theories as to the reasons for the bombing arose, including the idea that the US government itself had a role in the attack, since one report concluded that bombs had been placed within the building itself. According to this rather far-fetched theory, the government needed grounds for persecuting right-wing groups and thus had a hand in planning the attack in some way.

CONSPIRACY THEORIES

Another theory was that McVeigh belonged to a criminal group called the Midwest Bank Robbers, who had been active in the United States in the early 1990s. This group were outspoken racists with white supremacist views. The evidence for McVeigh's involvement was that the FBI found that the same type of explosive caps were used by both McVeigh and the Robbers. There was also evidence to show that McVeigh and the Robbers had held meetings in Arkansas a short time before the Oklahoma bombing occurred. Yet another conspiracy theory alleged is that McVeigh was part of a group of Islamic fundamentalists based in the Philippines, and was linked to the al-Qaeda network.

Whether or not McVeigh was working alone or in collusion with others, the Oklahoma bombing was one of the worst domestic terror attacks in US history, and he will be remembered as the man who planned and executed it, killing and injuring hundreds of innocent victims in the process.

THE UNABOMBER

The Unabomber was the codename that the FBI
gave to the terrorist Theodore (Ted) Kaczynski,
who perpetrated a series of mail bombings to universities and airlines starting in the 1970s and
ending in the 1990s. In the process, three people
were killed, twenty-three wounded and hundreds
more terrorised. His crimes prompted the most
expensive manhunt ever mounted by the FBI.

An extremely intelligent, well-educated man,
Kaczynski penned a paper called *Industrial Society
and Its Future* and sent it to various media outlets,
giving his reasons for his crimes. As he saw it, his
atrocities were committed to draw attention to the
problems of modern society, especially in terms of
technological innovation. He believed that his campaign would help to cause the downfall of civilisation and halt the progress of technology. However,
although he had a distinguished academic mind, it
soon became clear that he was mentally unbalanced, and his crude bombs, which killed and
maimed innocent victims, were obviously the work
of a deranged killer.

THE BRILLIANT LONER

Theodore John Kaczynski was born on May 22, 1942, in Chicago. He grew up in Evergreen Park, a working-class area in the suburbs of Chicago. One significant episode that happened in his childhood was that, while he was still a baby, he was given some medicine that caused an extreme allergic reaction and had to be taken in to hospital. As was the custom of the day, during the time he was there, his parents were only allowed to visit him occasionally. According to Kaczynski's mother, when he returned home, he had changed from being a contented baby into a fearful, withdrawn one, and he never again found it easy to establish relationships with other people. Today, the dangers of isolating babies and young children from their mothers or regular carers has been recognised, and it is known that such an experience can cause deep-rooted anxieties in adults.

Although he was very withdrawn and sensitive, the young Theodore, or Ted as he became known, was clearly very gifted and did brilliantly at school. Yet despite his intellectual prowess, he was lacking in social skills, and was unable to relate well to his peers or to adults. His academic success meant that he was able to skip several grades and graduate from high school early. Again, this process of fast-tracking gifted children and young people is now known to have some drawbacks, in that these individuals often find it difficult to establish relationships with their own age group, having been separated from them throughout their school career.

THE DROP-OUT

After leaving high school, Kaczynski went on to gain a degree in mathematics from Harvard, and then a master's degree and a PhD from Ann Arbor University, Michigan. His teachers were amazed by his ability to solve mathematical problems, and he soon reached a level that marked him out as something of a genius. He was offered a fellowship at the university, and began to teach students. He worked for three years as a lecturer there, and during this time published important papers on mathematics. After that, he completed two years as an assistant professor in mathematics at the University of California, Berkeley.

Still only in his twenties, Kaczynski now looked set to reach the top of his career as a mathematician. However, in 1969 he suddenly resigned from the job, without explaining why. Not only did he leave Berkeley, he severed all ties with the academic world, to the puzzlement of his colleagues, who could not understand why this mathematical genius should decide to walk away from his career for no apparent reason.

UNIVERSITY AND AIRLINE BOMBS

After quitting his job, Kaczynski had very little income, and went to live in a remote wooden cabin in the countryside. He began to do odd jobs for local people, but was earning very little money, barely eking out an existence and living without basic amenities in the cabin. His family tried to help, but he maintained a distance from them as well as everyone else. The more isolated he became, the more cranky and disturbed his behaviour was, until in 1978, he began to send bombs through the mail.

His first target was Professor Buckley Crist at Northwestern University, who received a package in May 1978. The package had been left at a car park in Chicago University with a return address to Professor Crist. When the professor received the package, he became suspicious and had the package opened by a campus police officer, Terry Marker. It exploded, but fortunately Marker was only slightly injured. The bomb had been crudely assembled, and as a result it was not very effective. Evidently, although Kaczynski was a mathematical genius, he was not so good at DIY.

Next, Kaczynski began to target airlines, sending bombs designed to explode in airports and on aeroplanes. In 1979, a bomb placed in the cargo hold of American Airlines Flight 444 began to smoke, but fortunately it did not explode before the pilot made an emergency landing. Because of the seriousness of the crime, the FBI was called in to investigate. From this time on, Kaczynski stepped up his campaign with bombs that, while still primitive, were now lethal. In 1985, he sent one to the University of California, which resulted in a student losing four of his fingers and the sight in one eye. In the same year, he began to target computer stores, leaving nail bombs in the car parks outside these stores. In one case, the store owner was killed outright.

THE UNABOMBER MANIFESTO

After this atrocity, Kaczynski's activities ceased for a while. However, in 1993 he targeted a computer science professor at Yale University, David Gelernter, who thankfully survived the bomb Kaczynski sent to him. Another academic, geneticist Charles Epstein, was not so lucky. He was maimed by one of Kaczynski's bombs in the same year. The following year, Kaczynski targeted an advertising executive, and the year after, the president of the California Forestry Association. Meanwhile, the FBI seemed unable to make any progress on catching up with the Unabomber, who by now was terrorising the general public with these random terror attacks.

More clues came in when Kaczynski began to write letters to the newspapers, threatening to strike again if his articles were not printed. He demanded that a manifesto he had written, entitled *Industrial Society and Its Future*, be printed in one of the US's major newspapers and promised that he would then end his bombing campaign. In order to try and resolve the situation, the *New York Times* printed his manifesto, which became known as *The Unabomber Manifesto*. A great deal of controversy surrounded this decision; in some quarters, it was felt that this was pandering to the murderer. However, the newspaper argued that printing the manifesto might help to solve the mystery for once and for all.

Kaczynski's writing showed signs of mental disturbance, in that it was essentially a rant, although obviously the work of an intelligent, well-educated man. In it, he argued that human beings suffer from the 'progress' of technology, which harms the majority of people on the planet, and causes immense environmental damage. Kaczynski believed that the only way forward was through bringing technological progress to an end and returning to live as our ancestors did.

THE NET CLOSES

As the *New York Times* editors had hoped, publishing the manifesto laid a trail of clues that led to the Unabomber's door. David Kaczynski, Ted's brother, recognised Ted's writing style and train of thought, and felt compelled to contact the police to let them know who the Unabomber was. At one time, David had been very influenced by his brother's ideas and had even helped to buy the plot of land where Ted now lived. However, since then he had distanced himself from his brother somewhat, feeling that Ted's reclusive life was unhealthy. Ted had few social contacts, only seeing people when he needed to buy food, and living in a very restricted way, without electricity or running water. In addition, Ted had begun to show signs of serious mental disturbance.

Reading the *Unabomber Manifesto* in the newspaper, David realised that Ted was responsible for the bombing campaign. He contacted the police and told them where Ted was living, asking them not to let his brother know that it was he who had turned him in. Police offers duly arrested Ted Kaczynski at his cabin in Montana in April 1996. Unfortunately, David's part in turning his brother in came to light. However, David used the reward money he received to pay his legal expenses, and also to compensate the victims' families.

At the trial, Kaczynski refused to plead insanity, which was the most obvious defence in his case. A court psychiatrist diagnosed him as suffering from schizophrenia, but fit to be tried. Kaczynski initially pleaded guilty, but later withdrew his plea; however, this was not accepted, and he was convicted. He was sentenced to life imprisonment and incarcerated at Florence, Colorado, where he remains to this day.

ABIMAEL GUZMÁN

Abimael Guzmán was the notorious leader of the Sendero Luminoso ('Shining Path'), a Maoist revolutionary group that developed a reputation as brutal, ruthless terrorists in Peru. The group was formed, ostensibly, to wage a 'people's war' against the injustices of the state, but went on to murder many ordinary citizens, including poverty-stricken peasants and left-wing political organisers such as trade unionists, simply because they had, in the eyes of the Shining Path, colluded with the state. The group was active as a guerrilla movement from the late 1970s until the 1990s, when Guzmán was finally captured and imprisoned. After his initial trial, which many considered to be undemocratically carried out, there was a rise in atrocities and massacres; however, in the longer term, the group became less active in Peru.

PHILOSOPHY PROFESSOR

Abimael Guzmán was born Manuel Rubén Abimael Guzmán Reynoso on December 3, 1934 in Mollendo, a coastal town about 1,000 km (620 miles) to the south of Lima, the capital city of Peru. His father was a rich man whose wealth had come from winning the national lottery, and who had fathered children by six different women. Guzmán himself was illegitimate, and when he was only five years old, his mother Berenice Reynoso died, leaving him to the care of his mother's family. He was raised by them until he was thirteen, when he went to live with his father and stepmother in the city of Arequipa. Here, he attended a private Catholic school, and did well in his studies. As a young man, he went on to take a degree at the San Augustin University in Arequipa, majoring in Social Studies.

It was at university that Guzmán became politicised. A shy, diligent, student who was obsessively well organised and hardworking, Guzmán soon became interested in radical politics. He was particularly influenced by a book written by the founder of the Peruvian Communist Party, José Carlos Mariátegui la Chira, entitled *Seven Interpretative Essays on Peruvian Reality* and published in 1928. In it, Mariátegui argued that a Marxist perspective could be applied not just to modern industrial societies, such as Great Britain, where Marx had predicted revolution would occur, but also to the conditions of an agriculturally-based Latin American society such as Peru. Just as Mao had envisioned in China, and Lenin in Russia, agricultural societies with a large, poverty-stricken peasantry could also undergo revolution – and, contrary to Marx's predictions, these were the countries where, in fact, the major communist revolutions took place, rather than in Europe.

REVOLUTIONARY LEADER

In Peru, the agricultural economy was controlled by large landowners, or 'latifundistas', who kept the peasant population in conditions of miserable poverty. Guzmán proposed that new, more egalitarian communities could evolve on the model of some aspects of the Incas' social organisation. In addition, Guzmán argued that, if the corrupt government of Peru could be destabilised, by whatever means possible, the situation would be ripe for revolution.

On gaining his degrees in law and philosophy, Guzmán took up a position as Professor Philosophy at a university in Ayacucho, a city in the Andes. Here, he became the protege of Dr Efraín Morote Best, who encouraged him to study Quechua, the language spoken by the Indians of the region. During this time, Best and Guzmán developed a wide circle of radical academics who were frustrated by the iniquities of the society they lived in, with a corrupt government and an oppressed peasantry. In 1965, Guzmán travelled to China to see communism in action, and returned determined to change the situation in Peru.

BURNING THE BALLOT BOX

In the mid 1970s, Guzmán left his post at the university and began to organise an underground revolutionary political group. At the same time, the Communist party in Peru split, with Guzmán heading the group that backed the Chinese form of communism rather than the Soviet. This faction became known as the 'Shining Path', named after a slogan of Mariátegui's: 'Marxism-Leninism is the shining path of the future'.

Calling himself Presidente Gonzalo, Guzmán went on to develop his theory of a Maoist revolution in Peru, criticising both US and Soviet imperialism and citing Lenin's theory that both would collapse in time. His teachings were influential in academic circles, and his followers believed him to be a major Marxist teacher, along with Lenin and Mao.

During the 1970s, the influence of the Shining Path moved outside the universities, and a guerrilla group was formed, operating in and around Ayacucho. The first major action of the group was to burn ballot boxes during an election at Chuschi, a village outside the city. This was ironic, since these elections were the first to be democratically run for almost a decade. However, the rationale of the Shining Path was that the Peruvian government, whether democratically elected or not, was presiding over a ruined economy in crisis, and that only a radical solution would succeed in freeing the peasantry from their oppression. The group's aim was to destabilise the country by any means possible so as to create a situation in which the government could be overthrown and replaced with a Marxist regime which – according to Guzmán – could begin the work of radically reorganising the whole of Peruvian society from top to bottom.

BLOODY CIVIL WAR

Despite the rhetoric, the Shining Path was in fact a very autocratic organisation that dealt with opposition of any kind by resorting to violence. Anyone who did not agree with Guzmán's point of view was targeted as an enemy, which included not only the army and the police, but ordinary citizens and peasants who co-operated with the state – even minimally, by such actions as voting in elections – and activists from rival left-wing groups, including the other major Marxist-Leninist group in Peru, the Tupac Amaru Revolutionary Movement.

Before long, the atrocities perpetrated by the Shining Path had escalated into a full-scale, bloody civil war in Peru. It is now thought that over 70,000 people died as a result of the fighting, over half of them murdered by the Shining Path. However, Guzmán continued to maintain that the Shining Path was promoting 'a people's war', and even went on to proclaim that his group was promoting a 'higher stage of Marxism' in which the old order would disappear and a new 'equilibrium' would become apparent. The reality was rather different: many witnesses reported acts of terrible vengeance wreaked on ordinary citizens and peasants and their families for 'collaboration with the state'; and the guerrillas of the Shining Path came to be feared throughout the Andes as brutal murderers, thugs and bandits. Many believe that, had the Shining Path managed to take over power in Peru, their atrocities and massacres would have reached the scale of Pol Pot's Khmer Rouge in Cambodia. Thankfully, however, this situation was prevented by the capture of Guzmán, the group's leader, in 1992.

CAPTURE AND CONVICTION

The President of Peru, Alberto Fujimori, was determined to root out the insurgents, and ordered the National Directorate against Terrorism (DINCOTE) to act. They began by ordering surveillance of several houses in Lima where terrorists were suspected of hiding. One of these houses was a ballet studio where dance teacher Maritza Garrido Lecca was living. The detectives checked the garbage of the house, noticing that a large amount was being taken out each day, and that it contained empty tubes of a skin cream used to treat psoriasis. Guzmán was known to suffer from this skin condition. Prompted by this clue, on 12 September, the house was raided, and eight members of the Shining Path, including Guzmán, were found.

Guzmán's computer was also found and confiscated. It turned out to contain a mass of incriminating evidence against him, and this later helped to secure his conviction. When it was checked, the computer showed a long list of the Shining Path's bases, soldiers and weaponry around the entire country. According to Guzmán's records, in 1990, the organisation had over 20,000 members, and a cache of over 1,000 weapons, including rifles, revolvers and hand grenades.

TRIAL AND CONVICTION

Unfortunately, the trial of Guzmán that followed was seen by many as unfair and undemocratic. The government tried to persuade the media and the public that Guzmán was a common criminal, whereas it was well known throughout the country that he was the leader of a political faction. In addition, Guzmán was tried under emergency terrorist legislation. After a trial that lasted only three days, Guzmán was convicted, receiving a sentence of life imprisonment.

The trial was so hasty that in 2003, an appeal was granted to retry the case, along with that of over 1,000 other prisoners convicted of terrorism. In November 2004, Guzmán was tried again, but the trial was abandoned because he and the members of the Shining Path ignored the judges and gave revolutionary salutes to the international press, also shouting Maoist slogans to the gallery. However, in October 2006, after several more aborted trials, Guzmán was finally sentenced, and received a life sentence, which he continues to serve.

PART SEVEN

SWINDLERS
AND
FORGERS

VICTOR LUSTIG

Count Victor Lustig is one of the great criminal masterminds of all time. Operating as a con man in the 1920s and 1930s, he secured his place in history as one of the most audacious swindlers the world has ever known by pulling off an outrageous scam: to sell the Eiffel Tower – which he did not own – to two different buyers. Lustig was a highly intelligent, well-educated man who spoke several languages, and he also had considerable personal charisma; however, he was completely without moral scruples and committed many frauds and swindles, until he was finally arrested and imprisoned.

THE MYSTERIOUS BOHEMIAN

Little is known about Lustig's early life, except that he was born in Bohemia, now the Czech Republic, on 4 January, 1890. His first encounter with the law was at the age of nineteen when he got into a fight with a man over a woman that they were both courting. In the process, the man brutally knifed him, so that the young suitor was left for the rest of his days with a huge scar that ran along the side of his face from his ear to his eye. In his later career as a con man, this scar would prove to be something of a handicap, making Lustig very easy to identify in police parades – of which, as it turned out, there were to be many.

As a young man, Lustig left home and settled in Paris, a city that at the time offered many opportunities for a bright young man without too many moral qualms about how he would earn his living. Despite his humble origins, Lustig became a popular figure in high society, a witty, intelligent companion who was much admired by women. He spoke five languages fluently, dressed well and had a great deal of charm. He was also adept at playing cards, and eventually began to earn his living as a professional gambler.

Lustig found work on the luxury ocean liners plying their way between Paris and New York, and in the process befriended some of the richest and most powerful socialites in both countries. For a while he earned a good living as a gambler, but this lucrative career was halted by by the outbreak of World War I, when liners like the ones he was working on were commissioned for war service; suddenly, pleasure cruises, along with other luxuries and fripperies of *fin de siècle* Paris, had become a thing of the past.

BIRTH OF A CON MAN

Ever resourceful, Lustig decided to leave war-torn Europe and head for the United States, so as to find other ways of making a living. Once there, he began to look into the property market, and in 1922, bought a tumbledown farm in Missouri. For this, he paid the bank Liberty bonds, which were a type of savings bond sold in the United States at the time to support the Allies in the war. These bonds could be used for making payments and redeemed for their original value plus interest. The bank was surprised to find Lustig making this offer, since the house was almost valueless, and to encourage him to make the purchase it offered to cash an extra ten thousand dollars' worth of bonds for him.

During the transaction, Lustig managed to switch envelopes of money and bonds in such a way that he made off with both. The bank pursued him, but when it caught up with him, he used his personal charm to convince the authorities that there had been a mistake, so the bank did not prosecute him. Moreover, he kept the ten thousand dollars that he had stolen.

Encouraged by the success of his new life of crime, Lustig moved his operations to Canada, where he went on to commit more frauds. One of these was a complex scam that involved stealing the wallet of a banker, Linus Merton, and then returning it to him, saying that he had found it in the street. Having gained the wealthy man's confidence, he now enacted the next stage of the plan. Lustig revealed a scheme of his to the banker, saying that he had devised a way of earning money by gambling on the horses. This involved a time delay whereby he had an accomplice intercept information coming by telegraph wire to the bookmakers, so that he could place a large sum of money on the horse that he had been told had won.

The banker was intrigued by this scheme, and his greed got the better of him. He gave Lustig 30,000 pounds to place a bet on the horse that was – so he thought – sure to win the race. Lustig assured him that his accomplice, whom he claimed was his cousin, would intercept the wire before it came into the bookmakers', so that the bet could be placed accurately. Unfortunately for Merton, however, the whole tale that Lustig had told him turned out to be a pack of lies. There was no cousin, no intercepted telegraph wire and no bet. Instead, Lustig absconded with the money and was never seen again.

SELLING THE EIFFEL TOWER

Further encouraged by the success of this escapade, for which he was never arrested, Lustig now turned his attention and imagination to the city where his good fortune had first begun – Paris. The idea for a new scam came to him as he was reading an article in a French newspaper about the Eiffel Tower.

According to the article, the famous landmark of Paris, the Eiffel Tower, was becoming extremely dilapidated. It was so expensive to maintain that the authorities were thinking of tearing it down. This news inspired Lustig: he would contact several scrap iron companies, posing as a government official, and ask them to put in bids for the job of demolishing it. He would then ask whichever of the businessmen seemed the most gullible for a bribe to secure the contract. Having done this, he would pocket the money and disappear. The plan had the added attraction that whoever had offered to bribe him would be in trouble, which would distract attention from finding the perpetrator of the crime.

So as to give his scam maximum credibility, Lustig sent letters on official-looking writing paper to the heads of several scrap iron companies. He then arranged a meeting with all of them at the same time, at the plush Hotel de Crillon, Place de la Concorde. The choice of venue was designed to reassure the businessmen that this was a bona fide meeting, since many high level government officials used the hotel for their business transactions.

THE SCAM IN ACTION

The directors duly assembled, and Lustig appeared,

playing the role of government official with gusto. He even made up a title for himself: Deputy Director General of the Ministry of Posts and Telegraphs. He told the assembled company that the government had, with regret, decided that the Eiffel Tower was now too expensive to maintain and had decided to sell it for scrap. He pointed out that the Tower had originally been built as a temporary structure as an engineering display for the Paris Exposition in 1889. He even took the group on a tour around the tower, showing them the many problems with its upkeep and pointing out how badly it needed to be repaired. He told the men that they would have to bid for the contract to destroy it, but that the whole affair should be conducted in the greatest secrecy, because it was a very controversial, potentially unpopular decision that would have to be broken to the French public with tact at a later date.

THE LONG ARM OF THE LAW

The directors agreed not to discuss the project with their families or colleagues and went home at the end of the day. The next day, Lustig chose his victim: a rather nervous man whose name was Andre Poisson. He contacted Poisson to ask for a bribe, so that Poisson's company could secure the contract. Having collected the money, Lustig then absconded, leaving the hapless Poisson to explain himself to his employers and the police.

As he had hoped, Lustig got away scot free with the scam. Poisson realised he had been made a fool of and was too embarrassed to call the police. Thus, Lustig was never pursued for the crime. Instead, he went to Austria, where he lodged in the best hotels and dining at the finest restaurants, before his money ran out and he decided to try his luck again.

Foolishly, as it turned out, Lustig went back to Paris and performed exactly the same fraud once again. This time, however, his victim went straight to the police. Lustig managed to escape to North America, where he continued to act as a con man until he was finally locked up. Even then, he managed to escape from prison, but was recaptured and sent to the high security prison at Alcatraz, where he died in 1947.

ELMYR DE HORY

Elmyr de Hory was one of the most talented art forgers of the twentieth century, whose paintings have now become valuable in their own right. Before he died, he claimed to have painted over 1,000 forgeries and sold them internationally. His forgeries of masters such as Picasso, Matisse, and Modigliani deceived some of the most respected experts in the art world, and at one time he made a great deal of money. However, when the forgeries were discovered, he was forced to go on the run, pursued by the FBI and Interpol.

A concentration camp survivor who had learned to paint forgeries to earn a living because he could not sell his own work, de Hory had been deeply scarred by his early experiences. In later life, when his forgeries were discovered and he became a wanted man, living in constant fear of capture, his mental health broke down. He committed suicide in 1976.

PRISON NIGHTMARE

De Hory was a Hungarian Jew, born Elmyr Dory-

Boutin into a wealthy family. His father, an Austro-Hungarian ambassador, was a highly successful man, and the family lived a comfortable, privileged life; however, there was little emotional warmth in the family, and Elmyr's parents left the care of their son to servants and governesses, so that he seldom saw them.

At the age of sixteen, Elmyr's parents divorced, and he moved to Budapest, where he began to move in bohemian circles and became aware that he was a homosexual. Two years later, he enrolled at the Akademie Heinmann in Munich, excelling at his studies as a classical painter. He then went to Paris to continue his studies at the Académie la Grande Chaumière under the painter Fernand Léger, and afterwards, returned to Hungary with the intention of making his living as an artist.

However, it was then that events took a turn for the worse. In Hungary, he was involved in a sexual relationship with a man suspected by the government of being a spy. As a result, he was thrown in jail in a remote part of the Carpathian Mountains. The conditions in the jail were abysmal, but de Hory found that he could gain small privileges by using his skill of painting. He painted a portrait of a senior camp officer and was rewarded for his labours, but life in the prison was still desperately harsh.

By the time Elmyr was released, World War II had broken out, and the Nazis had invaded Hungary. As a Jew and a homosexual, he became a target for Nazi persecution, and it was not long before he was arrested and sent to a concentration camp. Here he was brutally beaten and had to be sent to hospital to recover. Although one of his legs was broken, he nevertheless managed to make a daring escape from the hospital, making his way back to his parents' house in Hungary. However, when he got there, he found that another disaster had taken place: both his parents were dead, and the estate had been confiscated by the Nazis.

De Hory was left penniless but, ever resourceful, he escaped from Hungary to France. Here he was forced to find new ways of making a living, and thus tried his hand at forgery. His knowledge of art history and skill as a classical painter helped him to produce beautiful works that fooled even the sharpest art collector's eye, and in this way, he began to earn a good living make a new life for himself in his adopted country. He even created a history for his paintings, telling buyers that they had been in his parents' collection before the Nazi occupation of Hungary.

DOUBLE-DEALING

De Hory's first forgery was a Picasso, which he sold in 1946. From then on, he began to make substantial sums of money from his paintings. He found a partner in crime, Jacques Chamberlin, who agreed to operate as his dealer, and went on to become a rich man. He and Chamberlin travelled around Europe selling the forgeries and living in luxury. But this successful period of de Hory's life was not to last. Unbeknown to him, Chamberlin was double-dealing, keeping large sums of money for himself rather than sharing the profits. When de Hory found this out, the pair parted company on hostile terms.

De Hory then went on a visit the United States, and decided that there was a promising market for his line of work there. He now had a wide repertoire of styles to draw on, and had forged paintings by such masters as Matisse, Renoir and Modigliani. He also began to work in oils, expanding the range of his works – and the profits from them. To avoid recognition, he traded under a variety of names, including Louis Cassou, Elmyr Herzog, Elmyr Hoffman and Joseph Dory. At the same time, he tried to sell his own works, hoping that he could go straight and make a living as an honest painter; however, he soon found that there was no market in the United States for original paintings by an unknown Hungarian.

SUICIDE ATTEMPT

By the 1950s, de Hory was living in Miami, selling his works by mail order so that there would be little chance of his true identity being traced. But in 1955, his luck ran out. A Matisse that he had forged was sold to the Fogg Art Museum, and an expert there realised that the museum had been sold a fake. In addition, a Chicago art dealer named Joseph Faulkner had also realised that he had been duped and had begun court proceedings against him. De Hory went on the run again, using false identity papers to travel to Mexico City. However, complications of a different kind then ensued, when he was accused of murdering a British homosexual there. He was jailed for the murder, but it transpired that he was completely innocent, so he was eventually let out. De Hory returned to the United States, but by now his spirit was broken.

De Hory knew that his career as a forger was coming to an end: his style of painting was beginning to be recognised and it was only a matter of time before the orders for his work ceased. He also knew that he had few other options in life: painting was his only real skill. Moreover, he was terrified of being caught for his forgeries and thrown in jail again: his experiences as a prisoner – seldom for anything he had done wrong – had completely traumatised him. At a low point, he took an overdose of sleeping pills, intending to end his life; but, fortunately, he was discovered before he died and taken to hospital.

The next phase of de Hory's life began when he went back to Miami and began a relationship with

Ferdinand Legros, a man with great skill as a confidence trickster. Legros began to sell de Hory's paintings for him, but like Chamberlin, he turned out to be a double-dealer, keeping most of the money for himself and lying to de Hory about the prices buyers had paid for the paintings. In addition, Legros was a violently bad-tempered man who constantly argued with his lover, Real Lessard, who travelled with them. In the end, de Hory left the pair of them to battle it out together, travelling to Europe to try to find some peace of mind.

ON THE RUN

Sadly, however, de Hory found that he was unable to survive without Legros, so began a commercial partnership with him once more. This time, Legros installed de Hory in a luxury villa in Ibiza, Spain, where he could set up his studio and produce his forgeries. Meanwhile, Legros would sell them to museums and galleries in Europe's big cities. The plan worked for a while, but de Hory became unhappy at his island retreat. Legros kept de Hory on a tight budget, keeping the profits of his trans-actions for himself; also, de Hory was lonely and missed city life. He began to produce inferior paintings, and before long they were discovered as fakes. The police were notified, and soon de Hory was on the run again. He fled to Australia, but eventually returned to his home in Ibiza once more. In 1966, Legros and Lessard turned up at the house, also on the run. They asked de Hory to leave, and took over the house for themselves there, but police caught up with them over forgeries they had made to a Texas oil magnate, and they were arrested.

Next, it was de Hory's turn to be pursued by the police. Without any evidence to show that he had committed crimes in Spain, in 1968 the police managed to charge him with homosexual activities and consorting with criminals. Once again, he was sent to jail. However, when he came out, he un-expectedly found that a new phase of success had opened up in his life. Biographer Clifford Irving had written a best-selling account of his life, and he became a celebrity, appearing on television and in a film by Orson Welles. For the first time, he was able to sell his own paintings. However, he then found out that the authorities were planning to extradite him. Faced with more upheaval, he made another suicide attempt, and this time succeeded.

FRANK ABAGNALE, JR

Frank Abagnale, Jr was a con man whose extraordinary exploits, posing as an airline pilot, a doctor, a lawyer and a university lecturer, shocked the world when he was revealed as an impostor. A high-school dropout with no qualifications at all, he nevertheless managed to conterfeit documents and behave in such a way as to convince those around him that he was trustworthy and reliable. His bizarre adventures lasted for five years during the 1960s, after which he was arrested and brought to trial. Ever resourceful, after serving his prison sentence, he used his inside knowledge to set up a fraud consultancy company, which he still runs to this day.

EARLY LIFE

Abagnale was born in 1948 and grew up in Westchester County, New York. His father ran a stationery store. He received a religious education at a school run by The Congregation of Christian Brothers, an Irish Catholic sect, which later received a great deal of criticism for abuse of children in their care.

When he was sixteen, his parents divorced, and his life began to go off the rails. He began to spend money on his father's credit cards, running up huge bills and attempting to impress his girlfriends with his wealth. To begin with, his father was reasonably tolerant of his behaviour, but when he realised that Frank Jr was about to bankrupt him, he put a stop to the spending sprees. At this point, traumatised by his parents' split and all the financial problems he had created for his father, he ran away from home. He never saw his father again, but over a decade later, made contact with his mother once more.

'THE BIG NALE'

Thus it was that, at the age of just sixteen, Abagnale began life on his own in New York City. He had one advantage over the other runaways that came to the city: although he was young, he found it easy to get by: strangely enough, his hair had begun to turn gray, giving him a mature, authoritative air. Taking advantage of his looks, he altered his driving license to pretend he was ten years older than he was, and from then on began a career of crime in the city that later earned him the name 'The Big Nale'.

Realising that counterfeiting could earn him a living, Abagnale decided to make some changes to his bank account. He managed to alter the numbers on the deposit slips normally found at his bank in such a way that each time a client of the bank made a deposit into their account, it went into Abagnale's account instead. In this way, he amassed over 40,000 dollars before the bank discovered what was going on. However, not content with this sum, he also wrote hundreds of bad cheques that went unpaid. In addition, he ran up a huge overdraft on his account.

Realising that his frauds were going undetected, at least for a number of weeks, sometimes months, Abagnale went on to open a number of other accounts in several banks. He also developed a range of fraudulent banking activities, such as printing out counterfeit cheques, putting them into his account and then asking to borrow large sums of money on his account.

THE SKYWAYMAN

Eventually, his frauds were discovered, and Abagnale had to make a swift exit as a bank customer. He now had to look for new ways to earn a living. This time, he resolved to try his hand at a new type of fraud, which on the face of it, looked completely impossible: he took to impersonating aeroplane pilots so that he could ride around the country free of charge.

He had found out that, within the aviation industry, pilots often rode around on aeroplanes as passengers, using seats that had not been booked and were available for staff only. The pilots charged their expenses to the airline company that employed them. This practise was known as 'deadheading' and was a way in which airline companies helped each other out.

The way Abagnale operated was to get a sample pass sent to him, which he then altered. He managed to obtain an FAA pilot's certificate by buying a display plaque, copying it and resizing it to fit the ID form. He also got a Pan Am uniform by phoning the outfitters, telling them that he had lost his uniform and needed to buy another one in a hurry. The bill was charged to an employee of Pan Am. Armed with his new identity, and calling himself Frank Williams, he turned up at airports asking for a ride on TWA planes. The first time he did this, he did not know where the special seat for the pilots was located on the plane, and had to be shown where to sit by an air hostess; yet no one blew his cover. Indeed, airline pilots were so well respected in the 1960s that no one thought to ask him any questions at all, and he made many trips around the world as Pilot Frank Williams over a period of two years, earning the nickname, 'The Skywayman'.

DOCTOR AT LARGE

Abagnale made the most of his new career impersonating an airline pilot, using his authoritative position to live the high life. He cashed bad cheques everywhere, and had many romances with air hostesses who often did not realise he was many years their junior. In addition, he travelled the world, which had been a long held ambition since he was a child. However, after a while, he got tired of being permanently on the run and of being unable to confide in anyone about his true identity. He became very lonely and decided that wanted a more stable life. Also, he knew that sooner or later, his subterfuge would be discovered.

His next move was to rent an apartment in Georgia, which he did by pretending to be a doctor. Having secured the rental, he decided to take on the doctor's persona for keeps. Not long afterwards, he met another doctor, who asked him if he could help out at the hospital where he worked. Extraordinarily, he was allowed to begin work at the hospital without anyone asking to see any evidence of his qualifications for the job. Yet such was Abagnale's personal charm that he managed to cover his ignorance by joking and laughing with the staff, who found him to be a convivial character and who did not suspect for one moment that they were working with a man who did not even have a high-school diploma, let alone any qualifications in medicine.

THE WHEEL OF DECEPTION

By this time, Abagnale's behaviour was verging on the insane, yet he did – thankfully – still have enough sense to quit the job when he realised that he was endangering his patients' lives. He was also aware that soon enough he would be caught out and his lie exposed. Thus, he moved on again – this time to Louisiana, where he decided, overnight, to become a lawyer.

His new job went well for a time, and he earned a good living, managing to fool everyone around him that he was a qualified attorney. However, as before, he soon realised that time was running out for him, so he switched again – this time, to the relatively harmless position of sociology lecturer. And so it went on, changing occupations under a variety of aliases – including Frank Williams, Robert Conrad, Robert Monjo and Frank Adams – and amassing a huge fortune by forging cheques, until, finally, the wheel of deception came full circle and he returned to his first job, impersonating an airline pilot.

THE LONG ARM OF THE LAW

In the five years since he had first arrived in New

York City as a sixteen-year-old, Abagnale had committed hundreds of frauds. Not surprisingly, by this time, a number of law enforcement agencies, both within and outside the United States, were looking for him. In fact, he was a wanted man in every American state, and was also being pursued by international police from a total of twenty-six countries.

The end came when he was arrested while attempting to board an Air France plane in his guise as a Pan Am pilot. He was twenty-one years old. He was tried and convicted in a court of law in France, and given a prison sentence, before returning to the United States, where he also served a sentence. However, there was a twist to the tale: while in prison in the United States, he was approached by the US security services, which asked for help in solving a number of large fraud cases. In return for agreeing to help them, Abagnale was let out of jail and enabled to form his own company. He then paid off his debts and began a new career, this time for real – catching criminals guilty of fraud.

Abalagne has since married, had a family and used his remarkable skills to catch other criminals. In 1980, he recounted the bizarre story of his life in a book entitled *Catch Me if You Can*, which was a bestselling title in the United States, and later became the basis of a film of the same name.

HAN VAN MEEGEREN

Han van Meegeren was one of the most ingenious art forgers of his time, amassing a fortune for himself of around forty million dollars by the end of his career. He spent years developing techniques to produce perfect forgeries of Dutch masters such as Vermeer, Pieter de Hooch and Frans Hals, and was also a talented painter in his own right, as well as a skilled art restorer. His forgeries were so accurate that they would, most likely, never have been discovered as such until years after his death. However, during the occupation of Holland by the Germans in World War II, he sold one of his paintings to a leading member of the Nazi government, Hermann Goring. To begin with, nobody believed van Meegeren's story, but he went on to prove his case, whereupon he was hailed as a national hero.

RIDICULED ARTIST

He was born Henricus Antonius van Meegeren in

Deventer, Holland, in 1899. The third child in the family, he was brought up a Roman Catholic. He developed an interest in art, but his father did not approve and sent him to study architecture at university. However, van Meegeren rebelled against his father and decided to do his own thing and become a painter. He developed a passion for the style of the Dutch Golden Age painters of the seventeenth century, so much so that they inspired his own works. Instead of painting in a contemporary style, he made reference to the historical paintings of the Golden Age, using the same rich colours and complex perspectives, but these did not go down well with the art critics of the day, who complained that his work was derivative and old-fashioned. In some instances, he was even ridiculed for his classic style. This meant that he could not pursue his career as an original artist, as no one would buy his pictures.

PLAN OF REVENGE

Stung by the critics' panning of his work, van Meegeren plotted his revenge. He would paint a picture in the style of a Dutch master, present it to a gallery and then wait for the art critics of the day to praise it to the skies. He would then make it known that the painting was a fake, so that the critics would be revealed as stupid, ignorant and easily led. To confound them, he painted a beautiful Vermeer, using his by now well-honed skills as a painter of the period. It was entitled Christ and the Disciples at Emmaus and was a careful copying of Vermeer's style, down to the type of canvases, brushes, paints and glazes used in the seventeenth century. He made sure to give the painting the appearance of extreme age, baking the glaze so that the painting looked old and grubby.

Van Meegeren claimed that the painting was an unknown, early work by Vermeer, and it caused great excitement when it was first shown. In the absence of scientific dating techniques, to accurately measure the age of a painting, such as are available today, the critics declared the painting genuine. To van Meegeren's delight, one of the critics was Abraham Bredius, whose reviews of van Meegeren's work had been scathing. Van Meegeren had the pleasure of standing with a large crowd in front of the painting, and hearing Bredius praise it to the skies, declaring that it was Vermeer's 'masterpiece'.

Van Meegeren came up with a plausible story as to how he had acquired the painting, telling potential buyers that it had come from an aristocratic Italian family who had lost their money and needed funds, but they did not want it to be known who they were. Eventually, the painting was bought by the Boymans Museum of Rotterdam for the sum of two and a half million dollars.

LARGE FORTUNE

Van Meegeren had painted Christ at Emmaus to show up his critics rather than to make a fortune. However, his success in fooling the art world was such that he now realised he could make huge sums of money by continuing his career as a forger. Beginning with Christ at Emmaus, which fetched a huge sum, over the next few years he began a series of forgeries, including works by Pieter de Hooch, Frans Hals and – of course – Vermeer.

So accurate were they that nothing was suspected for years, and van Meegeren was able to amass a large fortune from the proceeds of the paintings. He was helped by the fact that the World War II broke out, causing a certain amount of chaos and bringing into being a busy black market trade in all kinds of valuable goods, including old masters, as currencies declined in value. One of his paintings became the most expensive ever sold in the world at the time, fetching over a million Dutch guilders.

Van Meegeren was now a very rich man, and he proceeded to spend his money with great abandon, developing a taste for the high life. Soon, he became renowned for his drink and drug-fuelled excesses. It became clear, however, that his wealth had not brought him happiness in his personal life. Commentators have suggested that the reason for this lay in the fact that he had never been taken seriously as an original artist, even though he was a highly skilled painter, and that despite his wealth, this lack of recognition continued to rankle with him.

NAZI COLLECTOR

Van Meegeren went on painting Vermeers, producing six more after the 'Christ and the Disciples at Emmaus'. In 1943, he sold the last one, entitled 'Christ and the Adultress' to Hermann Goring, one of the most prominent members of the Nazi regime. At the time, the Nazis were occupying Holland. At the end of the war, the Dutch authorities began the work of restoring the art works that the Nazis had plundered from the country, and the Vermeer was found in Goring's collection. It came to light that the Vermeer had been sold to him by van Meegeren, so the authorities contacted van Meegeren to find out more. He was arrested and charged with collaboration, which was a serious crime at the time, amounting to treason and carrying with it the death penalty.

Because of the situation van Meegeren found himself in, he was forced to confess the fact that the painting was a forgery executed by him, and not a Vermeer at all. To begin with, the authorities did not believe him, but while in prison, van Meegeren conceived a plan to convince them that this was the truth.

THE SAD DEMISE

He asked for his art materials to be brought to him and proceeded to paint a picture under surveillance by his jailers. To everyone's amazement, he produced a painting that looked exactly like the work of Vermeer, entitling it 'Jesus among the Doctors'. It was clear that van Meegeren had the skills to produce an extremely persuasive forgery, and one that would fool even the most highly regarded art expert. As a result, the authorities changed the charge against him, from treason to forgery.

The fact that he had not been let off the charges infuriated van Meegeren, and he refused to finish off the painting by glazing it and rubbing dirt into the glaze to give it the appearance of age. Even so, he was brought to trial and convicted, receiving a prison sentence of one year. The trial attracted massive press attention, and van Meegeren emerged as something of a national hero. The public warmed to the forger as the man who had cheated the hated Nazi figure Hermann Goring, although it later transpired that Goring had paid for the fake painting with fake currency!

Sadly, however, van Meegeren was by this time a sick man, and in no position to enjoy his new-found fame and popularity. His abuse of drink and drugs had taken its toll on his health, and instead of serving out his sentence, he was sent to hospital. He died there on December 30, 1947.

After his death, his works sparked a debate in the art world about the status of forgeries. Commentators such as Arthur Koestler argued that if a copy or forgery is so good that it fools even the experts and delights visitors at museums and galleries where it is shown, there is no real basis to reject it. However, others have pointed out that, sooner or later, it becomes clear that forgeries are not the real thing, however good they are: in van Meegeren's case, his Vermeer paintings now look like artefacts from the 1930s and 1940s, with elements of film noir in the way the faces are lit, rather than originals from the seventeenth century.

CLIFFORD IRVING

Clifford Irving is notorious for faking an auto-biography of Howard Hughes, the eccentric millionaire who had become a complete recluse after living a highly public life as a movie mogul and businessman in the 1950s. Irving and his co-writer Richard Suskind believed that Hughes' aversion to publicity was such that he would never step forward to condemn the autobiography as a hoax. However, as it turned out, Hughes broke his silence to do exactly that, and Irving's ruse was discovered.

FASCINATION WITH FORGERY

Irving was born on November 5, 1930, the son of talented media people. His mother Dorothy was a magazine cover artist and his father Jay was a celebrated cartoonist. Irving grew up in a creative environment and attended Manhattan's High School of Music and Art before going on to study at Cornell University. As a young man he worked at the *New York Times*, while writing his debut novel, *On a Darkling Plain*. He also married his first wife,

Nina Wilcox, but the marriage broke up after only two years. The novel was published in 1956 and received good reviews, but it did not sell many copies. Irving took time off to travel in Europe and write a second novel, *The Losers*. This was published in 1958. He lived on the island of Ibiza, remarried, then returned to the United States with his new wife Claire Lydon. Sadly, she died soon afterwards in a car crash. Irving then published a third novel, *The Valley*, and in 1962 returned to Ibiza. He married again, this time to a British model, Fay Brooke, but the marriage was short-lived. With his fourth wife, artist Edith Sommer, he had two sons.

While in Ibiza, he became friends with the notorious art forger Elmyr de Hory, and wrote a biography of de Hory's life entitled *Fake!* Published in 1969, the book was an immediate success. Both Irving and de Hory appeared in a documentary by Orson Welles called *F For Fake* in 1974, which helped make de Hory a well-known figure.

Encouraged by this success, and fascinated by the world of forgery, fakes and frauds, Irving came up with a daring plan: to fake an autobiography of the world's most famous recluse, Howard Hughes.

THE HOWARD HUGHES LEGEND

During the 1950s, Howard Hughes was one of the United States' most brilliant public figures, a pioneer of the movie industry and an entrepreneur whose personal charisma and legendary wealth made him a constant focus of attention for the media. By 1958, however, Hughes had tired of the constant glare of publicity and had become completely withdrawn, refusing any contact with the outside world. Reports that he was mentally ill, and would not, for instance, cut his hair or his nails, fuelled public curiosity as to his personal life. There were even reports that he was terminally ill, or possibly dead. As a result, many writers and film-makers had attempted to enquire into what was really going on in Hughes' world, but Hughes had always managed to bribe them to stop publishing or broadcasting anything concerning him. Irving reasoned that, since Hughes had such a deep aversion to drawing attention to himself, he would not make a fuss when the fake autobiography appeared, but would simply retreat further into his reclusive environment. He was wrong.

Together with author Richard Suskind, Irving decided to concoct the autobiography, using material from news archives to document the different periods in Hughes' life. Suskind was in charge of the research for the book, while Irving used his creative talents to forge letters in Hughes' handwriting. Together, they produced a series of letters, purportedly from Hughes to Irving, in which Hughes expressed interest in the idea of allowing Irving to assist him in writing his autobiography. According to the forged letters, Hughes knew of Irving's work, in particular the de Hory biography, and would let Irving conduct a series of interviews that might lead to a book. However, Hughes insisted that, for the moment, the project should remain secret.

THE HOAX

Armed with the letters, Irving got in touch with McGraw-Hill, his publishers, and told them that Hughes had expressed an interest in letting him work on his life story. Excited by this news, the publishers invited Irving to show them the letters, which Irving did. They were fooled and drew up contracts between Irving, Hughes and themselves, promising an advance of over 800 dollars, most of which was due to be paid to Hughes. When the cheque arrived, Irving's wife put it in a Swiss bank account. The deal was set, and Irving had been paid. All he had to do now was to write the book.

The fact that Hughes was so secretive about every aspect of his life helped enormously to keep the truth from the publishers while the book was being written. Irving and Suskind reported meetings with Hughes in remote spots far from anywhere, enjoying themselves with tall stories about where and when they had met Hughes – for example, in one instance, on the top of a pyramid in Mexico.

The book itself was a highly imaginative account of Hughes' life, using material culled from a variety of sources, such as the private files of *Time-Life* magazine, and an unpublished manuscript by author James Phelan, who was engaged on ghost-writing the memoirs of Hughes' former business manager, Noah Dietrich. Phelan did not know that a mutual acquaintance, Stanley Meyer, had given Irving the manuscript to look at, in the hope that he could rewrite it in a more accessible style.

In 1971, the manuscript arrived at the publishers, McGraw-Hill. The story of Hughes' life was somewhat lurid and far-fetched, but it was written in a gripping style, and executives at McGraw-Hill were delighted with it. To check its veracity, an expert graphologist was called in to study the handwritten notes on the manuscript, supposedly from Hughes, and the letters were declared to be genuine. McGraw-Hill announced that the book would be published, to great excitement in the literary world.

However, those who had contact with some of Hughes' business interests expressed doubts, saying that they had heard nothing about it from the Hughes organisation. Irving argued that the book had been kept a secret, and that Hughes had not told anybody about it while it was being written. Others, however, expressed their belief that the autobiography was authentic: for example, the last journalist ever to have interviewed Hughes, Frank

McCullough, read the manuscript and pronounced it to be a true story. To attempt to authenticate the autobiography further, McGraw-Hill called in a new team of graphologists, Osborn Associates, who also found Hughes' handwritten notes to be authentic, and asked Irving to undergo a lie detector test, which he passed. It looked to Irving and Suskind as though they had pulled off their scam.

ENDGAME

But then Hughes spoke. To everyone's amazement he contacted seven journalists whom he had worked with in former times, and conducted a telephone conference with them, which was filmed for television. Speaking down the line, Hughes announced that the autobiography was a hoax, and that he had never met Clifford Irving in his life. He said that he, Hughes, was living in the Bahamas and had not left to meet anyone anywhere. This was sensational news, and the world's press were, of course, riveted. Irving immediately countered this claim by saying that Hughes' voice, heard on television, was a fake, and that the journalists had rigged up the whole story to discredit him. However, by this time, his claims were beginning to sound far-fetched, as indeed they were.

Before long, Hughes' lawyers were suing not only Irving and his publishers. Swiss police investigated the bank where the cheque from McGraw-Hill to Irving had been deposited, and found that a bank account had been opened in the name of Helga R Hughes. The cheque to H R Hughes had been received shortly afterwards. Police were sent to Ibiza to interview the couple, but once again, Irving denied that he had been involved in the fraud. In the meantime, author James Phelan had noticed that some of the facts from his own book had been lifted from the text. Then the Swiss bank revealed that their account holder was a woman, and the deposited cheque was traced to Edith Irving, Clifford's wife. Finally, Irving's cover was blown.

On January 28, 1972, Clifford Irving and his wife, along with Richard Suskind, confessed everything. They were charged with fraud and went to trial in March of the same year. Irving was convicted and received a prison sentence of fourteen months. His co-author Suskind received a lighter sentence of six months, but in the event only served five. Irving returned the money to his publishers. He spent his time in prison getting fit, also gave up smoking while he was there. After he came out of jail, Irving went on with his career as an author, writing a number of bestselling titles and earning substantial advances for his work.

JOYTI DE-LAUREY

Joyti De-Laurey is remembered as the personal assistant who stole over four million pounds from her employers at the bank of Goldman Sachs in the City of London. Starting in 2001, she siphoned money from her bosses' personal bank accounts into her own, enjoying a lifestyle of reckless spending that would have been completely beyond the means of someone on a personal secretary's salary. However, such was her charm that her bosses suspected nothing, and it was only after she became greedy and stole too much money at once, that she drew attention to herself. She was found out, arrested, brought to trial and convicted.

The whole affair attracted a great deal of media attention, especially when it was pointed out that the large amounts of money that De-Laurey had stolen from her employers had gone undiscovered simply because the individuals concerned were so rich that they did not notice the loss of a few million here or there. Thus, in a sense, when the De-Laurey affair hit the headlines and the astronomical incomes of those at the top of the financial elite began to emerge, it was the banking world, as much as De-Laurey herself, that was put on trial, at least in terms of media and popular opinion.

MONEY LAUNDERING

Joyti De-Laurey was a thirty-five-year-old Hindu woman married to a fifty-year-old chauffer named Tony. The couple lived in a suburban house on relatively modest means. De-Laurey worked as a personal secretary at Goldman Sachs, one of the leading investment banks in London, on a modest salary of around 20,000 pounds. Her bosses were millionaire banker Jennifer Moses and Moses' husband Ron Beller. As well as dealing with normal office arrangements, De-Laurey undertook to organise all aspects of their busy personal lives, such as arranging birthday parties, holidays abroad, shopping trips, beauty sessions and so on. De-Laurey was extremely hard-working and went to great lengths to please her employers, so much so that as time went on, they began to leave everything to her, congratulating themselves on having found such a helpful personal assistant who could work on her own initiative. They even awarded De-Laurey substantial bonuses for what they thought was her loyal service to them.

Unbeknown to them, however, De-Laurey was swindling them on an almost daily basis, forging their signatures on their personal cheque books, and helping herself whenever she liked to money from their personal accounts. She began cautiously, signing cheques for small amounts of money at first, but when her bosses appeared not to notice what was going on, she became more daring. She began to take out bigger and bigger amounts, making over seventy withdrawals in a period of only four months. To hide what she was doing, she opened bank accounts abroad under her maiden name and enlisted the help of other members of her family in her money-laundering venture.

THE HIGH LIFE

Strangely enough, although De-Laurey began to live the high life as the money poured in, nobody at the bank noticed what was going on. Her neighbours were surprised to see a fleet of luxury cars parked outside her house, and they noticed that her husband Tony was driving around on an expensive motor bike complete with personalised number plates. De-Laurey also made a lot of alterations to her house and took holidays whenever she could. She and her husband loved holidaying in Cyprus and bought a luxurious villa and a boat there. The villa alone was worth 700,000 pounds. She also bought a Range Rover and a custom-built Aston Martin. Not only this, the couple began to take flying lessons, spending at least 2,000 pounds on a course for herself and her husband. According to De-Laurey's neighbours, who were watching all this with amazement, and were interviewed later, they thought she had won the lottery and so no questions were asked.

De-Laurey's next scam was outrageous, and later attracted a great deal of criticism in the press. She told her employers that she had contracted cervical cancer, and needed to have expensive treatment at a hospital in the United States. Such was the warmth of her bosses' affection and concern for her that they paid for the trip. What they did not know was that, instead of going to hospital, De-Laurey was spending the time away from work in a luxury hotel in Beverly Hills, shopping on Rodeo Drive and eating out in the finest restaurants in the area.

TWO MILLION MISSING

On her return, De-Laurey began to work for Edward Scott Mead, a director at Goldman Sachs. She came with glowing references from her previous bosses, Jennifer Moses and Ron Beller. Her new boss Mead was even richer than Moses, and De-Laurey resolved to steal ever larger amounts of money from him, aware that he was too wealthy to notice what was going on. However, it was at this point that she made her mistake. She became too greedy, and her behaviour became reckless. Amazingly, she stole two million pounds out of Mead's account, but it was only four months later that he became aware of it, when he dipped into his funds to make a charity donation to his former college.

When Mead found out what had happened, he was naturally furious and had De-Laurey arrested and charged. When the case came to trial, De-Laurey was convicted and sentenced to seven years' imprisonment. The others received shorter sentences. Mead called De-Laurey a liar and a thief, and announced that she had abused the trust of the bank directors in the most cynical, calculating way. However, the press were less than sympathetic to Mead, particularly when it emerged that he had so much money in his account that he had not noticed the loss of two million pounds for several months.

SORDID DETAILS

As the trial progressed, sordid details about Mead's personal life began to come out, including the fact that he was having an affair. De-Laurey had tried to defend herself by claiming that Mead had paid her the money to cover up details of the affair, but this proved to be untrue; however, during the course of the trial, Mead was forced to admit that he had, as De-Laurey claimed, indeed been unfaithful to his wife. In addition, it emerged that the salaries paid to the bank's top executives were exorbitantly high, and the press became extremely critical of this aspect of the bankers' personal lives as well. The picture that emerged in the newspapers and on television was one of over-paid, over-privileged capitalists at Goldman Sachs and other banks in the city, living a life of ease and luxury while their minions did all the work. Because of this, journalists expressed a certain amount of sympathy with De-Laurey's attempt to redress the balance by helping herself to their inflated salaries whenever she had the opportunity.

The De-Laurey affair also prompted discussion of some of the more shady dealings of the banking world, which some argued were not very different to the type of activities that De-Laurey had engaged in. Such was the hostility in the press towards Mead, in particular, that he complained to the newspapers that he often felt as though he, not the defendant, was on trial. And when De-Laurey was given a seven-year prison sentence, many felt that this was overly harsh; she had been shown to be a thief, they argued, but her actions had not caused any real hardship to anyone, and therefore she should have received a more lenient sentence.

FINAL SCANDAL

De-Laurey began to serve her sentence, but the scandals were not over. It was later reported that while in prison, she had struck up a relationship with an elderly Sikh chaplain, asking him to bring her make-up, magazines, perfume and other luxuries to her cell in Send prison, Woking, Surrey. The chaplain, eighty-two year old Makhan Singh Roy, was humiliated by the incident and had to step down from various committees that he worked on, even though it was never confirmed that he had actually complied with De-Laurey's demands. Afterwards, De-Laurey was transferred to another prison. Her husband Tony commented that she had done nothing wrong.

The De-Laurey case remains memorable as an instance of a personal assistant stealing huge sums of money from her bosses, but attracting very little condemnation from the press and public, simply because her wealthy City employers were so unpopular.

MARTIN FRANKEL

Martin Frankel was a financier who pulled off frauds worth two million dollars all over the United States. He had no formal qualifications whatsoever, and had a record of abject failure in his business ventures, yet he seemed able to persuade people to give him money for his 'investments', and even to involve them in his underhand dealings. He was unconcerned about the morality of his behaviour, and showed no regrets that he had stripped so many people of their assets and livelihood. But as time went on, his life of crime began to take its toll, and he became paranoid to the point of madness. Eventually, the law caught up with him and he was arrested, brought to trial and convicted in 2002 of insurance fraud, racketeering and money laundering.

STEALING AND CHEATING

Frankel was born in Toledo, Ohio, in 1954, the son of a Lucas County judge, Leon Frankel. Martin was the second child of the family, and he showed intelligence from a young age. At school, he did well in his studies, but was socially awkward.

On leaving high school, he went on to attend the University of Toledo, but it was here that his personality problems began to become evident. He became frightened of taking tests, to the point that he developed a complete phobia about them. He also found it difficult to organise himself for studying. It became clear that, although Frankel had done well at school, his success had been achieved without a great deal of effort on his part; now that the work had become more difficult, he was terrified of failure, and had become completely phobic about any situation in which his inadequacies would be revealed.

His problems grew more and more difficult to handle, until he eventually dropped out of college. Soon afterwards, he began to take an interest in finance and the securities market. He believed he could make a lot of money quickly by speculating on the market, and that this was an easy way to earn a living, especially now that he had few prospects of gaining formal qualifications. However, he appeared to pay little attention to the risks involved in financial gambles, particularly for a person like himself with limited funds to play with, and he also seemed entirely unconcerned about lying, stealing and cheating to get what he wanted.

BOGUS COMPANIES

Frankel began to frequent brokerage houses, soaking up as much information as he could learning about the world of finance. He was especially fascinated by large frauds that had taken place within the financial world and avidly studied these cases. One of the cases that interested him was that of Robert Vesco, a US financier who had made a great deal of money taking over failing businesses and who had fled the country when his dealings came under government investigation.

Frankel made it his business to meet as many people as possible in the finance world, forging a friendship with John and Sonia Schulte. The Schultes owned a securities business that was affiliated to a larger New York company, Dominick & Dominick. Frankel persuaded them that he had a sure-fire way of predicting the stock market, and impressed them with his knowledge of the way the financial markets operated. Frankel was particularly close to Sonia Schulte, who persuaded her husband to take him on as an employee in their firm.

FIRED FOR INCOMPETENCE

It was not long, however, before Frankel became something of a liability to the Schulte's business interests. Frankel seemed unable to conform to the requirements of working in an office, and often came to work wearing jeans and a T-shirt rather than a suit. Schulte would have been prepared to overlook this had Frankel's business acumen been impressive, but once he was working at the firm, it became clear that Frankel did not know what he was doing. Although he had a good theoretical knowledge of trading on the financial markets, he did not have the personal qualities to actually do the job. Being a trader requires an immense amount of confidence and the ability to make important decisions very quickly. As was the case in his high school and university days, Frankel could not stand to be tested on his performance. So great was his fear of failure, he avoided actually doing the work of trading on the markets.

While conducting a business deal, Franklin had pretended to be an agent from Dominick & Dominick, the company's parent firm. Schulte knew that this kind of behaviour from one of his employees could put him out of business for good. He duly fired Franklin. But this was not the last Schulte would hear of his former employee; for unbeknown to him, Franklin was now having an affair with his wife, Sonia.

VATICAN SCAM

Franklin was now out of a job and had returned to live at his parents' house while he tried to set up a new business. Working from their home, he set up an imaginary business, Winthrop Capital, advertising in the telephone book. Amazingly, he managed to wheedle a substantial sum of money from various clients who called for advice on investments. He then proceeded to place the money on the financial markets and lose almost all of it. Yet, still believing he was a financial genius, he went on to set up a series of other ventures. Sonia Schulte then left her husband and together, the pair followed the example of Franklin's hero Robert Vesco and began to buy up failing companies specialising in the insurance sector.

Their dealings became ever more questionable, but the couple began to enjoy a luxurious lifestyle. One of Franklin's strangest scams was with the Vatican. In order to pull this off, he posed as a rich Jewish philanthropist, setting up an organisation called the St Francis of Assissi Foundation. He contacted two well-respected Catholic priests in New York, Emilio Colagiovanni and Peter Jacobs. He also made contact with Thomas Bolan, the founder of a body known as the Conservative Party of New York. From them, he managed to obtain large funds that apparently belonged to the Vatican, and promised to make investments that would yield large profits. With the money, he made a series of complex deals buying and selling insurance companies, and this time his business acumen – and his shady dealings – paid off: he, and his clients, made large profits. But that was by no means the end of the story.

DIAMONDS AND DAMES

Frankel was now a rich man, with assets of over four million dollars. He and Sonia had also set up home together with her two daughters. Sonia had alleged that John Schulte, the girls' father, had molested the daughters, and thus had gained custody of them. Thus Frankel, Sonia and her daughters now lived together in a large house in Greenwich, Connecticut. But family life with Frankel turned out to be far from blissful. Frankel's mental illness, which had been an issue since his school days, came to the fore once again, this time in a more disturbing, aggressive form. He began to hold large parties, flaunting his wealth, and little by little these turned in to sadomasochistic orgies. Before long, Sonia had had enough, and removed herself and her two daughters from the home. Left on his own, Frankel continued his debauchery, inviting young women to live in the house, and engaging in more and more bizarre sexual practices. Eventually, in 1997, one of the women hanged herself in the house.

Two years later, the law finally caught up with Frankel. His underhand business dealings were legion by now, and the authorities had more than enough evidence to assemble a case against him. All his companies were put under state supervision, and a thorough investigation began. At this point, Frankel realised that the game was up and fled to Europe in a hired private jet. In a scenario worthy of James Bond, he took with him a fortune in diamonds, plus two of his lady friends as companions. But by now his mental condition was deteriorating, and he had become intensely anxious and paranoid.

THE FINAL DEBACLE

It was not long before the two young women who had accompanied him from the United States decided to leave. Frankel then found a former employee of his, Cynthia Allison, who was willing to take their place, and holed up with her in a luxury hotel in Hamburg, Germany. But it was only a matter of time before he was tracked down, arrested and brought to trial.

Frankel was charged by the US federal government with fraud, to the tune of two million dollars. But before he was extradited, he faced more charges from the German government, of using a false passport and of smuggling diamonds into Germany. He was put on trial for these crimes in a German court, and pleaded guilty, but asked for exonerating circumstances to be taken into account.

Unfortunately, his excuse was rather feeble: he claimed that he had brought the diamonds in so that he could help with charity work in the future. As one might imagine, the courts were not convinced of this sudden change of personality on Frankel's part, and convicted him of the crimes. He received a three-year sentence and was sent to jail in Germany. During this time, he made an escape attempt, but this was not successful.

After serving his prison term, he returned to the United States where he was charged with twenty-four counts of fraud and racketeering. Once again, he was convicted and given a prison sentence of sixteen years. Monsignor Colagiovanni and Sonia Howe (formerly Schulte) also pleaded guilty to lesser charges and were convicted of their crimes.

NICK LEESON

Nick Leeson was a high-flying financial trader whose unorthodox, speculative and sometimes fraudulent deals caused the complete collapse of his employer, Barings Bank, in 1995. In a series of complicated and extremely risky deals, he began to lose more and more money, just as a gambler does in a casino – only this time, he was dealing in millions, not thousands, and using the bank's money rather than his own.

METEORIC RISE

Leeson was born on February 25, 1967. The son of a plasterer, he grew up in Watford, Hertfordshire, an area north of London. His father took little interest in his son, but his mother recognised his intelligence and drive, and she made sure that he received a good education. She even typed out the application for his first job, at the prestigious Coutts Bank in London, where he was employed as a school leaver at the age of eighteen.

In his new job, Leeson showed himself to be remarkably adept at understanding the complex world of finance, and he was soon promoted, earning a high salary. At the same time, his friends from school were working as builders and mechanics.

Leeson had a lot of money to spend, and was enjoying a life of ease, when, unfortunately, disaster struck. His mother who had been diagnosed with cancer, but was expected to live for another decade. However, she died suddenly. Leeson's mother had been the centre of family life and still had young daughters that needed to be looked after. Leeson promised himself that he would take care of the family, and he was spurred on by the memory of her support to progress further in his career.

RISKY VENTURES

By the early 1990s, Leeson had landed a job as manager of a new operation in futures markets on the Singapore International Monetary Exchange with Barings Bank. Barings was oldest investment bank in London, whose history went back to the time of the Napoleonic wars. Leeson was part of a new wave of quick-witted, young, working-class men who became stock market traders in the volatile financial climate of the 1980s, making – and his case, losing – fortunes for the banks and businesses that employed them.

Leeson's speciality was trading in derivatives, that is, speculating on assets rather than buying and selling assets themselves. Derivatives consist mainly of options, futures and swaps, all of them involving speculation on the prices of assets rising or falling in the future, and all of them risky ventures. Options or futures are contracts in which one party agrees to pay another an agreed fee for the right to buy or sell. So, for example, a person who owns stock in a company may pay a fee to another at an agreed, fixed rate, so that if the value of the stock goes down, the other party must buy the stock at that rate. The person selling may gain an advantage in that, if the value of the stock goes down, he can sell without losing too much money; the person buying may end up better off by getting a good price on the stock. Swaps are agreements based on cash flows, in which businesses agree loans with each other, balancing out interest rates to each other's advantage.

GAMBLING MILLIONS

These complex business deals are essentially a form of gambling on assets: however, the assets themselves are not necessarily based on solid material goods or commodities, but may be in the form of changeable financial arrangements such as equities, bonds, interest or exchange rates, and indices (the stock market or consumer price index). Thus, the situation is one in which gamblers are gambling on the future behaviour of the financial markets, which is to a large extent unknown, with no back-up in the form of saleable goods. Moreover, the deals are so complicated and move so fast, that very few people on the boards of companies and banks understand exactly what is going on at any one time, and the traders are left very much to their own devices.

To play this game, which involves enormous sums of money, traders need tremendous confidence, nerve and skill. Enter Nick Leeson. Although he was still only in his twenties, he impressed his superiors not only with his confidence, but with his knowledge of the financial markets.

From 1992 on, Leeson began to make deals that were not authorised by his superiors, but because he was making so much money for the bank – his deals accounted for ten per cent of the bank's income at one time – his employers failed to keep a track of what he was doing. He was both Chief Trader at the bank and also responsible for settling his accounts, jobs that are usually separate in most establishments. In this way, he was able to hide losses on bad trades: at first, these involved only a few thousand pounds here and there, but by the end of 1994, he had lost over two hundred million pounds.

THE BUBBLE BURSTS

To recoup the situation, Leeson placed what is

called a 'short straddle' deal involving 'call and put' options on the Singapore and Tokyo stock exchanges. This complex deal was basically a bet that the Japanese stock market would not go up or down overnight. Unfortunately for him – and for Barings – an unforeseen disaster occurred, in the shape of the Kobe earthquake, which happened early on the morning of January 17, 1995. Undeterred, Leeson began to bet on the likelihood of the markets recovering, gambling on the possibility that the Nikkei Stock Average would go up rapidly. However, it did not. Leeson ran up a phenomenal bill of over 800 million pounds, which was twice the amount that the bank allocated for trading purposes. Realising that the game was up, Leeson decided not to confess, but instead ran away, leaving a note to say he was sorry.

Now on the run, Leeson went first to Malaysia, then to Brunei, and then to Germany, where he was arrested. He was extradited and taken to Singapore, where he was charged with fraud. As it transpired, he had obtained authorisation for his 'short straddle deal' but had hidden his previous losses from his superiors, and he made deals that were far too speculative, involving sums that he, and the bank, did not have at their disposal. He was charged, brought to trial and convicted of fraud. The judge sentenced him to six and a half years in a Singaporean jail, in conditions that were far from civilised. While he was serving his term, he was diagnosed with colon cancer and was released in 1999.

BACK FROM THE BRINK

Although Leeson had undoubtedly acted in a reckless manner as a trader, there were many who felt that Barings Bank was also to blame for the debacle. The bank had failed to keep any checks on their employee, allowing him all sorts of privileges because he had initially earned them so much money, including being allowed to settle his accounts himself, rather than having involvement from auditors and others who would have noticed what was going on and put a stop to it.

Not only the bank, but the whole financial systems of options, futures, swaps and so on was also criticised, since it encouraged gambling on extremely volatile markets in a way that was far too risky and could lead – as it did in the case of Barings – to the complete collapse of financial institutions that employed hundreds of people and dealt with thousands of investors' savings. It was also pointed out that although Leeson earned a high salary, he did not personally profit from these financial dealings. Instead, he was only trying to make as much money as he could for the bank, albeit in a way that was extremely risky.

The next phase of Leeson's career began when he

returned to Great Britain and published an auto-biography, *Rogue Trader*. In it, he described his humble beginnings, his rise to become Chief Trader at Barings, his eventual fall from grace and the nightmare of his prison term in Singapore. He also recounted how, under the strain of all this, his marriage fell apart. During the time that he was in jail in Singapore his first wife, Lisa, had stood by him. She had even taken a job as an air hostess so that she could visit him regularly in jail. However, it then emerged that, unbeknown to her, Leeson had had a number of affairs with geisha girls while on visits to the far east. After these revelations, Lisa divorced him. Shortly afterwards, Leeson developed colon cancer, losing a great deal of weight, and undergoing chemotherapy, during which period most of his hair fell out.

However, Leeson was not a quitter, and after these awful disasters, he confounded all expectations by surviving his cancer and remarrying. His new wife, Leona Tormay, was an Irish beautician who already had two children. The couple then had a baby boy together.

Leeson went on to forge a new career for himself as an after-dinner speaker and became the commercial manager of Galway Football Club in the west of Ireland. In 2005, he wrote a book entitled *Back from the Brink: Coping with Stress*, in which he described how he fought his way back from the total breakdown of his world.

PART EIGHT

BANK ROBBERS

BUTCH CASSIDY

Robert LeRoy Parker, alias Butch Cassidy, was a notorious outlaw who, in the early years of the twentieth century, committed some of the most famous robberies and heists in North America. Together with his sidekick Harry Longabaugh, also known as The Sundance Kid, he and his gang The Wild Bunch managed to evade the law for many years. Later in their career, the pair had to decamp to South America to avoid arrest, and lived there for several years before they were killed in a shoot-out. Butch Cassidy and The Sundance Kid have gone down in history as the last of a dying breed of outlaws and migrant cowboys whose flamboyant flouting of the law made them folk heroes of the Wild West.

CATTLE RUSTLER

Parker was born in 1866 and grew up in a Mormon family. His parents, Maximilian and Ann, were immigrants from England who had travelled to Utah Territory to escape persecution for their Mormon faith. The family were hardworking owners of a ranch at Circleville, Utah, about 125 kilometres (200 miles) away from Salt Lake City. Robert began to help them at an early age, but his parents' strict Mormon principles appeared to have little appeal for him, and he became rebellious. As a boy, he met an old cattle rustler called Mike Cassidy, who impressed him greatly. He adopted the man's surname, and under the influence of his new mentor, he stole a horse, much to his parents' anger. Afterwards, he left home and began to travel around the country as a free agent.

Parker worked at any job he could find, including as a butcher, which is where he derived the name 'Butch' (the term 'butch' is also used to describe a borrowed gun). 'Butch' Cassidy, as he was now known, soon tired of earning an honest living and took to stealing cattle. It was not long before he was caught and thrown in jail, at Laramie in Wyoming, where he served a sentence of two years.

THE OUTLAW LIFE

When Cassidy emerged from jail, he was a seasoned criminal and began to live the life of an outlaw in earnest. He had all the attributes of a leader: he was quick-witted, confident, fearless in a fight and had a natural charisma that drew people to him. He soon gathered a team of desperadoes around him, and became leader of a gang that was known and feared across North America: 'The Wild Bunch'.

Cassidy's right-hand man was The Sundance Kid. Like Cassidy, Sundance had grown up in a strongly religious family. He had been born Harry Alonzo Longabaugh in Philadelphia, Pennsylvania, and was the youngest of five children in a poor family. As a young man, he had left home and travelled around the country trying to earn a living. However, there were frequent periods when he had no job and no money, and during one of these, he stole a horse in the town of Sundance, Wyoming. He was caught, thrown in the town jail, and served eighteen months there, before emerging with a new nickname: The Sundance Kid.

THE WILD BUNCH

The partnership between Cassidy and Sundance became unshakeable, and they stayed together through many exploits as the leaders of the Wild Bunch. Other members of the gang included Harvey Logan, alias Kid Curry, who joined the gang after pulling off a string of robberies with his own gang, and who was the scourge of the detective agency, Pinkerton's. William Pinkerton, head of the agency, once described him as 'the most vicious outlaw in America' and said of him: 'He does not have one single redeeming feature. He is the only criminal I know of who does not have one single good point.' However, many of those who met Curry described him rather differently, as a gentleman: a quietly spoken, polite man who had many friends and was popular with women because of his courteous way of behaving.

There were also several women among the Wild Bunch. One of these was Etta Place, about whom very little is known. She was Sundance's woman, but there were rumours that she and Cassidy were also lovers. There has been much speculation about the relationship between the three, but it is known that she stayed with the outlaw gang for many years. Others who travelled with the gang included Ann Bassett, a young woman from a ranch in Brown's Park, whose family had at one time been cattle rustlers.

Other characters in the gang were Ben Kirkpatrick, known as 'The Tall Texan', who had a reputation as a womaniser, 'Deaf' Charlie Hanks, Tom 'Peep' O'Day, Bill Tod Carver and 'Wat the Watcher' Punteney. Together, with Butch Cassidy and The Sundance Kid at their head, the outlaws committed the longest sequence of successful robberies ever to take place in the Wild West.

HEISTS AND HOLD-UPS

Their first bank robbery took place at Montpelier, Idaho, in 1896, and after that, they continued their heists in Wyoming. Here they robbed an Overland Flyer train and, after a shoot-out, got away with

$30,000. Encouraged by this success, the gang robbed another train, but this time they only managed to get away with about $50. So the Wild Bunch turned their attention to banks again and went to Nevada, where they stole over $30,000 from the bank at Winnemucca. The gang continued their robberies until 1901, when they held up a Northern Pacific Train in Montana and came away with $40,000.

However, this was to be their last heist. For years, the Wild Bunch had been pursued by the private detective agency Pinkerton's, and now they were coming close to being caught. With the agency hot on their heels, they decided to split up. Butch Cassidy, The Sundance Kid and Etta Place travelled to South America, where they bought a ranch.

Meanwhile, the rest of the gang were captured. Ben Kirkpatrick, 'The Tall Texan', was caught and jailed. When he had served his sentence, he took to robbing trains again, and was later killed in a shoot-out. 'Deaf' Charlie and Carver also met their ends in this way. Kid Curry was captured and held in jail in Knoxville, Tennessee, but he managed to escape. He is thought to have been shot to death in a train robbery, but some believe that, like Cassidy and Sundance, he escaped to South America and bought a ranch. Legend has it that he lived peacefully in Patagonia with a Spanish wife, who bore him eight children, until he finally died of old age.

THE END OF THE LINE

Butch Cassidy and The Sundance Kid are believed to have lived quietly with Etta Place on their ranch in South America for several years before running out of money. When this happened, they reverted to their old way of life – robbing banks, trains and travellers. The story goes that they held up a payroll transport in the mountains of Bolivia and were pursued by troops in an attempt to recover the money. It is not entirely clear what happened after that: some maintain that the pair were shot by the troops, others that they committed suicide after being wounded. There is also a theory that the two outlaws who were shot were not Cassidy and Sundance at all, but a pair of common criminals whose names were unknown.

After their death or disappearance, Butch Cassidy and The Sundance Kid were remembered as folk heroes. Despite the fact that they and their gang, The Wild Bunch, were often ruthlessly violent during the course of their robberies, and often directed their violence against ordinary people such as bank clerks and train drivers, they were held in great affection by the public. This was mostly because they and the Wild Bunch represented an outlaw spirit, of men and women who were not prepared to live by small-town morality or conform to a dreary bureaucracy. They were also regarded as rebels fighting against the greedy profiteering of the banks and railroads, offering an alternative way of life – albeit rough and dangerous – that harked back to the early days of the Wild West.

HEROES OR VILLAINS?

Although Cassidy, The Sundance Kid and the Wild Bunch were essentially criminals, they were seen in a romantic light by the public, who viewed them as carrying on a valued tradition at the heart of the American Dream. They represented the last of the pioneers, frontiersmen and early settlers who were born with nothing, but who staked their claims in the deserts and prairies of the land, took what they wanted from it, and built lives for themselves, free from government and state interference.

Obviously, this was an idealised picture, and the reality of Cassidy's life, and that of his associates, was somewhat more sordid, involving as it often did the brutal treatment, even murder, of innocent people. However, today, their legend lives on as tough, freedom-loving outlaws and rebels who helped to keep the independent spirit of the pioneers alive. Since their death, they have period-ically been immortalised in popular culture, such as in the George Roy Hill film of 1969, *Butch Cassidy and the Sundance Kid*, starring Robert Redford and Paul Newman.

DILLINGER

The bank robber John Dillinger was branded Public Enemy Number One by the FBI in the early 1930s. Regarded by the authorities as a violent, dangerous man, to others he became a hero, a latter-day Robin Hood, and even something of a celebrity. Along with other famous criminals of the day, such as Bonnie and Clyde, he was admired by the press because he was a thorn in the side of the establishment. This was a time of economic depression, when many banks had collapsed, taking their clients' savings with them. In many cases, banks were foreclosing on their debtors and making people homeless by claiming their houses in return for debts. The banks were thought of as ruthless in pursuit of their own interests and lacking in sympathy for the poverty of the people, and thus the general public had become hostile to them. When outlaws such as Dillinger robbed the banks, many supported them, especially when records such as bank lists of mortage holders were destroyed in the process.

Another aspect to Dillinger's fame was that the media had expanded during the 1930s, ushering in the age of mass communication. For the first time, whenever news broke, radio reports and film newsreels could instantly be broadcast all over in North America. The exploits of the bank robbers were followed just as keenly as those of Hollywood film stars. The culture of celebrity had begun.

RECKLESS LIVING

John Herbert Dillinger was born into a poor, hard-working family on June 22, 1903 in Brightwood, Indiana. His mother died of a stroke when he was only three years old. His father, a grocer, John Wilson Dillinger, treated him harshly but also spoilt him from time to time, buying him expensive toys. He was largely raised by his sister, sixteen-year-old Audrey, who ran the family after her mother died.

John Herbert grew up to be a difficult, rebellious child. From a young age, he formed his own street gang, known as the Dirty Dozen. These children were the scourge of the neighbourhood, stealing coal from passing freight trains and getting up to all kinds of mischief. In one incident, he and a friend terrified another boy by taking him to a wood mill, tying him down and turning on the circular saw, stopping it only inches from his body. At the age of thirteen, he was involved in gang-raping a local girl. Thus, even from his childhood days, it was clear that he was a violent individual.

Dillinger's first job, came at the age of sixteen, when he was employed as a mechanic. With his new-found earnings, he lived a wild life of reckless drinking, and it became even more difficult for his father to discipline him. In despair, his father moved the whole family to a small farm near Mooresville, Indiana. However, it was not long before his wayward son was in trouble again. He was arrested for stealing a car in the neighbourhood, and subsequently had to join the Navy to avoid a court case.

BANK ROBBERIES

Dillinger's rebellious spirit earned him no favours in the navy, however, and within months he had deserted his ship. He returned to Mooresville and married a local girl, sixteen-year-old Beryl Hovius. He attempted to settle down, but he could not hold down a job, and ended up throwing his lot in with a man named Ed Singleton, the town pool shark. Together, the pair tried to rob a grocery shop in the town, but were caught doing it. Singleton pleaded not guilty, but was convicted and sent to prison for two years. Dillinger, on his father's advice, pleaded guilty, was convicted and received a prison sentence of ten to twenty years, despite the fact that he had no previous convictions. The harshness of his term, especially as it had been increased because he had been honest about his crime, seems to have embittered him against society, and from that time on he lived outside the law. While in prison, he learned to become a criminal, meeting some of the most notorious bank robbers of the period while serving his sentence.

Much of his time in prison was spent planning his escape, which finally came on May 10, 1933, when he was paroled because his stepmother was ill. While at home, Dillinger laid plans to help his friends escape from jail, and he also robbed a bank in Bluffton, Ohio. He was arrested and sent back to jail, but while he was inside, eight of his prisoner friends escaped, using guns that had been smuggled into their cells and shooting two guards on their way out. Later, on October 12, these friends helped Dillinger escape, shooting a sheriff in the process. Bound together by these experiences, The Dillinger Gang, as it now became known, embarked on a series of daring bank robberies around the country.

ESCAPE ATTEMPTS

First, the gang raided police arsenals at Auburn and Peru, Indiana, stealing machine guns, rifles, ammunition and bullet-proof vests. They then committed several bank robberies, but it was not until a police officer was killed at a raid in Chicago, Illinois, that the heat was on. From that point, the FBI swore to track down the killers.

However, it was not so easy to catch up with them. The robbers now had plenty of money and spent Christmas in Florida, living the high life. They then headed down to Tucson, Arizona, robbing a bank in Gary, Indiana, on the way. As he made his getaway, Dillinger shot and killed a policeman. By the time they got to Tucson, the word was out and the gang were arrested. They were found in possession of three sub-machine guns, two rifles, five bullet-proof vests, and more than $25,000 in cash. Not even Dillinger could argue his way out of that one: they had been caught red-handed.

Dillinger was taken to an 'escape-proof' prison in Crown Point, Indiana, to await trial. However, despite the high security, he managed to escape, making a replica gun out of wood and then colouring it black with boot polish. Waving the replica gun, he managed to force a prison officer to surrender his own gun, and then, with the help of another inmate, took several hostages before making off from the prison in the governor's own car.

SHOOT-OUT

J. Edgar Hoover, head of the newly formed FBI , was incensed by the news of what Dillinger had done and ordered his capture as a number one priority. A massive manhunt began. Dillinger teamed up with his old comrades and formed a gang, this time including

Lester Gillis, also known as Baby Face Nelson. Gillis was known as something of a psychopath, a man who liked machine guns, liked shooting and liked killing. The new gang set off on a series of ever more outrageous bank heists. On one memorable occasion, they engaged in a massive shoot-out with the FBI, in St Paul, Minnesota.

Time was running out for Dillinger and his band of desperadoes. He had been wounded in the St Paul shoot-out and his health was failing. The band robbed another police arsenal, taking more guns and bullet-proof vests, and headed out to a resort lodge at Rhinelander, Wisconsin. Their plan was to hide out there until the heat had died down. However, news of their whereabouts reached the FBI, and soon officers arrived in large numbers at the lodge. Outnumbered by police, it looked as though the game was up for Dillinger and his men: but once again, they got away.

In the chaos of the shoot-out that ensued, three innocent onlookers were killed. Baby Face Nelson also shot an FBI agent. The gang members all managed to escape, making the FBI look foolish indeed. Afterwards, there was a public outcry against the FBI, not only for letting the small band of robbers go free, but also for shooting the bystanders through sheer incompetence. Hoover's FBI was now at the nadir of public opinion, while Dillinger's gang was enjoying celebrity status.

FINAL AMBUSH

It was at this point that Dillinger let fame go to his head. He went to Chicago and underwent minor plastic surgery to change his looks, and began to frequent the nightclubs and brothels of the city right under the nose of the authorities. He also appeared in public to watch baseball games, supporting the Chicago Cubs. Even then, the FBI somehow failed to find grounds to arrest him.

But the end was near, and on July 22, 1934, Dillinger attended a film, *Manhattan Melodrama*, in Lincoln Park. With him was his girlfriend, Polly Hamilton, and a brothel-keeper, Ana Cumpanas, also known as Anna Sage. Sage was facing deportation charges, and unbeknown to Dillinger, had worked out a deal with the FBI so that the charges would be dropped. When the friends left the theatre, Sage tipped off the FBI by wearing a dress that showed up red in the night. The FBI, who had set up an ambush, opened fire, shooting Dillinger in the back and killing him instantly. They had finally got their man.

Dillinger was buried at Crown Hill Cemetery, Indianapolis. The FBI afterwards reneged on the deal with Sage, and she was deported back to Romania, where she lived until her death in 1945.

WILLIE 'THE ACTOR' SUTTON

William Sutton made his name with a string of
notorious bank robberies, totalling about 100,
between the 1920s and the 1950s. He had two
nicknames, 'Willie the Actor' and 'Slick Willie'. The
first was derived from his habit of disguising himself
to make a raid; the second from his dandified style of
dress. Sutton was far from the stereotype of the bank
robber as a brutal thug; instead he was charming,
well-dressed and polite, which made him a favourite
with women. During his thirty-year career, he stole
about two million dollars, a phenomenal amount of
money for the period he lived in.

EXPERT SAFE CRACKER

Sutton was born into an immigrant Irish family in
Brooklyn, New York. The fourth of five children, he
left school after he had completed the eighth grade,
and went on to work in a series of jobs: as a driller,

a gardener and a clerk. A restless soul, he never stayed in a job for much more than a year, and eventually quit working to concentrate on his main talent in life: stealing.

From the age of nine he had a reputation as a thief and as a teenager began to break into houses. In one instance, he broke into his girlfriend's father's place of business and stole enough money and goods to elope with her. Not surprisingly, the father was furious and Sutton ended up in the dock, charged with robbery. He received a short prison sentence for the crime, during which time he did as much as he could to learn more about the world of professional robbery.

In prison, Sutton met a seasoned safe cracker called Doc Tate, who introduced him to the world of organised crime. He now graduated to robbing banks and jewellers, becoming an expert safe cracker like his mentor Tate. He carried a pistol or a sub-machine gun on his escapades, but he always swore that it was not loaded and he had no intention of hurting anyone. Asked why he still carried the gun, given that he was not prepared to use it, he quipped, 'You can't rob a bank on charm and personality'.

MASTER OF DISGUISE

Sutton continued with the traditional approach of storming banks waving a gun until, one day, he had a better idea. While staking out a bank, he watched as uniformed guards drove up outside with a marked van, then walked inside to pick up the day's takings. He realised that if he could disguise himself as a guard or other official, he would not have to go to the trouble – and risk – of robbing banks by threat of violence. Thus, he began to mount a series of raids dressed in a variety of disguises: as a security guard, a mail man, a messenger and a maintenance worker. This was how he gained his nickname, Willie 'The Actor' Sutton, attracting admiration from the press and media by showing a modicum of intelligence and flair in the execution of his robberies, rather than committing them by using the usual brute force.

From this time on, whenever Sutton committed a bank robbery or raided a jewellery shop, he made a habit of dressing up for the occasion. As befitted the characters he was disguised as, whether mailmen or maintenance workers, he was polite to all those he met. He still carried a gun, but he prided himself on never having to use it. One of his victims commented that, far from being traumatised by the robbery, he felt as though he was in a movie during the experience – except that the usher had a gun.

DARING ESCAPE

Sutton was living the high life, spending his stolen money and jewels on expensive clothing and other luxuries. In 1929, he got married, but by now his luck was running out. He was finally caught, and in June 1931, he was convicted of assault and robbery. He received a sentence of thirty years, and his wife promptly divorced him.

Sutton was sent to the notorious Sing Sing Prison in New York, which was thought to be a high security institution. But Sutton thought otherwise, and had no intention of spending the next thirty years of his life languishing in jail. Instead, after serving only a year of his sentence, he made a daring escape. On December 11, 1932, using a smuggled gun, he held a prison guard hostage and then managed to climb up a thirty-foot prison wall, using two ladders joined together. Amazingly, he got clean away, and once back in circulation, he returned to his previous way of life.

Sutton's next bank raid was on February 15, 1933, when he made an attempt on the Corn Exchange Bank and Trust Company in Philadelphia, Pennsylvania. He arrived disguised as a mailman but a passer by noticed what was going on and raised the alarm. The police were called, but Sutton managed to escape.

The following year, on January 15, 1934, he and two associates broke into the same bank through a skylight. The robbery was successful, but a month later, the police caught up with him. Sutton was arrested, charged, brought to trial and convicted. He received a prison sentence of twenty-five to fifty years in Eastern State Penitentiary, Pennsylvania.

LIFE SENTENCE

Once again, Sutton tried to escape from prison – four times, to be exact. Each time, he was caught and punished until finally, on April 3 1945 he and twelve other prisoners managed to escape through a tunnel. However, his freedom was short-lived; once outside the prison, he spent a day on the run, and was then captured by the Philadelphia police and returned to the prison.

As a punishment, Sutton received a life sentence and was transferred to the Philadelphia County Prison in Homesburg, Pennsylvania. Undeterred, he continued his escape attempts, and finally managed to break free on February 10, 1947. That night, Sutton and his friends dressed up as prison guards and walked across the prison yard to the high wall on the other side. They carried two ladders with them. Unfortunately for them, just as they were walking across, a searchlight caught them in the act. With his characteristic panache, Sutton called out, 'It's okay,' hoping that the searchlight operator would take them for prison officers. He did, and they were allowed to continue. Once again, 'the actor' had calmly persuaded everyone, in the heat of the moment, that he was a normal workman going about his everyday business.

TEN MOST WANTED

By now, Willie Sutton was a well-known figure in the press, much admired for his cool demeanour under pressure, and for the fact that he seldom resorted to actual violence in his bank robberies and prison escapes. He continued to rob banks and jewellery shops, and became such a menace that the FBI added him to their list of Ten Most Wanted Fugitives. When his picture was released, his stylish way of dressing was noticed – but not in the way that Sutton had intended, unfortunately for him.

Sutton's photograph was circulated to tailors in New York, as well as the police, and one day Arnold Schuster, a twenty-four-year-old tailor's son, recognised the notorious criminal on the subway. He alerted the police, and on February 18, 1952, Sutton was arrested. With the glare of publicity now on him, Sutton enjoyed his last few moments of freedom. Asked by a press man why he robbed banks he replied simply: 'Because that's where the money is.' (This line was later attributed to a journalist.) The public loved him, and found his ease in front of the cameras beguiling. Such was his popularity that he gained a reputation as a kind of latter-day Robin Hood, although in actual fact he never gave any of his money away and clearly loved spending it – on himself.

But while Sutton was playing the role of gentleman thief to the gallery, a more tragic tale was unfolding. Schuster, the young man who had turned Sutton in, was murdered by mob assassins, who wanted to let the world know that informing on wanted criminals carried with it a heavy price.

NEW CAREER

Sutton was brought to trial once more and convicted. He was sent to Attica Prison in New York to serve the rest of his life sentence, and received an additional sentence of 105 years. This time, when he went to prison, he did not escape. In fact, he went on to spend most of his adult life in jail.

On Christmas Eve 1969, Sutton was finally released from Attica Prison. He was ill with emphysema and other health problems, but he was too poor to get proper medical attention. For some months he lived on welfare payments, but he later regained his health and began to rebuild his life. In his later years, he began to lecture about prison reform and also advised banks on how to protect themselves from robbery. He even made a television commercial for the New Britain Bank and Trust Company, promoting their new photo credit card.

Willie Sutton spent his declining years in Spring Hill, Florida, with his sister. He finally died at the age of seventy-nine, and was buried quietly in his family's plot at a cemetery in Brooklyn.

GREAT TRAIN ROBBERY

The Great Train Robbery took place in Buckinghamshire, England, on August 8, 1963, and became one of the most famous crimes in British history. A total of £2.3 million was stolen, most of it in used bank notes. To the outrage of the nation, the bulk of this money was never recovered. (Today, the equivalent amount would be about £14 million.) One of the most remarkable aspects of the heist was that no guns were used; however, although it was often painted as a victimless crime, it was not: during the heist, the train driver was hit over the head with an iron bar, which left him bruised and bleeding. To the delight of the tabloid press, who saw the robbery as an exciting adventure story, the fifteen-strong gang of London criminals who had hijacked the train, led by Bruce Reynolds, made a successful getaway, and later hid out at nearby farmhouse. Here, they passed the time by playing the board game Monopoly, and ironically, it was this that proved to be their downfall: their fingerprints on the paper money were later discovered by police, and led to the identification and arrest of thirteen members of the gang.

HEIST AT THE BRIDGE

The train that the robbers made their target was a 'travelling post office' train, or TPO, that was operated by the Royal Mail on the London to Glasgow line. The plan had been initiated by Bruce Reynolds, an antique dealer who drove an Aston Martin and liked to show off his wealth. Also prominent in planning the robbery and putting it into operation was John Wheater, a solicitor, who came from a middle-class background and was able to act as front man for the group. It was Wheater who rented the farmhouse where the gang hid out after the robbery. Another member was Buster Edwards, a con man who had had a previous career as a boxer; Phil Collins later played Edwards in the film *Buster*, based on the robber's life. Charlie Wilson, a bookmaker, also featured in the gang, along with the 'brawns' of the operation, Gordon Goody and Jimmy Hussey. Also part of the gang was Ronnie Biggs, a junior member with a fairly insignificant role, who was later to become one of the most notorious Great Train Robbers when he escaped from prison.

Bruce Reynolds made it his business to study the comings and goings of the postal trains in and out of London. He also managed to get hold of information concerning large amounts of cash that were occasionally carried on the trains. He chose a spot to hold up the train, near a bridge known as Bridego Bridge, which was situated outside Cheddington in the county of Buckinghamshire. This was a quiet place, and it was thought that the train would slow down as it came to the bridge, so that the robbers could flag it down and climb aboard. Another advantage to the spot was that it was near a military base; large supply trucks were often to be seen on the roads nearby, so the robbers' truck would not seem particularly conspicuous as it drove away from the train loaded with money.

TRAIN DRIVER ATTACKED

In the early hours of August 8, 1963, the robbers drove to the spot and set up the ambush. It was a few minutes after three o'clock in the morning when the raid began. Dressed as railway men, wearing overalls, the gang rigged up some temporary signals on the line, using large batteries to power the lights. As the train driver, Jack Mills, neared the bridge, he noticed a red 'stop' light, and slowed the train down to a halt. David Whitby, a fireman, got out of the train onto the track to see what was going on. Buster Edwards, one of the robbers, pulled him off the track and into the scrub nearby. Once Whitby realised what was going on, he offered no resistance and was left by the side of the track. However, Mills, the train driver was not so lucky. When he got off the train, the robbers attacked him, hitting him over the head with an iron bar. Mills collapsed by the side of the track.

HIDEAWAY FARMHOUSE

Up to that point, the robbery had been committed without violence, as had been the plan. There had been no real need to attack Mills, but in a panic, the robbers had beaten him over the head. Next, they made another mistake. Ronnie Biggs had brought in a retired train driver to drive the train into a place where the mailbags of money could be easily shifted onto the robbers' truck. But the elderly driver did not understand how the train worked, as the design had changed since the days when he was employed. Thus, Mills was brought back in to drive the train, even though he was injured.

Once the train was in position, the gang worked as quickly as they could, forming a human chain to unload over 100 sacks of money into the truck. Then they drove away, leaving Mills to his fate. They drove to their hideout at Leatherslade Farm, and here they sat tight until the fuss had died down, playing Monopoly and drinking cups of tea. However, the police were soon on their trail.

Eventually, the gang left the farmhouse, when they felt it was safe to do so. But they foolishly left their fingerprints all over the paper money on the board game. When the police raided the farmhouse, this gave them a very useful set of clues. Most of the gang members had been involved in crime before, and were well known to the police. It was a simple enough matter to identify the fingerprints and match them to the ones held on their records. In this way, thirteen members of the gang were caught. In a highly publicised trial, the robbers were brought to justice, convicted and sentenced on April 16, 1964.

DRAMATIC ESCAPES

That was by no means the end of the story. Charlie Wilson and Ronnie Biggs were both imprisoned, but they later made dramatic escapes from jail. Wilson went to Montreal, Canada, and lived quietly there until he was tracked down via a telephone call that his wife made to her parents in the UK. Buster Edwards fled to Mexico, but gave himself up in the end. Bruce Reynolds went on the run for five years, but the law caught up with him and he served a ten-year prison sentence.

Ronnie Biggs had not played a large part in the Great Train Robbery, but eventually he became the most notorious member of the gang. After serving a year of his prison sentence, he escaped from prison by scaling a wall with a rope ladder. He underwent plastic surgery and travelled around the world, eventually settling in Rio de Janeiro, Brazil, with his Brazilian wife and child. Under Brazilian law, as the father of a Brazilian child, he could not be extradited to the UK, so he lived openly in Rio with them.

However, in later years, Biggs became seriously ill, and announced his intention to return to the UK. He had become tired of living abroad, with mounting health-care bills, and said that he was prepared to risk being imprisoned once he arrived in the UK. He was duly imprisoned when he arrived back, even though he had suffered several strokes and was in a very poor state of health.

THE AFTERMATH

The legacy of the Great Train Robbery makes sad reading. The train driver, Jack Mills, died from leukaemia in 1970. There was never enough evidence to convict any of the train robbers with the attack, so his case was never brought to court. Buster Edwards, on his release from jail, became a flower seller in Waterloo train station until he committed suicide in 1994.

Today, the Great Train Robbery is viewed in some quarters as an exciting adventure story involving colourful members of the London underworld, and in others as a rather shameful episode in which an unarmed man was brutally attacked for no reason. For many people, whether sympathetic to the robbers or not, it continues to hold a fascination. For years, the exploits of Ronnie Biggs and the other train robbers were constantly recounted in the tabloid press, while one of the detectives on the case, Chief Superintendent Jack Slipper (known as 'Slipper of the Yard') became so involved in it that he continued to try to track down the culprits long after he had retired from the police force.

One of the post office carriages that was targeted for the robbery was restored and went on display at Nene Valley Railway. As a result of the Great Train Robbery, the rule book of the British rail postal train services was changed, so that instead of climbing out onto the track at an unexpected red 'stop' signal and walking across the line to see the signalman, train drivers were directed to stay in their cabs with the doors locked. Had Jack Mills done that, the Great Train Robbery would quite probably never have happened.

MESRINE

Jacques Mesrine was a notorious French bank robber who operated in the 1960s and 70s. He committed a string of burglaries, jewellery shop robberies and bank robberies during that time, and was also involved in kidnapping and arms smuggling. He was also known for his audacious escapes from prison, in one case attempting to help over fifty inmates of a prison escape. He became 'public enemy number one' in France and remained the scourge of the authorities, until eventually, the French police unified their efforts to track him down, and ambushed him in his car on the outskirts of Paris. On November 2, 1979 police opened fire and gunned him down, killing him instantly.

Mesrine was born in Clichy, France, into a middle-class family. He was educated at the Catholic College of Juilly, but was expelled from there, and from another school, for violent behaviour. As a young man, he married – briefly – and served in the French army in Algeria during the war of independence there. On his return to France in 1959, he embarked on a career of crime.

RUTHLESS AND VIOLENT

Mesrine was a persuasive, charismatic person who was charmed those around him and was very attractive to women. He dressed fashionably and had a series of beautiful girlfriends who shared his taste for glamour and adventure, and who often accompanied him on his criminal escapades. He liked to live well and enjoyed eating at expensive restaurants, cutting a dashing figure in Paris, so that among some sections of the press and the public, he was regarded as something of a hero. The reality was a little different. In actual fact, Mesrine was a ruthless, violent man who boasted about murdering scores of victims. Although he liked to maintain that his crimes were motivated by radical political ideas, he showed no sign during his criminal career of being motivated by anything other than personal greed.

In 1962, Mesrine attempted to rob a bank with three accomplices, but was arrested, convicted and sent to jail. After serving a year of his sentence, he began work for a design company, but soon resumed his criminal activities again, this time in Spain. He was arrested in Spain after only six months, and then opened a restaurant in the Canary Islands, but this too was short-lived. He went back to his life of crime once more, robbing a hotel in Chamonix, France, and then attempting a kidnapping in Canada.

KIDNAPPING PLOT

The Canadian fiasco was a plot hatched between him and his girlfriend, Jeanne Schneider. Their aim was to kidnap a textile and grocery millionaire, Georges Deslauriers, and pick up a ransom for him. The reason they chose Deslauriers was that he had hired them as domestic servants and then sacked them. Fortunately for their victim, the plot failed, and Mesrine and Shneider were sentenced to ten years' imprisonment. Amazingly, they managed to escape from custody, capturing a prison warder, stealing his keys and locking him in a cell. They then hid out in the woods, until they were captured and brought to justice once more.

Mesrine was sent to a high-security prison outside Montreal, Saint Vincent de Paul. But, as it turned out, the prison was not high security enough. Within a short time, he had mounted a daring escape with five other inmates. The prisoners stole a pair of pliers from the prison workshop and proceeded to cut through a maze of fences. They climbed out, flagged down cars on the road and got away. As if this was not enough, Mesrine decided to help the other fifty-three inmates of the prison, who were still inside, by going back to liberate them. Before doing so, he robbed several banks to raise enough money, and bought an arsenal of shotguns and wire cutters. He devised a complicated plan to break through the security systems at the prison, but when he put it into operation, he failed. He had to make a quick getaway, and the prisoners remained inside; but once again, he had escaped capture.

JUDGE HELD HOSTAGE

Now on the run, Mesrine and an accomplice, Jean-Paul Mercier, fled to Venezuela to escape the long arm of the law. But, as seemed to be the pattern with Mesrine, he could not stay away from France – and his life of crime – for very long. He returned to his home country and began to rob banks again until in 1973 he was caught and tried. The trial attracted a great deal of interest from the press, and it became sensational when Mesrine jumped up in court, as the judge was reading out the charges, and took him hostage. He was brandishing a gun that had been hidden for him in a nearby toilet by an accomplice, which he had concealed under his clothes when he attended the court. He put the gun to the judge's head, held onto his victim and used him as a human shield. In front of amazed onlookers, Mesrine made his way out of the courtroom into the street, still holding on to the judge, and jumped into a getaway car. The police opened fire, but he got clean away.

A few months later, Mesrine was arrested once again. He was brought to trial, convicted and sent to jail, this time to the maximum security jail at La Sante de Paris. To the horror of the authorities, and the delight of the press – who used the incident as an opportunity to vent their hatred of the French police and security services – Mesrine managed to escape again, causing an absolute furore all over the country. The French police were harangued for being so incompetent that they let him go, while Mesrine was lauded as a folk hero, a kind of latter-day Robin Hood – a rather romantic view of him, which did not tally with his violent personality, or his self-indulgent tastes.

MAXIMUM SECURITY?

The sensational escape from La Sante de Paris, hitherto regarded as maximum security, was effected by Mesrine and two accomplices, both prisoners at the jail. Together, they held up the guards, stole their uniforms and locked the guards in the prison cells. Using threats, they demanded ladders and climbed over the high prison walls, using grappling irons and ropes. In this way, they managed to escape, becoming the first prisoners from La Sante de Paris ever to do so.

Mesrine's escape from La Sante de Paris infuriated the French authorities, which now redoubled their efforts to capture him. However, Mesrine evaded arrest, and went on to step up his exploits, robbing banks and jewellery shops, and smuggling arms. He also kidnapped wealthy individuals and held them to ransom. He boasted during this period that he had killed over thirty people, most of them pimps, but this claim was never verified. Yet even though he was apparently a murderer, the popular French press continued to view him as a loveable rogue and a thorn in the side of the authorities, rather than as a dangerous criminal.

SHOT TO DEATH

After the humiliation of La Sante, the French government decided to act and put a stop to Mesrine's criminal activities for once and for all. A manhunt was ordered, and ministers instructed police departments across France to search for him. Eventually, his home in the outskirts of Paris at Clignancourt was located. A truck loaded with armed police was dispatched there, and it followed Mesrine as he drove his BMW. This time, as instructed, the police were taking no chances. Instead of trying to flag Mesrine down and arrest him, they pursued him and shot nineteen rounds of bullets through the windscreen of his car, killing him dead.

Mesrine's death was hailed as a victory in some circles, and the President of France, Valéry Giscard d'Estaing, congratulated the police operation. Others, however, claimed that it was illegal and unfair to treat any citizen in this way, whatever their crimes. Mesrine had not been given any warning, or told to slow his car down, before the police opened fire on him. The police action, the critics claimed, was unwarranted, since they were not acting in self-defence and Mesrine had not opened fire on them.

THE LEGACY

During his life, Mesrine had been concerned about the type of publicity he received. He often gave interviews to try to persuade the press that his criminal activities were politically motivated, although this was not true. He took great exception to negative publicity, threatening to kill journalist and former policeman Jacques Tillier because he had written hostile articles about him. After Mesrine's death, his flamboyant career inspired many musicians to write songs about him; one band from Quebec even named themselves after him. But it was as a comedy act that he was finally immortalised, in the 1980 film *Inspecteur la Bavure*, which starred the French comedian Coluche and Gerard Depardieu, whose portrayal of the character Morzini was apparently directly inspired by Jacques Mesrine.

ANTHONY PINO

On January 17, 1950, the Brinks building in Boston, Massachusetts, was broken into by armed robbers, who stole over $2 million worth in cash and securities. The size of the haul was so big that the Great Brinks Robbery, as it was called, became the largest bank heist ever to take place in the history of the USA up to that time. Billed as 'the crime of the century', the robbery was seen as the work of a criminal mastermind since it had been minutely planned down to the last detail and very few clues were left at the crime scene. For years, police came no closer to finding the culprits, who undertook not to spend their ill-gotten wealth, to avoid attracting suspicion. However, eventually all nine members of the gang were tracked down and brought to justice, including the man behind the plan, Anthony 'Fats' Pino.

AUDACIOUS ROBBERY

Pino was Italian by origin, and had been born in Italy in 1907. As a child, he had immigrated to the USA with his parents, and the family had settled in

Boston. His parents did not register him to become a naturalised American citizen. Exposed to the rougher elements · of the city, Pino soon found himself involved in a life of crime, operating as a burglar, among other nefarious activities. In 1928, he was charged with sexual abuse of a minor and convicted of the crime. He was later charged with having burglar equipment in his possession, and with breaking and entering a property with the intent to commit a felony.

Once the Immigration and Naturalisation Service realised that he was not an American citizen, they began proceedings to have him deported back to Italy. On his release from prison in 1944, he was taken into custody by the immigration authorities, but he managed to get the deportation order dropped by appealing for a pardon. Had the Immigration Service known that Pino was, at the same time, in the process of planning the biggest bank robbery in US history, they might have revised their decision.

For over a year, Pino had been staking out the target for his robbery, the new Brinks building in Boston. He assembled a team of criminals drawn from the Boston underworld around him to help him do the job: among them were Joseph O'Keefe (nicknamed 'Specs'), Joseph 'Big Joe' McGinnis, and Stanley Gusciora (nicknamed 'Gus'). Over a period of months, the gang became as familiar as they could with the layout of the building, and with the comings and goings of the staff who worked there. On one of his visits, Pino discovered that staff on the second floor routinely counted up the takings for the day, much of it in cash. He also found out that the amounts of money they were dealing with were huge and realised that, if he could only access this money, he could get away with $1 million or more.

THE BIG DAY

However, there was just one problem: security. To get to the money, the robbers would have to pass through five locked doors, all of which set off alarms when an intruder made the slightest noise. It was here that Pino's experience as a burglar came in. He devised a plan whereby members of his team would, over a period of months, become familiar with the times the doors were left open and unattended. Then, at a given time, the robber would take the lock out of the door and give it to a locksmith to make extra copies of the key that would open it. Afterwards, the robber would return the lock to the door and screw it back in. As can be imagined, it took a long time for the robbers to find opportunities when no one was looking, unscrew the door lock and take it to a locksmith to copy the key. But eventually, with immense patience, the job of copying keys for all five doors was done – and still no one at the bank had noticed what was going on.

The day came when all the right factors were in place to put the plan into action. The area around the bank was peaceful, so that there would not be too many witnesses; there were only a few employees left in the premises; and, most importantly, the bank's takings that day were high. This was the moment that Pino and his team had been waiting for. They had called the robbery off six times at the last minute, due to some hitch or other, but now, at last, the moment was right.

HALLOWE'EN MASKS

The robbers were dressed alike, in navy suits and chauffeurs' caps, an outfit similar to the uniform of the Brinks' employees. To disguise themselves, they wore Halloween masks; to make sure they left no fingerprints, they donned gloves. At 6.55 p.m. on January 17, 1950, they drove up to the bank.

Pino and the driver stayed in the car while seven of the team entered the building. Using their copied sets of keys, they gained access to the second floor and held up five Brinks employees who were counting the takings. They then bound and gagged the victims, and piled up the money ready to take it away. So far it had all gone to plan, it seemed; but then a Brinks employee buzzed on the door to be let in. The robbers looked at each other in horror, wondering what to do, but before they could act, the Brinks employee walked off, apparently having given up his errand. The robbers redoubled their efforts, loading up the money as fast as they could, and within half an hour, they had left.

THE USUAL SUSPECTS

Naturally enough, as soon as their attackers disappeared, staff called the police. It was only a matter of minutes before the police arrived, along with agents from the FBI. However, they found few clues that would help them find the robbers. None of them could be identified, because of the Halloween masks that they had worn; and there were no fingerprints anywhere, because the attackers had worn gloves. The only evidence that the robbers had left behind was the rope and sticky tape they had used to bind and gag the staff – and a chauffeur's cap. As well as the money, the robbers had stolen four revolvers, so the serial numbers of these were noted down by the FBI, in case this information might be useful at a later date. Other than the obvious fact that the heist had been carried out by professionals, this was all the police had to go on at this stage.

Initially, the police turned to the usual suspects in the city, career criminals who had long been a thorn in their side. However, there was no evidence to show that any of them were guilty. In desperation, the police began to interview older criminals, such as former members of the 'Purple Gang' of the 1930s, who had been bootleggers in the days of Prohibition, but they seemed to know nothing about what was fast becoming known as 'the crime of the century'.

FINAL ARRESTS

When news of the robbery appeared in the press, the public were fascinated. The bank offered a reward of $100,000 for information that would lead to the culprits, and soon the police began to receive hundreds of calls, but none of these yielded any useful information. Of course, the police had their suspicions; but until some evidence was found, nothing could be done.

Then there was a breakthrough, or so it seemed. Children playing on a sandbar in Mystic River, Somerville, found one of the revolvers. In Stoughton, Massachusetts, parts of the truck the gang had used were found, and as a result, police visited Gus Gusciora and 'Specs' O'Keefe at their homes in the area, but no evidence to connect them to the robbery could be unearthed.

It was not until O'Keefe was arrested in connection with another burglary that the truth began to come out. While he was in prison, officials became aware that he was involved with a wealthy gang on the outside. In 1955, O'Keefe was released, and a rift between the gang members developed, as O'Keefe accused the others of cheating him over the proceeds of the robbery. In response, Pino hired a hitman to kill O'Keefe, a man named Elmer 'Trigger' Burke. Burke shot O'Keefe several times, but did not manage to kill him. While in hospital, and bitter about his treatment at the hands of the gang, O'Keefe agreed to give evidence against them.

As a result, Anthony Pino was arrested on January 12, 1956. All the remaining members of the gang, except Gusciora, who had died, were also arrested. At the trial, which began on August 12, 1956, all the gang members except O'Keefe were convicted and given life sentences. In return for his cooperation, O'Keefe only received a four-year sentence. As to the money, it was never recovered.

PART NINE

FICTIONAL
MASTERMINDS

BLOFELD
(JAMES BOND)

Ernst Stavro Blofeld is the creation of Ian Fleming, author of the *James Bond* series of spy novels. The evil genius behind the fictional terrorist organisation SPECTRE, which is dedicated to the destruction of the British Secret Service in general, and top spy James Bond in particular, Blofeld spends his time trying to outwit his opponent, and usually fails. He has been memorably depicted on film: in early James Bond movies, he is referred to only as Number One; his face is never seen and we only see his arm and hand as he strokes a Persian cat on his knee. We also hear his voice, speaking in a soft and rather sinister manner. Later in the series, we find out that Number One is in fact Blofeld. A number of different actors played Blofeld, with varying degrees of credibility. He usually appears wearing a Nehru jacket and fondling a cat. In the novels no mention of a cat is made, and Blofeld is described as having black hair and a crew cut. None of the actors playing Blofeld to date has fitted this description; however, today the film image of Blofeld, rather than that of the book, is the one that has impacted on the public imagination as Fleming's famous criminal mastermind.

TREACHEROUS VILLAIN

According to the life history that Fleming gives in his novel *Thunderball*, Blofeld was born on 28 May, 1908. (This was also, as it happens, Fleming's birth date; and it seems that the name Blofeld was inspired by one of Fleming's schoolmates, father of the British cricket commentator Henry Blofeld.) As Fleming tells the story, Blofeld grew up in Gdynia, which was then in Germany, but is now part of Poland. His father was Polish and his mother Greek. The child, who was named Ernst Stavro to reflect his mixed parentage, became a Polish national after World War I. Fleming imagines that, as a young man, Blofeld attended the University of Warsaw and gained a wide-ranging education in political history and economics. He also credits him with degrees in radionics and engineering at Warsaw's University of Technology. (Radionics is a theory, popular around the turn of the twentieth century, according to which all forms of matter have 'energy frequencies' – vibrations and harmonic patterns. These frequencies also occur in human beings and determine their state of health. According to the theory of radionics, or pseudoscience as some believe it to be, patients can be medically diagnosed by studying these 'energy frequencies', and a cure for their condition can be found by rebalancing the frequencies, thus restoring them to good health.)

Blofeld's career of crime began at the Ministry of Posts and Telegraphs in the Polish Government. He began to wheel and deal on the Warsaw stock exchange, using his knowledge of what was going on at government level to make huge amounts of money buying and selling stocks and shares. His treachery reached dangerous proportions when he copied and sold top-secret information gained from the Ministry to the Nazis, prior to World War II.

TERRORIST ORGANISATION

In 1939, knowing that the Germans were about to invade Poland, Blofeld disappeared, destroying all records of his life there. He went to live in Turkey, where, under the guise of working for Turkey's national radio station, he set up an intelligence organisation, selling secret information to both the Nazis and the Allies. Ever the pragmatist, when he realised that the Allies were about to win the war, he began to back the Allied war effort, and was rewarded in the post-war period with many medals and honours. After the war, Blofeld moved to South America for a short time, and went on to his terrorist organisation, SPECTRE (the Special Executive for Counter-Intelligence Revenge and Extortion).

Blofeld makes his first appearance in *Thunderball*, Ian Fleming's ninth novel, but is still only a minor character at this period, as his dastardly plans to rule the world and in the process, to kill James Bond and incapacitate MI5, are mainly carried out by underlings. In Fleming's subsequent novels, Blofeld's role as an evil genius becomes more central, and we follow his progress as he goes underground, living in Switzerland under the disguise of the Comte de Bleuville, and plotting to destroy the UK's agricultural economy. When Bond manages to foil Blofeld's plans, Blofeld gets his revenge by murdering Bond's new bride, Tracy, thus also ensuring that our hero continues to be an eligible bachelor for his next series of adventures. Blofeld's many villainous escapades continue, with Bond in hot pursuit, until they are brought to an end in *You Only Live Twice*. Here, Blofeld makes his appearance living in Japan under the guise of one Dr Guntram Shatterhand. Bond hunts him down and finally strangles him to death, bringing his opponent's evil reign to a close.

THE EVIL GENIUS

The film versions of the James Bond novels contain many different, and sometimes inconsistent, images of Blofeld, and do not always tally with the narratives in the novels. In *From Russia With Love*, Blofeld is presented as a powerful but shadowy enemy: we only see his hand, wearing a ring, and petting a large white Persian cat, while hearing his voice, which is soft-spoken and menacing. Throughout *From Russia With Love*, Blofeld is simply referred to as Number One. Later, in *Thunderball*, Blofeld's face continues to remain unseen, and this time, to add to the sense of mystery, his name is omitted completely from the credits. In both these films, *From Russia With Love*, and *Thunderball*, Number One's body is played by Anthony Dawson, while his voice is played by Eric Pohlmann.

It is only when Bond finally meets his nemesis, in *You Only Live Twice*, that we find out what Blofeld looks like. Blofeld is played by Donald Pleasence, who replaced Slovakian actor Jan Werich in the part. (Werich had afilmed several scenes but had to retire due to illness.) Unlike Fleming's original hero, Blofeld as played by Pleasence is short and bald, and has a scar over his right eye. The scar was added to give the character a more unusual appearance and to convey a sense of his bitterness and resentment against the world; apparently, other ideas, such as giving Blofeld a hump back, a limp, or a lame hand, were ruled out as excessive. Pleasence's portrayal of Blofeld as a petulant, childish character with a quick temper was somewhat at odds with the quiet menace of the character in previous films, but proved to be a memorable performance. Since then, the character of Blofeld has been widely parodied, especially in films such as the Austin Powers series.

WANTED FUGITIVE

As Bond actors for the films changed, so too did the major characters, including Blofeld. In the film version of *On Her Majesty's Secret Service*, Blofeld is played by American actor Telly Savalas, who brings a tough, hands-on quality to the role he plays as a man obsessed with building a super-human race in the mountains of the Alps. By this time, according to the story, Blofeld has become a wanted fugitive, and Bond has been looking for him all over the world. Bond manages to foil the evil Blofeld's plans, but as always, Blofeld escapes his clutches and lives to fight another day.

In the follow-up film, *Diamonds Are Forever*, Blofeld is played by English actor Charles Gray, and he has now developed a sense of humour and a penchant for cross-dressing. Moreover, Blofeld is no longer bald, but has sprouted a luxurious head of hair. As part of his latest plan to destroy civilisation, Blofeld is stockpiling diamonds so that he can make a laser satellite capable of destroying targets on the earth; Bond's mission is to stop him before he can do so. In a typical action-packed scene, Bond gains control of a crane that is launching the submersible Blofeld is trying to escape in, and smashes it from side to side in such a way that, by the end of the film, we are not sure whether Blofeld is alive or dead.

MEMORABLE VILLAIN

In later films, a character similar to Blofeld appeared in *For Your Eyes Only*, with a body provided by John Hollis and a voice courtesy of Robert Rietti. In *Never Say Never Again*, Max Von Sydow plays a cool, calm version of Blofeld, now sporting a beard, but still fondling a cat as in previous incarnations.

Fleming also created other flamboyant villains in his novels, including *Dr Julius No*, a cold, calculating doctor of half-Chinese, half-German origin, who is plotting to rule the world by launching US space ships from his West Indian retreat. Auric Goldfinger is an eccentric millionaire obsessed by gold, who wants to bomb Fort Knox so that he can destroy the American gold standard and increase the worth of his own hoard. However, the most popular of Fleming's villains is undoubtedly Blofeld, who has become one of the most memorable criminal masterminds in contemporary popular culture, inspiring many imitators in fiction, on film, and on television around the world today.

RAFFLES

Arthur J. Raffles is the late nineteenth-century creation of E.W. Hornung, brother-in-law to Arthur Conan Doyle, the author of the Sherlock Holmes stories. Just as Conan Doyle created a gentleman detective, Hornung created a gentleman thief; and just as Holmes' sidekick was Doctor Watson, Raffles' partner in crime is Harry 'Bunny' Manders. Hornung dedicated his first collection of Raffles stories, entitled *The Amateur Cracksman* to Conan Doyle, who later wrote: 'I think I may claim that his famous character Raffles was a kind of inversion of Sherlock Holmes, Bunny playing Watson. He (Hornung) admits as much in his kindly dedication. I think there are few finer examples of short-story writing in our language than these, though I confess I think they are rather dangerous in their suggestion. I told him so before he put pen to paper, and the result has, I fear, borne me out. You must not make the criminal a hero.'

Conan Doyle was worried that having a thief as the central character, indeed hero, of a fictional piece would corrupt the reader. However, the real problem with Raffles was more that he confused the readers, in the sense that the motivation for his actions was not entirely clear. Add to the confusion, Raffles' circumstances were constantly changing, to the point that he almost became a different character – in contrast with Sherlock Holmes, who remained virtually the same throughout all the stories.

THE GENTLEMAN THIEF

Hornung's gentleman thief, A. J. Raffles lives in Albany, a wealthy area of London, among the wealthy establishment figures of his day. To add to his cachet, he is a well-known cricketer, playing for a team called *The Gentlemen of England*. Because of this, he has many friends, and is often invited to social functions. However, despite his appearance of wealth in his upper-class milieu, he actually earns his living by carrying out ingenious burglaries, often robbing his friends and acquaintances in high society. He is known by professional criminals from the lower classes as 'the Amateur Cracksman', and likes to give the impression of thieving for the fun of it, as a hobby rather than a serious enterprise. At the same time, he earns a substantial amount of money from his ill-gotten gains, and enjoys duping those around him, especially individuals that he feels are stupid, ignorant and mean.

Raffles' partner in crime is Harry 'Bunny' Manders. Raffles and Bunny were at a prestigious

English public school together. Their partnership goes back to a time when Bunny was in financial trouble and was contemplating suicide because of his massive debts. He had written a number of bad cheques to cover his gambling losses, and knew that he would never have enough money to pay them. Faced with being publicly scorned for his behaviour, he had decided to end it all.

By chance, just as he was planning his final exit, Bunny ran into his old chum from school, Raffles, who persuaded him that thievery was the way forward. After expressing some reservations, Bunny realised that this was the only way to get out of the jam he was in, and joined his former schoolmate him in a life of crime. Since that time, the pair have been inseparable. They form a close partnership, just as Sherlock Holmes and Doctor Watson did. Occasionally, Raffles mistreats Bunny, taking advantage of his naivety, and being impatient with his slow-wittedness; but at heart, Raffles knows that in Bunny he has found a brave and loyal follower, who will always help him get out of the many scrapes they find themselves in.

OUTCASTS FROM SOCIETY

Like Sherlock Holmes, Raffles is a master of disguise. He can speak English with many different accents, and has an apartment where he keeps clothes and other items for dressing up. Together, Raffles and Bunny embark on a series of burglaries, made easier by the fact that Raffles is so well connected, and because of his prowess at cricket, he is a popular figure at social functions. The pair often commit their burglaries wearing immaculate evening dress, which helps them to go undetected as they go about their nefarious business.

The stories of Raffles and Bunny's escapades were first published as collections under the name *The Amateur Cracksman*. After this, the Raffles stories changed, which some critics regard as a weakness in the series. In the second phase of stories, published under the name of *The Black Mask*, we meet Raffles and Bunny as professional thieves who are now outcasts from polite society. It appears that they were eventually caught stealing from the rich guests on an ocean liner, and that this is the reason for their disgrace. According to the story, Bunny was arrested for robbery on board the ship, while Raffles escaped by jumping into the sea, and was presumed to have drowned.

However, when Bunny is released from prison after serving his sentence, he receives a call from a rich invalid asking for help. When Bunny visits the house, it turns out that the invalid is Raffles in disguise. The pair are thrilled to be reunited again, and once more resume their life of crime, this time as professional thieves who are no longer trusted as part of high society, and whose must keep their identities secret. They commit a number of audacious robberies, but eventually, their luck runs out and they volunteer as soldiers in the Boer War, where Bunny is seriously injured, and Raffles dies in battle.

THE PSYCHOLOGY OF RAFFLES

Critics have pointed out that, although the stories are well-written and entertaining, they do not measure up to the standard of Arthur Conan Doyle's creation, *Sherlock Holmes*. Partly, this is because the plots are not so satisfying, but it is also because the motivation of the Raffles character is rather unclear. To some degree, Raffles is cynical about society: he remarks at one point, 'We can't all be moralists, and the distribution of wealth is all wrong, anyway.' There is a suggestion in the stories that a trip to 'the colonies' changed Raffles' mind about belonging to the upper classes; he found himself without funds in a foreign country, and had to resort to stealing to survive. When he did, he found that he became addicted to the activity: 'I'd tasted blood,' he says, 'and it was all over with me. Why should I work when I could steal? Why settle down to some humdrum un-cogenial billet when excitement, romance, danger and a decent living were all going begging together.'

Thus Raffles turns away from the respectable values of society to indulge his taste for danger, rather than because of some basic disagreement with the social world around him. Indeed, many of his views are contradictory. Although he appears to be critical of the elite, he is a staunch supporter of the monarchy and appears to uphold the values of the status quo; and although in some ways he has a strong sense of loyalty to his friends, he is not above stealing from them.

Raffles despises the social milieu he is part of on the grounds that people want to befriend him only because he is a famous cricketer. He claims that he himself has lost interest in the game, preferring his occupation as a thief because he finds it mentally stimulating to work out a clever plan for a robbery, and also finds it exciting to go out on the job. However, he does have some scruples: he tries to avoid killing people (although he does so once, and does not rule out such an eventuality in the future), and he will never steal from his host (although he often steals from other guests at the social functions he attends). He is also somewhat ashamed of the way he abuses Bunny's loyalty to him, and when he finally dies, he speaks of his regret at introducing his innocent friend to a life of crime.

Although Raffles steals for profit, he also does so as a form of sport. In one case, he steals a gold cup from the British Museum and sends it to the Queen by post, on the occasion of her Diamond Jubilee. In another instance, he steals from a former schoolmate and makes a donation to the school, shaming the man into making a donation himself. His last adventure is to steal a collection of memorabilia connected to his crimes from Scotland Yard. Yet this motivation seems, at times, strained, and it is never entirely clear why Raffles behaves in the way he does, other than to satisfy a lust for adventure.

THE LEGACY OF THE GENTLEMAN THIEF

The Raffles stories by E. W. Hornung appeared in several collections: *The Amateur Cracksman, The Black Mask* and *A Thief in the Night.* In the twentieth century, several authors took up where Hornung left off and wrote stories about Raffles. John Kendrick Bangs' novel *R. Holmes & Co* concerned a character called Raffles Holmes, who was related to both the original Raffles and Sherlock Holmes. In the 1960s, author Barry Perowne wrote a series of Raffles stories. The famous literary figure Graham Greene wrote a play called *The Return of A. J. Raffles,* and author Peter Tremayne also wrote a novel called *The Return of Raffles.* American writer Philip Jose Farmer included Raffles and Bunny in a science fiction story entitled *The Problem of the Sore Bridge* and, in more recent times, Raffles made it into the movies. The part was played by several well-known actors, including John Barrymore and David Niven.

MORIARTY

One of the first criminal masterminds to be
depicted in modern fiction is Sherlock Holmes'
adversary, Professor James Moriarty. Moriarty is a
genius mathematics professor whose writings are so
abstruse that no one is able to understand or
criticise them. He is admired for his brainpower but
has a 'diabolical' nature, making him extremely
dangerous. Moriarty is the head of a secret criminal
organisation, and Sherlock Holmes' task is to
destroy his evil plans. However, Moriarty remains
elusive until Holmes finally comes face to face with
him in a story called *The Final Problem*. In the story,
Holmes and Moriarty fight hand to hand on the
edge of a great waterfall called the Reichenbach
Falls, until they both fall to their deaths, still locked
in mortal combat.

A DIABOLICAL NATURE

Although Moriarty is often represented as Holmes'
nemesis and his greatest adversary, Moriarty in fact

only appears in two of Conan Doyle's stories (there are sixty Sherlock Holmes stories in all). He is mentioned in five other stories, but only in passing. However, the character of Moriarty so appealed to the reading public that he has become far more central than he actually was in the Sherlock Holmes tales. One of the reasons that Conan Doyle did not make Moriarty a more important character was that he wanted to avoid a situation in which Holmes was constantly outwitted, as this would have detracted from the idea of his hero's brilliance as a detective. Thus, Moriarty made few appearances in the Holmes literature – but when he did appear, he proved to be unforgettable, and he has inspired many writers, film-makers, actors and others since Conan Doyle's time.

From the Sherlock Holmes stories, we learn that Moriarty is a man of good birth who had a privileged education. As a student, he showed a 'phenomenal mathematical faculty', and aged only twenty-one, he wrote a treatise about the binomial theorem in mathematics that astounded his professors. This treatise earned him a chair at a small British university, and at an early age he seemed set to have a brilliant academic career. As well as mathematics, he wrote on astronomy, and his book *The Dynamics of an Asteroid* was so brilliant and difficult to understand that no one could be found to review it in the scientific press.

However, before long it transpired that Moriarty had 'hereditary tendencies of the most diabolical kind'. As Sherlock Holmes puts it, 'a criminal strain ran in his blood, which, instead of being modified, was increased and rendered infinitely more dangerous by his extraordinary mental powers'. In the university town where Moriarty lived, 'dark rumours' about him began to circulate, until he was forced to leave and live in London, where he sets up his criminal organisation and becomes known to the police as 'the Napoleon of Crime'. Conan Doyle borrowed this phrase from police inspector Robert Anderson at Scotland Yard, who used it to describe Adam Worth, a German-born gentleman criminal who was the real-life scourge of the London police at the time. Other critics have suggested that aspects of Moriarty's character were based on another famous London criminal, the celebrated eighteenth-century thief Jonathan Wild. What characterised all these characters, both real and imagined, was that they were all highly intelligent, as well as morally corrupt.

A FEARFUL PLACE

There are two Sherlock Holmes stories in which Moriarty appears, *The Valley of Fear* and *The Final Problem*. In *The Valley of Fear*, set before *The Final Problem* but published after it, Holmes is trying to prevent Moriarty's agents from committing a murder. He never actually meets Moriarty, but in the final part of the story, Moriarty sends him a note. In *The Final Problem*, Holmes almost succeeds in his task of destroying Moriarty's underground organisation, but he has to leave London in a hurry to escape being killed by Moriarty's men. Moriarty follows him, and eventually catches up with him in the Swiss Alps, where they finally meet at the Reichenbach Falls. Conan Doyle was obviously impressed with the waterfall, which is over 180 metres (600 feet) high, and is one of the highest cataracts in the Alps. He imagined the scene on a particular ledge, accessible only by climbing a path to the top of the waterfall, crossing a bridge over it, and following a trail down a hill. Today, there is a memorial plaque at the ledge which reads: 'At this fearful place, Sherlock Holmes vanquished Professor Moriarty, on 4 May, 1891'. (Interestingly, Mary Shelley was also inspired by the great waterfall, and had her monster Frankenstein follow a similar route in 1818.)

Unusually for a detective series, Conan Doyle had his hero plunge to his death along with the villain. The reason for this, he later explained, was that he felt he was writing too many Sherlock Holmes stories, instead of trying his hand at serious literature. Of course, the fact that he was being well paid for the stories, and that they were extremely popular, made it all the more difficult for him to stop. However, according to a letter he wrote to his mother, when he wrote *The Final Problem* he had decided to kill of Sherlock Holmes. He had realised, 'I must save my mind for better things, even if it means I must bury my pocketbook with him'. Despite his best intentions, however, Conan Doyle could not resist resuscitating his hero, and eventually brought him back to life in *The Adventure of the Empty House.*

INTELLIGENCE AND EVIL

In Moriarty, Conan Doyle created a memorable character who is frightening not just because he is evil, but because he is super-intelligent: a scientist, with a knowledge of mathematics, astrophysics and technology that is well beyond most people's grasp. This idea of science and technology as potentially destructive goes back to the eighteenth-century Romantics, to authors like Mary Shelley, who were alarmed at the rapid progress of technology and had lost faith in the rationalism of the Enlightenment period. The Romantic writers stressed the power of the supernatural and were fascinated by the irrational, rather than rational, aspects of human nature. Conan Doyle brought this strand of thought, in which intelligence is no longer linked to rationalism and but has become dangerously intertwined with subterranean emotions of hatred, lust for power and violence, into popular literature in the nineteenth century with his Sherlock Holmes series. Although he did not see the stories as having great literary merit, they touched on some of the important themes of European literature up to that time, such as the place of the irrational, of dark emotions, in the minds of intelligent people. The fact that he made his hero an opium-smoking intellectual and his arch-villain Moriarty a scientific mastermind made his stories all the more fascinating to the general public, who had been used to detective fiction in which the heroes and villains were somewhat two-dimensional 'goodies' and 'baddies'.

A LIVING LEGEND

Despite Conan Doyle's attempt to kill off Moriarty, he survived well into the twentieth century and beyond, as new generations of writers took inspiration from the idea of a criminal mastermind presiding over an evil worldwide organisation that threatens to destroy civilisation. In addition, Moriarty was represented on film by a number of actors in the 1930s and 40s, including George Zucco, Lionel Atwill and Henry Daniell. In 1985, Moriarty was played by Anthony Higgins in the film *Young Sherlock Holmes*, which elaborated on Moriarty's life history. In 2003's *The League of Extraordinary Gentlemen*, a film adaptation of the comic book by Alan Moore, which casts Moriarty as the head of British Intelligence, the supervillain finally meets his end at the hands of Fu Manchu, another fictional master criminal.

Moriarty has also been parodied in various comedies, including the seminal 1950s British radio show, *The Goon Show*, in which a character called Count Jim Moriarty appears as an incompetent criminal mastermind. In the 1988 movie *Without a Clue*, Sherlock Holmes and Doctor Watson reverse roles, with Holmes emerging as a bumbling fool and Watson as the true genius of the piece. In this story, Moriarty attempts to undermine the British economy by counterfeiting money, but, during an action-packed finale, he meets his end when gas pipes explode in a theatre fire. In yet another incarnation, Moriarty appears in cartoon form as the evil Professor Ratigan in *The Great Mouse Detective*. Here, he and the Holmes character, Basil of Baker Street, fight to the death on Big Ben, the famous clock tower at the Houses of Parliament. Both the characters fall off the clock, but in true Disney style, only the villain dies.

Today, the fictional character of Moriarty continues to fascinate writers, film-makers and cartoonists, as well as the general public in many countries all over the world. The fact that he remains such a shadowy figure in the Sherlock Holmes stories has only served to intensify speculation about him, making his legend all the more inviting for new generations of storytellers to elaborate upon.

FANTOMAS

Fantomas is a fictional master criminal who was created by hack writers Marcel Allain and Pierre Souvestre at the turn of the twentieth century. The first appearance of this character, who went on to become one of the most famous villains in French crime fiction, was in 1911. After that, he appeared in forty-three stories, most of them written by the Allain–Souvestre team, but some of them written by Allain after Souvestre died in 1914. In later years, the Fantomas series inspired a number of television series, films, and comic strips.

Commentators have pointed out that in some respects, Fantomas is a typical villain in the old-fashioned, Gothic novel style, but, as a serial killer, he also represents a modern anti-hero. In this respect, Fantomas as a character represents an important development in the history of crime fiction. Fantomas is also fascinating as an instance when popular fiction, churned out as trashy, commercial writing, developed a serious following among artists and critics, inspiring many of the surrealist painters, writers and film-makers of the day.

INFANT SADIST

The background of Fantomas emerges piece by piece in the stories that feature him. We are told that he is of British and French ancestry, and that he was probably born in 1867. French writer Jean-Marc Lofficier has speculated that the creators of Fantomas may have imagined him to be the son of Rocambole, a fictional adventurer, who was also important as a link between the Gothic novel style and modern crime stories. According to this theory, Fantomas' mother was Ellen Palmure, a British aristocrat who was Rocambole's lover for a while. Ellen gave birth to twins, Fantomas and his nemesis, Juve, in 1867. Ellen did not keep either of the children: Juve was raised in a French state orphanage, while Fantomas was taken into the care of the Rev. Patterson, a friend of Ellen's, in the UK. As a child, Fantomas displayed a sadistic nature, and his original family shunned him.

As an adult, Fantomas grew into a monstrous individual, who would stop at nothing to commit his evil, destructive crimes. A master of disguise, Fantomas leads his arm of street thugs, known as 'apaches', wreaking havoc on the inhabitants of the city at any opportunity. He also has an army of spies and henchmen and he commands a shadowy underworld of outcasts committed to the downfall of civilised society. Although he is a member of high society and moves with ease among the rich and powerful, in his secret life as Fantomas, he wages war against the status quo and attempts to spread chaos and terror wherever he goes.

TORTURE AND TERROR

Some of his most dastardly crimes include: releasing dozens of plague-infested rats on a ship to infect the passengers; putting sulphuric acid in perfume dispensers in a Parisian department store; and crashing a passenger train, killing all those inside. He also enjoys torturing and terrorising individuals. In one story, a rebellious underling is hung as a human clapper in a large bell; in another, a victim is placed face up in the guillotine so that he can watch the blade come down on him before he dies. Fantomas has no mercy, and nobody really understands what motivates him.

Inspector Juve, a Parisian police inspector, carries out a single-handed crusade against the evil genius Fantomas. Only Juve realises the extent of Fantomas' evil nature, but on the whole he is powerless to do anything about it. Although Juve does his best to capture Fantomas, he usually fails, for Fantomas is 'everywhere and nowhere', and constantly slips through the net. In the end, Juve finds himself becoming obsessed with Fantomas, to the degree that he wonders if he is going insane. Whether or not Juve is actually Fantomas' twin brother, there is a deep connection between them, and this picture of the psychological link between the police inspector and the criminal he is trying to catch is a very modern one, predating much of twentieth-century crime fiction.

DEATH'S HEAD TATTOO

Other characters in the Fantomas novels include Jerome Fandor, who helps Juve in his campaign against Fantomas. Fandor, also known as Charles Rambert, is a journalist on a newspaper called *La Capitale*. There is some suggestion that Fandor may be Fantomas' son, just as Juve may be Fantomas' brother. Fantomas' mistress is Lady Beltham, the widow of one of his victims, who has strong misgivings – as well she may – about the relationship. She wants to break away from Fantomas, but each time she tries, she is drawn back to him. Thus, the liaison persists over many years.

The character of Helene, Fantomas' daughter is again a very modern one. Helene sports a lurid death's head tattoo, smokes opium and wears men's clothing. She is in love with Jerome Fandor, and he with her, but for a long time their passion for each other is never requited. If Fandor really is Fantomas' son, a sexual relationship between them would be incestuous, but it is never made clear whether this is the case.

The shadowy existence of Fantomas, and the fact that we never find out his exact history, allowed his creators to constantly play with his identity, bringing in all sorts of unlikely connections between the characters. In various stories, it is hinted that in the past Fantomas was a man called Archduke Juan North, who lived in the German principality of Heisse-Weimar, and fathered a child, Vladimir. Next, we hear that he lived in India, where he fathered another child, Helene. Helene's mother was a European woman, who had also been having an affair with an Indian prince, so it is possible that Fantomas may not be her father after all.

DEATH ON THE *TITANIC*

We also hear that, in the late 1890s, Fantomas travelled to North America, Mexico and South Africa, where he fought in the Boer War under the name of Gurn. It was at this time that he met Lady Beltham, the wife of Lord Edward Beltham, and the pair became lovers. When they came back to Europe, Lord Beltham discovered their affair and tried to shoot his wife. To prevent this happening, Gurn hit Lord Beltham with a hammer and then strangled him. Lady Beltham stays with Fantomas, but she is deeply unhappy about the relationship, and after helping to kill one of Fantomas' victims, she commits suicide.

Fantomas' son, Vladimir, appears in 1911, only to have his lover murdered by his father. Vladimir, who turns out to be almost as evil as his father, is eventually shot by Juve. The following year, both Fantomas and Juve meet their end aboard the famous *Titanic*.

SURREALIST VISIONS OF EVIL

The Fantomas series was hugely popular in France and elsewhere in Europe, and it also attracted praise from artists and writers of the period. The surrealist writer Guillaume Apollinaire praised it highly, saying: 'From the imaginative standpoint Fantomas is one of the richest works that exist', while the film maker Jean Cocteau referred to its 'absurd and magnificent lyricism'. Certainly, the Fantomas books are more surrealist than realist: the central character himself seems to have an unearthly existence, and extraordinary scenes abound in the stories. For example a horse-drawn cab gallops at dawn through the Parisian streets, with a corpse riding it as coachman; blood, sapphires and diamonds rain down from the sky; victims are poisoned with deadly bouquets of flowers; and the gold is stripped from the dome of the Invalides each night. In addition, there is the constant interplay of shifting identities in the books. Fantomas' nemesis is Juve, who may or may not be his twin brother;

Juve's partner is Fandor, who may or may not be Fantomas' son; and Fandor's lover Helene may or may not be Fantomas' daughter. To make matters more complicated, Fantomas also dons a myriad of disguises, for example impersonating a tramp, Bouzille, who sometimes helps him in his escapades. But Bouzille sometimes helps Juve, and Juve also dresses up as Bouzille on occasion. Thus, in the Fantomas series, we are constantly confronted with characters and their mirror images in a way that does not remotely describe day-to-day reality but which has great resonance in describing the tortuous relationships between people on a psychological level. To this extent, Fantomas is not run-of-the-mill crime fiction, but accurately portrays the lurid fantasies of the mind, and the way human beings always move between good and evil, in a series of relationships and actions that question their basic morality.

Amazingly, the authors of the Fantomas series wrote the novels at the rate of one a month. They were published for thirty-two successive months, and were eagerly awaited by Parisians of all social classes. There were many reasons for their popularity: the low price of the books (65 centimes each); the lurid covers by Gino Starace, the first of which showed the ghoulish Fantomas hovering over Paris holding a knife dripping with blood; the gruesomeness of the crimes; the fact that the hero always escaped; and also, that his motivation for committing the crimes was never clear. The novels were made into a series of films directed by Louis Feuillade, which were also extremely popular. However, World War I then intervened. Feuillade was wounded, and although he later resumed film-making, he never made another Fantomas film. Souvestre died in the influenza epidemic at the end of the war. Allain married his widow and went on to write more stories, but the Fantomas novels never achieved the same popularity again.

HANNIBAL LECTER

Of all the criminal masterminds in fiction, Dr Hannibal Lecter is perhaps the most memorable. The creation of author Thomas Harris, Lecter is a highly intelligent, cultured man who trained as a psychiatrist but became a serial killer. He is a cannibal, devouring parts of his victims in the most gruesome ways, but is also renowned as a gourmet and talented cook. This combination of primitive savagery and sophisticated *savoir faire* is what makes Lecter such a chilling character. He is at once the most base of men, and the most high-minded.

TRAUMATIC CHILDHOOD EVENTS

The first novel in which Lecter appears, *Red Dragon*, was published in 1981, and five years later, this was adapted for the screen under the title of *Manhunter*, starring Brian Cox in the role of Lecter. There followed a run of movies starring Anthony Hopkins that made Lecter into a household name, and he was also played by actor Gaspard Ulliel.

Hannibal Lecter's background emerges piece by piece in the novels by Thomas Harris. According to Harris, Lecter was born in 1933, the son of a wealthy aristocrat, Count Lecter. Lecter's ancestry went back to a warlord, Hannibal the Grim, who was the victor at the Battle of Grunwald, a real battle that took place in 1410. In the battle, which became one of the most famous in medieval times, the Poles and Lithuanians defeated the Teutonic Knights, a crusading military force of German Roman Catholics.

Hannibal Lecter's mother, Madam Simonetta Sforza, was equally aristocratic, being connected to the Italian Sforza and Visconti families, who ruled Milan at different times over a period of two-and-a-half centuries. Rumour also suggests that among the family's antecedents was Giuliano Bevisangue ('blood drinker'), a notorious tyrant in Tuscany during the twelfth century, but this is never confirmed.

Hannibal's sister Mischa is three years younger than him, and the siblings share a very strong bond. However, with the onset of World War II, their childhood is brutally disrupted. The family are forced to leave their country house and hide in a forest lodge to escape from the Nazis, and at the age of twelve, Hannibal finds himself an orphan when his parents and their servants die in the fighting. The lodge is overrun by desperate looters who round up the children to eat them. Hannibal's sister

Mischa is eaten, however, Hannibal manages to escape, with a wound on his neck where the skin has been stripped away.

Hannibal then finds himself back in his original family home on the estate, which has now been turned into an orphanage. The orphans are a violent, bullying crowd and he begins to engage in the same behaviour, but he is then rescued and taken to his uncle's home. There, he falls in love with his aunt, Lady Murasaki, who teaches him about Japanese culture. At the age of thirteen, Hannibal beheads a local butcher who has insulted his aunt, bringing him to the attention of the authorities in the shape of Inspector Pascal Popil. Hannibal is set free and continues his education, training as a doctor.

THE CHESAPEAKE RIPPER

As a young man, Hannibal returns to the forest lodge where his family died, unearths his sister Mischa's remains, and buries them properly. He then traces one of her killers, Enrikas Dortlich, and murders him, eating the cheeks of his dead body in revenge for his sister's murder. Hannibal also drowns another member of the group, Zigmas Milko, in formaldehyde, and eviscerates a man named Grutas by carving his sister's initial into his body, again and again. Popil pursues Hannibal brings him into custody. He wants Hannibal to be brought to justice, but there is little motivation for the authorities to do this, since all of his victims appear to be war criminals.

When Hannibal is released, he sets out on a campaign of evil that defies belief. He travels to Montreal, and there kills another member of the group, Bronys Grentz, before settling down to practise psychiatry in Baltimore. He becomes wealthy and is celebrated as a world-renowned psychiatrist. However, he has also become a serial killer, known as the 'Chesapeake Ripper', and has nine victims to his name. Many of these are clients who have come to him for advice, sometimes as part of a court order for various crimes. Molson Verger, for example, is a successful businessman who raped his sister. In revenge for this, Hannibal drugs Verger and persuades him to cut parts of his face off and feed them to his dogs. He then tries to hang Verger, but Verger survives, hideously disfigured and in need of a life-support machine. Another victim, Benjamin Raspail, is a flautist who has dared to irritate Hannibal by playing badly with the Baltimore Philharmonic Orchestra. Hannibal kills Raspail and then serves his heart, pancreas and thymus to the orchestra's board of directors.

LURID EXPERIMENTS

Lecter is eventually caught in 1975 by FBI detective

Will Graham, but it proves difficult to charge him. One of the reasons for this is that Lecter is ahead of the game when it comes to psychological tests; he remains impossible to classify, and as a result becomes more and more dangerous. At one point, he is admitted to hospital only to bite a nurse's tongue off and tear out her eye. Lecter and the hospital's director, Chilton, have a mutual loathing for one another, although Lecter gets on well with his immediate captor, Barney Matthews. During his stay at the hospital, Lecter helps to solve four FBI murder cases, one involving Will Graham, whom he double crosses, and one involving FBI trainee Clarice Starling. Eventually, he manages to escape, making a 'mask' from the torn-off face of a police officer and pretending to be a victim.

The next phase of Lecter's life takes place in Florence, where he becomes Doctor Fell and has plastic surgery. He also has a distinctive sixth finger removed from his hand. In Italy, he continues his career of disembowelling and cannibalising his enemies, performing ever more lurid experiments on them. He attempts to brainwash Clarice Starling into thinking she is his dead sister, but Starling resists; however, in the end she seduces him. More adventures follow, but Lecter remains at large, an ever more terrifying presence whose perversity and appetite for violence know no bounds.

In the films based on the Thomas Harris novels,

Lecter develops from being a sociopath into a more mythical monstrous character. Some explanations for his psychology are given, such as that he saw his sister being decapitated at the moment when he prayed to God for her survival, but in the end it is made clear that Lecter's evil streak is a mystery: 'they don't have a name for what he is,' says Clarice Starling. Lecter reiterates this, responding to attempts to explain his behaviour by saying, 'Nothing happened to me. I happened.'

REAL-LIFE INSPIRATION

The first movie actor to play Lecter was Brian Cox in *Manhunter*. After this, the role was taken by Anthony Hopkins, in *Silence of the Lambs* and a remake of *Manhunter*, filmed under the title *Red Dragon*. Although Harris' novels were successful, Hopkins' film portrayal of Lecter made the character world famous, and he became the archetype of the modern-day serial killer.

Harris is thought to have taken his inspiration for Lecter from real-life serial killers such as the infamous cannibals Albert Fish, Andrei Chikatilo and Jeffrey Dahmer. However, since the author rarely gives interviews, there is little information available on his sources for this most memorable of literary and screen monsters. What is clear is that Lecter's appeal lies in the contradictions of his nature. He is at once a charming, educated, sociable man with a concern for others and a tender affection for family members, such as his sister, and others, such as Clarice Starling, who later becomes his lover, and his jailer Barney Matthews. He has a brilliant mind, and is scathing about the lower intelligence of the many police officers and psychologists who try to typecast him. At the same time, he is a primitive savage who enjoys torturing his enemies and inflicting horrific violence on others, and who also indulges in the basest of human activities such as eating body parts.

Lecter's creator, Thomas Harris, gives us some pointers to the reasons behind his character's behaviour, such as Lecter's traumatising childhood experiences (in particular, his sister being killed and cannibalised in front of him). However, Harris makes it clear that, in the end, nobody can understand Lecter, and shows that, despite Lecter's superior intellect, he is not able to understand himself and must remain unable to contain or control his baser impulses. The inference is that, no matter how clever our psychologists become, some human beings are subject to unfathomable evil, and at the heart of humanity lies a mystery that we can never solve. Only by trying to put ourselves in the place of the evil-doer – as Clarice Starling and others do – can we hope to understand what makes a killer, and that is a dangerous game indeed to play.

DON VITO
CORLEONE

Don Vito Corleone, otherwise known as The God-father, is the fictional head of a New York Mafia family, both in the novel by Mario Puzo and the trilogy of films made by Francis Ford Coppola. The story follows the fortunes of the Corleone family, including Don Vito's final death and the inheritance of his position by his youngest son Michael. It also chronicles the lives of Don Vito's sons Santino and Fredo, his daughter Connie and his adopted son Tom Hagen, as well many other characters in the family. According to some sources, the character of Don Vito Corleone is based on real-life Mafia dons such as Vito Genovese, Frank Costello, Nicanor Fulgencio and Joseph Bonanno. Both the novel and the films portray the life of a Mafia don as one of excitement, glamour and power but also stress the darker side of it, revealing the personal torments of the Don as he tries to build a stable family life in a world where murder, extortion and crime is the norm.

THE MAKING OF A MAFIA BOSS

As Vito's life story emerges in the Godfather saga, he was born at the turn of the twentieth century in Corleone, a small town in Sicily. His father, Antonio Andolini, and his older brother Paolo, are murdered by Mafia boss Don Ciccio. Ciccio now plans to kill Vito, still only a boy, but Vito's mother calls on him and begs for his life. Ciccio refuses to let the boy go, reasoning that Vito will later seek revenge and kill him, whereupon Vito's mother threatens Ciccio with a knife. Vito is able to escape from Ciccio's house, but has to leave his mother to her fate.

Vito then boards a cargo ship loaded with immigrants bound for North America. When he arrives on Ellis Island, New York, the immigration officers there give him the name Vito Corleone, since he comes from that town. In New York, the boy is adopted by the Abbandando family and works in the family grocery store. As a young man, he marries and has children, but loses his job in the grocery store because of intimidation by Mafia boss Don Fanucci, who wants his nephew to take over the job. Little by little, Vito learns that the only way to survive in his world is to become involved with the Mafia, and he embarks on a life of petty crime. He sets up an olive oil business, using it as a front for organised crime, and becomes rich – but at a price. He murders Don Fanucci, and later his father's killer, Don Ciccio, in the process establishing the Corleones as one of the most powerful Mafia families in New York.

VORTEX OF CRIME

In his personal life, Vito is kind and generous. He is extremely loyal to his family, and he expects the same loyalty in return. He has four children, one of whom, Michael, has excelled both at college in the army. His greatest desire is that Michael should escape from the 'family business' and succeed in a more respectable field. However, the fact is that the family fortunes are based on criminal activities such as bootlegging and gambling. Their deals are enforced by intimidation; murder and violence are their stock in trade. Before long, Michael too becomes sucked into the vortex of crime, and he eventually succeeds his father as Don.

In Francis Ford Coppola's film trilogy, Michael is the main character of the story, and he is memorably played by actor Al Pacino. (Marlon Brando plays Vito in *The Godfather*, and Robert De Niro in *The Godfather II*, where we meet Vito as a younger man.) Michael enrols in the army to get away from the family and fights as a Marine in the Pacific during World War II. However, when his father is almost assassinated, Michael murders the men in revenge, afterwards fleeing to Sicily. During his period of exile, his brother Sonny is murdered, and he returns to take his place as heir to Vito's place as head of the family. When Vito dies, he becomes the new Don and begins a career as ruthless as his father's, murdering many leaders of rival families. Moreover, unlike his father, Michael is unable to keep the peace within the Corleone family itself, and bitter rivalries surface, resulting in more deaths. Eventually, Michael's beloved daughter Mary is murdered, and Michael retires to Sicily, heartbroken, where he dies of a stroke.

SEVERED HEAD

The Godfather was released in 1972, *The Godfather, Part II* in 1974, and *The Godfather, Part III* in 1990. It received rave reviews, and has become a classic of modern cinema. It also engendered a certain amount of controversy over its violent depiction of life in the Mafia; in particular, a scene involving the severed head of a horse shocked the public. Director Coppola was criticised by animal-rights activists, and in his defence, insisted that the horse's head had been destined for a dog food company and had not been killed for the purposes of the film. Coppola also came in for a great deal of criticism from the studio, Paramount Pictures, who questioned his decision to use Marlon Brando and Al Pacino in the lead roles, and almost replaced him as director several times.

However, Coppola managed to defend his actors and direct the movie as he wanted to, with tremendously successful results. When the film appeared, it was hailed as a masterpiece and revived the ailing career of one of the US's major stars, Marlon Brando.

Brando's performance as the elderly, mumbling, yet charismatic Vito Corleone was extraordinary. The Godfather as Brando portrayed him – with his often quoted line about 'making an offer you can't refuse' – became an icon of popular cinema. Once more, Brando appeared to have rewritten the rules of performing, creating a character that was at once idiosyncratic and archetypal, as he had done in his younger days, both on stage and screen.

THE 'REAL' GODFATHER

Marlon Brando, the 'real' Godfather, was born on April 3, 1924 in Omaha, Nebraska. As a young man, he was expelled from military school, and then went to New York to become an actor. He studied the principles of Stanislavsky, known as method acting, in which the actors try to create an entire emotional picture of their character, immersing themselves in the part and attempting to identify with him or her in every way possible. Brando went on to perform on Broadway, creating a sensation with his role as Stanley Kowalaski in *A Streetcar Named Desire*. His brooding sexuality and emotional intensity were a revelation to the theatre world, and before long he became a screen idol too, with the film adaptation of *Streetcar*.

During his long career, Brando gained a reputation as a rebel, both on and off screen. His portrayal of an angry young motorcycle gang leader in 1954's *The Wild One* established him as a major Hollywood star. The same year, his performance as a former boxing star in *On the Waterfront* was hailed as a masterpiece. He went on to make many more movies and became one of the most respected actors in Hollywood. However, his reputation for taking risks, coupled with his difficult behaviour off stage, made many producers and directors wary of working with him. By the end of the sixties, after a series of unsuccessful movies, it seemed that Brando's star was beginning to wane - until he took on the role of The Godfather in Coppola's film.

FAMILY TRAGEDY

Brando's performance in the title role was brilliant, and he received rave reviews. However, he angered the industry by refusing to collect his Academy Award, instead sending a Native American spokeswoman to the ceremony. She delivered a speech attacking the US government's treatment of the Native American population. It turned out later that the woman, supposedly called Sacheen Littlefeather, was not a Native American at all, but a Hispanic actress hired for the occasion.

Brando continued to court controversy with his next film, *Last Tango in Paris*, in which he gave another extraordinary performance as a depressed, lonely widower who becomes sexually involved with a much younger woman. In later years, he again drew criticisms, and confounded his fans, by making a number of unimpressive cameo performances, for which he was paid vast sums. Eventually, he retired to an island in the Pacific, where he became reclusive and overweight. Tragedy then struck when his son, Christian, killed the lover of his pregnant daughter, Cheyenne. Christian was found guilty of the murder and given a prison sentence, while Cheyenne committed suicide.

In need of money, Brando returned to the screen in a number of movies. Stories of his bizarre behaviour on the set abounded, and it appeared that his mental health was deteriorating. In 2004, after an absence from the screen of three years, Brando's physical health gave way, and he died of pulmonary fibrosis.

Today, Marlon Brando is remembered as one of the greatest actors in the history of American cinema. His role as Mafia boss Don Vito Corleone was one of the high points of his career; moreover, certain aspects of his personal life – such as the murder that took place in his family and his eventual isolation – uncannily echo that of his screen persona as the Don.

FU MANCHU

The character of Dr Fu Manchu appeared in a series of novels by Sax Rohmer, whose first novel *Pause!* was published in 1910. Rohmer's main character in the books, a fiendish oriental mastermind, was an immediate success, coinciding as it did with a wave of anxiety in Europe and the USA about the threat of Chinese immigration. The evil genius Fu Manchu came to embody the 'Yellow Peril' as it was known, with the supposed characteristics of cruelty, inscrutability and cunning ascribed by Westerners to the people of the East.

Along with Professor Moriarty from the *Sherlock Holmes* stories by Arthur Conan Doyle, Fu Manchu became one of the earliest criminal masterminds in fiction, continuing to fascinate readers throughout the twentieth century and into the new millennium. To some critics, Fu Manchu represents an offensively racist caricature of Eastern culture, while others see him as an entertaining mythical figure whose exploits are the stuff of harmless, often rather silly, old-fashioned horror stories.

THE DEVIL DOCTOR

Arthur Henry Sarsfield Ward, the real name of the creator of Fu Manchu, was born into a working-class family in Birmingham. Despite his lack of education, he rose to become a writer, earning his living by writing comedy sketches for performers in music hall. He also wrote short stories for magazines, some of which were serialised. In 1910, his first novel, *Pause!* appeared, but it was published anonymously. Two years later, a series of short stories were published under the name of Sax Rohmer, beginning with *The Mystery of Dr Fu Manchu.* The series was an immediate success and Rohmer became one of the best paid and most successful writers of his generation, eventually moving to the USA, where he set up home in New York with his wife, Rose.

Rhomer's Fu Manchu character was the devilishly cunning leader of the Si-Fan cult, dedicated to destroying the Western world and ruling the entire planet in an Eastern empire. Fu Machu has an incredible mind and he has been able to extend his lifespan by means of chemical potions. The drug he uses to maintain his youth and strength is called Elixir Vitae, and he is also able to hypnotise his victims merely by looking them in the eye.

As well as being a master of ancient Chinese arts, Fu Manchu is also able to Understand and utilise modern scientific inventions of all kinds. His Si-Fan devotees are extremely loyal to him, but his evil daughter Fah Lo Suee plots against him, creating all kinds of difficulties for him as she attempts to build her own sinister following. (A son, Shang Chi, later appeared in Marvel comic versions of *Fu Manchu*.) Known as The Celestial One and The Devil Doctor, Fu Manchu operates in China but has underground cells around the world's major cities. In London, his organisation is situated in Limehouse, a working-class area of East London. Ranged against him, and representing the forces of Western civilisation, stiff upper lips and 'decent values', are Sir Denis Nayland-Smith, a British spy, and his assistant Dr Petrie of Scotland Yard, who engage in constant battles with the evasive, but ubiquitous overlord of the East.

Despite the fact that he is a master of disguise, Fu Manchu has a very striking appearance. Sax Rohmer describes him thus: 'Imagine a person, tall, lean and feline, high-shouldered, with a brow like Shakespeare and a face like Satan, a close-shaven skull and long, magnetic eyes of the true cat-green.' The evil doctor also embodies all the most evil aspects of Chinese culture and government: 'Invest him with all the cruel cunning of an entire Eastern race, accumulated in one giant intellect, with all the resources of science past and present, with all the resources, if you will of a wealthy government – which, however, already has denied all knowledge of his existence. Imagine that awful being and you have a mental picture of Dr Fu Manchu, the yellow peril incarnate in one man.'

SPIDERS, PYTHONS AND POISONOUS MUSHROOMS

Fu Manchu's plots to take over the world are characterised by an array of horrific devices such as using animals, insects and biological weapons to murder his opponents. Among his arsenal of weapons are spiders, pythons, poisonous mushrooms and bacteria, used by an army of Eastern bad guys such as dacoits (armed robbers) and Thuggees (members of a secret society dating from the seventeeth century, who robbed and murdered travellers). He is also not above using beautiful women to lure his victims to their doom. One such is Karamaneh, a 'seductively lovely' double agent who works for him and is rumoured to be his lover.

The origins of Fu Manchu are shrouded in mystery, but it is thought that he was once a member of the Imperial family, who fell from power in the Boxer Rebellion, a Chinese rebellion at the turn of the century. During this period, many Chinese people, including Christians, rebelled against the Qing Dynasty's policy of allowing foreign influence to prevail in China in areas such as trade, politics, religion and technology. In his early books, Rohmer portrays Fu Manchu as a mere hired assassin who is sent out on missions by the Si-Fan terror organisation. Later, Fu Manchu rises to power, and he becomes head of the organisation, thus attempting to wreak his revenge on the forces of civilisation.

THE 'YELLOW PERIL'

Commissioner Sir Denis Nayland Smith and his side-kick Dr Petrie from Scotland Yard are Fu Manchu's sworn enemies. They are very much in the tradition of Sherlock Holmes and Dr Watson from the Arthur Conan Doyle series. However, instead of Holmes' intellectual brilliance, Nayland Smith tends to carry the day by force of sheer dogged persever-ance. In Rohmer's work, the stories are narrated by Dr Petrie and describe Nayland Smith's battle to combat the forces of evil, as epitomised by Fu Manchu. Rohmer describes Nayland Smith and Fu Manchu as having a grudging respect for each other, and each of them believe that a man's word is his bond, even when dealing with an arch enemy.

To some readers, Rohmer's stories are harmless enough, using the tried and tested clichés of adventure stories to entertain the readers. However, others note the racist language of Rohmer's descriptions, in particular his use of the term 'yellow peril', which harked back to anti-Chinese sentiment of the late nineteenth century and was still prevalent in the early twentieth. The 'yellow peril', also known as the 'yellow terror', was a phrase thought to have been coined by Kaiser Wilhelm II in 1895, when he referred to 'gelbe Gefahr'.

Beginning in the nineteenth century, thousands of Chinese labourers, often referred to as 'coolies', had travelled all over the world, particularly to the USA, to work as labourers. This mass immigration prompted a wave of anxiety on the part of people already living in the USA, which was encouraged by the press, particularly in William Randolph Hearst's newspapers, which often referred directly to the new arrivals as the 'yellow peril'. The 'yellow' referred to the skin colour of the Chinese, and the 'peril' to the imagined danger that these immigrants would not only take labouring jobs from white people, but would also import a different, and supposedly sinister, way of life and culture into Western civilisation. In Europe, where immigration from China was less of a problem, the fear of the east centred on Japan's rise as a major world power rather than on the Chinese immigrant population.

THE FU MANCHU MOUSTACHE

Despite, or perhaps because of, the fact that the character of Fu Manchu was in many ways a racist stereotype, the stories became extremely popular.

Several films were made featuring the evil genius, and on screen he was played by Boris Karloff and Christopher Lee. There were also many send-ups of the character, most notably by Peter Sellers. As time went on, he became a comedy villain and appeared in many comic strips such as Marvel comics *Master of Kung-Fu.* His trademark facial hair, a long, thin moustache extending either side of the face and hanging past the jawline, was worn by many Eastern characters in Western films, associated as it was with Chinese wise men, kung fu teachers and Mongol warriors. It also became a fashionable style of moustache for men in the USA during the 1970s, sported by all kinds of stars, from baseball players and heavy metal singers to wrestlers and television actors. (However, Rohmer himself never described his villain as having such a moustache!)

Fu Manchu also inspired many other evil Eastern masterminds in fiction. These include characters such as Ming the Merciless in the *Flash Gordon* comic strip of the 1930s, the *Pao Tcheou* series of novels written by Edward Brookner in the 1940s and 1950s, *Yellow Claw* from Marvel Comics in the 1950s, and *Dr No* in the 1960s James Bond novels by Ian Fleming. Today, although to some extent a figure of fun, Fu Manchu has undoubtedly taken his place in the pantheon of fictional criminal masterminds and remains the archetypal evil genius of the East.